UNBROKEN

AN OLYMPIAN'S JOURNEY
FROM AIRMAN TO CASTAWAY TO CAPTIVE

UNBROKEN

AN OLYMPIAN'S JOURNEY
FROM AIRMAN TO CASTAWAY TO CAPTIVE

LAURA HILLENBRAND

ADAPTED FOR YOUNG ADULTS

EMBER

Text copyright © 2014 by Laura Hillenbrand
"In Conversation" copyright © 2014 by Laura Hillenbrand
Cover photographs copyright © 2014: ocean and sky Joel Sartore/National Geographic Stock;
plane Getty Images/123RF

All rights reserved. Published in the United States by Ember, an imprint of Random House
Children's Books, a division of Penguin Random House LLC, New York. Originally published
in hardcover in the United States by Delacorte Press, an imprint of Random House Children's Books,
New York, in 2014. This work is based on *Unbroken: A World War II Story of Survival, Resilience,
and Redemption*, copyright © 2010 by Laura Hillenbrand, published by Random House,
a division of the Random House Group, a division of Penguin Random House LLC.

Ember and the E colophon are registered trademarks of Penguin Random House LLC.

Visit us on the Web! randomhouseteens.com

Educators and librarians, for a variety of teaching tools, visit us at RHTeachersLibrarians.com

The Library of Congress has cataloged the hardcover edition of this work as follows:
Hillenbrand, Laura.
Unbroken : an Olympian's journey from airman to castaway to captive / Laura Hillenbrand.
pages cm.
"Adapted for young adults."
Original version published: New York : Random House, c2010.
Includes bibliographical references and index.
ISBN 978-0-385-74251-1 (trade : alk. paper) — ISBN 978-0-375-99062-5 (lib. bdg. : alk. paper) —
ISBN 978-0-307-97565-2 (ebook)
1. Zamperini, Louis, 1917–2014—Juvenile literature. 2. World War, 1939–1945—Prisoners and prisons,
Japanese—Juvenile literature. 3. Prisoners of war—United States—Biography—Juvenile literature.
4. Prisoners of war—Japan—Biography—Juvenile literature. 5. World War, 1939–1945—
Aerial operations, American—Juvenile literature. 6. Long-distance runners—United States—
Biography—Juvenile literature. 7. Olympic athletes—United States—Biography—Juvenile literature.
I. Title. D805.J3 Z365 2014 940.54'7252092—dc23 [B] 2014014794

ISBN 978-0-385-74252-8 (tr. pbk.)

Printed in the United States of America
20 19 18 17 16 15 14 13 12 11
First Ember Edition 2017

Random House Children's Books supports the First Amendment and celebrates the right to read.

For the wounded and the lost

Contents

Map   x

Introduction   1

PART I

Chapter 1: The One-Boy Insurgency   5

Chapter 2: Run Like Mad   13

Chapter 3: The Torrance Tornado   21

Chapter 4: Plundering Germany   31

Chapter 5: The Red Circle   41

PART II

Chapter 6: The Flying Coffin   49

Chapter 7: "This Is It, Boys"   60

Chapter 8: Dying in Droves   69

Chapter 9: Five Hundred and Ninety-Four Holes   78

Chapter 10: "The Whole Island Was Blowing Up"   87

Chapter 11: "Nobody's Going to Live Through This"   95

PART III

Chapter 12: Downed   103

Chapter 13: Missing at Sea   107

Chapter 14: Thirst   112

Chapter 15: Sharks and Bullets   118

Chapter 16: Singing in the Clouds   125

Chapter 17: Typhoon   131

PART IV

Chapter 18: A Dead Body Breathing   139

Chapter 19: "No One Knows You're Alive"   145

Chapter 20: Farting for Hirohito   152

Chapter 21: Belief   160

Chapter 22: Plots Afoot   165

Chapter 23: Monster   171

Chapter 24: Hunted   176

Chapter 25: "He's Alive!"   183

Chapter 26: Madness   190

Chapter 27: Falling Down   196

Chapter 28: Enslaved   201

Chapter 29: Two Hundred and Twenty Punches   207

Chapter 30: The Boiling City   212

Chapter 31: The Naked Stampede   219

Chapter 32: Cascades of Pink Peaches   225

Chapter 33: Mother's Day   232

PART V

Chapter 34: The Shimmering Girl   243

Chapter 35: Coming Undone   251

Chapter 36: The Body on the Mountain   257

Chapter 37: Twisted Ropes   261

Chapter 38: The Promise   265

Chapter 39: Daybreak   271

Epilogue   275

In Conversation: Laura Hillenbrand and Louie Zamperini   285

Acknowledgments   293

Index   300

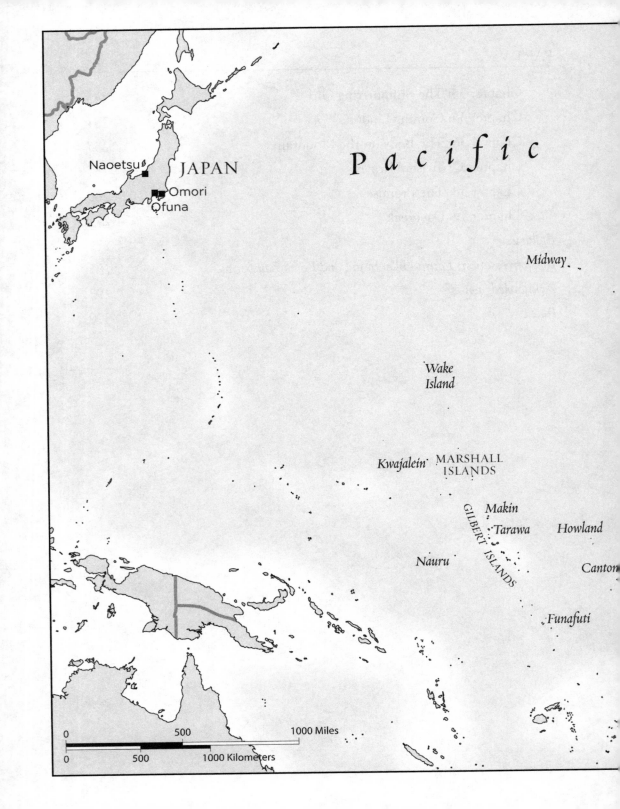

O c e a n

UNITED
STATES

CALIFORNIA

Torrance

HAWAIIAN ISLANDS

Kauai   Oahu

Hawaii

Palmyra Atoll

Introduction

All he could see, in every direction, was water.

It was June 22, 1943. Somewhere on the Pacific Ocean, American military airman and Olympic runner Louie Zamperini lay on a small raft, drifting. Slumped beside him was another crewman. On another raft, tethered to the first, lay the pilot, a gash zigzagging across his forehead. Their bodies, sunburned and stained yellow from the dye of the rafts, had shrunken to skeletons. Sharks glided in lazy loops around them, dragging their backs along the rafts, waiting.

The Second World War was raging, and in the Pacific, America and Japan were locked in a bloody struggle. Zamperini and his crew had been searching for a lost warplane when their bomber had crashed into the ocean.

They'd been adrift for twenty-seven days and had floated at least one thousand miles. The rafts were turning to jelly. The men's bodies were pocked with salt sores, their burned lips so swollen they pressed into their nostrils and chins. They spent their days watching the sky, singing "White Christmas." They were alone on sixty-four million square miles of ocean.

A month earlier, twenty-six-year-old Zamperini had been one of the greatest runners in the world. Now his body had wasted to less than one hundred pounds and his famous legs could not lift him. Almost everyone outside of his family had given him up for dead.

On that twenty-seventh day, the men heard a distant, deep strumming. Their eyes caught a glint in the sky: a plane, high overhead. Zamperini fired two flares and shook powdered dye into the water, enveloping the rafts in a circle of vivid orange. The plane kept going, slowly disappearing. The men sagged.

Then the plane reappeared. The crew had seen them.

Overjoyed, the castaways shouted, waving arms starved to little more than bone and skin. The plane dropped low and swept alongside the rafts. Zamperini saw the crewmen's profiles, dark against bright blueness.

Suddenly, there was a terrific roar, and the ocean seemed to boil. It was machine-gun fire. This wasn't an American rescue plane. It was a Japanese bomber.

The men pitched themselves into the sea and hung under the rafts, cringing as bullets pierced the rubber and sliced lines in the water around their faces. The firing blazed on, then sputtered out as the bomber overshot them. The men dragged themselves onto the one raft that was still mostly inflated. The bomber circled toward them again, the machine guns taking aim.

Zamperini's crewmates were too weak to go back into the water. As they lay down, hands over their heads, Zamperini splashed overboard alone.

Somewhere below, the sharks were done waiting. They bent their bodies in the water and swam toward the man under the raft.

PART

I

CHAPTER 1

The One-Boy Insurgency

In the predawn darkness of August 26, 1929, in a small house in Torrance, California, a twelve-year-old boy sat up in bed, listening. There was a huge, heavy rushing sound, growing ever louder, coming from directly above the house. The boy swung his legs off his bed, raced out the back door, and loped onto the grass. The yard was otherworldly, shivering with sound. The boy stood beside his brother, head thrown back, spellbound.

The sky had disappeared. An object he saw only in silhouette, reaching across a massive arc of space, was suspended low over the house. It was longer than two and a half football fields and as tall as a city. It was putting out the stars.

It was the German airship *Graf Zeppelin*. Nearly 800 feet long and 110 feet high, it was the largest flying machine ever crafted. It was the wonder of the world.

The airship was three days from completing a sensational feat, a journey around the globe. It had begun on August 7, when the *Zeppelin* had slipped its tethers in New Jersey and headed for Manhattan. On Fifth Avenue that summer, construction was soon to begin on a new skyscraper, the Empire State Building. At Yankee Stadium in the Bronx, Babe Ruth prepared to hit his five hundredth home run. On Wall Street, stocks raced toward an all-time high.

After a lap around the Statue of Liberty, the *Zeppelin* banked north, then turned over the Atlantic. In time, it reached Europe. The ship passed over Nuremburg, Germany, where an obscure politician named Adolf Hitler had just called for the killing of the "weakest" babies to strengthen the German race. Then it flew east of Frankfurt, where a Jewish woman was nursing her newborn, Anne Frank. Sailing northeast, the *Zeppelin* crossed over Siberia, where villagers, so isolated they'd never even seen a train, fell to their knees at the sight of it.

On August 19, as four million Japanese waved handkerchiefs, the *Zeppelin* circled Tokyo and sank onto a landing field. Four days later, the ship rose into a typhoon that whisked it over the Pacific, toward America. Passengers gazing from the windows saw the ship's shadow, following it on the clouds "like a huge shark." When the clouds parted, they glimpsed giant creatures, turning in the sea, that looked like monsters.

On August 25, the *Zeppelin* reached San Francisco, where crowds thronged the streets to see it. Turning south, it slid through sunset, across midnight, and over Torrance, where the boy in his pajamas stood.

Under the airship, his feet bare in the grass, he was transfixed. In the dark, he felt the rumble of the craft's engines but couldn't see the ship itself. He saw only blackness so vast, it seemed to swallow heaven itself.

———

The boy's name was Louis Zamperini. The son of Italian immigrants, he'd come into the world in Olean, New York, on January 26, 1917, an eleven-and-a-half-pound baby with black hair as coarse as barbed wire.

From the moment he could walk, Louie couldn't be corralled. The instant his mother thumped him down and told him to be still, he vanished. If she didn't have her squirming boy clutched in her hands, she usually had no idea where he was.

In 1919, when two-year-old Louie was sick with pneumonia, he climbed out his bedroom window, descended one story, and went on a naked dash

Pete (left) and Louie Zamperini, circa 1919. Courtesy of Louis Zamperini

through town with a policeman chasing him and a crowd watching in amazement. Soon after, during the family's move to California, Louie bolted, ran through the train, and leapt from the caboose. Frantic as the train rolled backward in search of her lost boy, Louie's mother spotted him strolling in perfect serenity. Swept into her arms, Louie smiled. "I knew you'd come back," he said in Italian.

In California, the family settled in the Los Angeles suburb of Torrance. Louie was as wild as ever. At five, he started smoking, picking up cigarette butts while walking to kindergarten. He began drinking one night when he was eight; he hid under the dinner table, snatched glasses of wine, drank them all dry, staggered right off the front porch, and fell into a rose bush. Leaping around one day, he impaled his leg on a bedpost; on another day, a neighbor had to sew his nearly severed toe back on. When Louie came home drenched in oil after diving into an oil rig well and nearly drowning, it took a gallon of turpentine and a lot of scrubbing before his father recognized him again.

Thrilled by the crashing of boundaries, Louie was untamable. In Torrance, a rebel was born.

Louie (left), Virginia, and Pete Zamperini on their front lawn in Torrance, California. COURTESY OF LOUIS ZAMPERINI

———

If it was edible, Louie stole it. Housewives who stepped from their kitchens returned to find their suppers gone. Residents looking out their windows saw a long-legged boy dashing by, a stolen cake balanced on his hands. He broke into his neighbors' house, bribed their Great Dane with a bone, and cleaned out their icebox. He picked the lock at the town bakery, snatched pies, ate until he was full, and used the rest as ammunition for ambushes.

Years later, when Louie told of his youth, most of his stories ended with ". . . then I ran like *mad*." People he robbed often chased him, and some threatened to shoot him. To minimize the evidence found on him when the police habitually came his way, he set up loot-stashing sites, including a cave he dug in the forest. Louie's older brother, Pete, once found one of his stolen wine jugs under the Torrance High bleachers. It was teeming with drunken ants.

In the Torrance Theater lobby, Louie crammed the pay-phone coin slots with toilet paper, then returned later to feed wire behind the coins stacked up inside, hook the paper, and fill his palms with change. A metal dealer never guessed that the grinning kid who often came by to sell him copper scrap had stolen the same scrap from his lot the night before. Discovering, while scuffling with an enemy, that adults would give quarters to fighting kids to pacify them, Louie declared a truce with the enemy and cruised around staging brawls.

When a teacher stood Louie in a corner for spitballing, he deflated her car tires. He set a Boy Scout state record in friction fire ignition by mixing his tinder with gasoline and match heads, causing a small explosion. He stole a neighbor's coffee percolator tube, set up a sniper's nest in a tree, spat pepper tree berries through the tube, and sent girls running.

His greatest feat became legend. Late one night, Louie climbed a church steeple, tied piano wire to the bell, strung the wire into a nearby tree, and roused the police, firefighters, and all of Torrance with apparently spontaneous pealing. Some townsfolk called it a miracle.

During a raucous childhood, Louie made more than just mischief. He shaped who he'd become. Confident that he was clever and bold enough to escape anything, he was almost incapable of discouragement. When history carried him into war, this resilient optimism would define him.

———

Louie was two years younger than his brother, who was everything he wasn't. Pete Zamperini was handsome, popular, and silky smooth with girls. He ushered his mother into her seat at dinner, went to bed at seven, and rose at two-thirty to run a three-hour paper route, tucking his alarm clock under his pillow so it wouldn't wake Louie, who shared a bed with him. He had a gallant habit of carrying pins in his pant cuffs, in case his dance partner's dress strap broke. He once saved a drowning girl. Pete radiated a gentle authority that led everyone, even adults, to be swayed by his opinion. Louie idolized Pete, who watched over him and their younger sisters, Sylvia and Virginia, with a parent's protectiveness. But he was overshadowed, and he never heard the end of it, even from his mother, who wept as she asked Louie why he couldn't be like Pete.

Louie didn't fit in with other kids. He was a puny boy, and thanks to the lingering effects of his pneumonia, in picnic footraces, every girl in town could dust him. His earlobes leaned off his head like holstered pistols, and above them waved the riotous hair that mortified him. He tried to smooth it with his aunt Margie's hot iron, hobbled it in a stocking every night, and slathered it in so much olive oil that flies trailed him around. It did no good.

Then there was his ethnicity. In Torrance in the 1920s, there was so much prejudice against Italians that when the Zamperinis arrived, the neighbors petitioned the city council to keep them out. Louie, who knew little English until grade school, couldn't hide his heritage. He survived kindergarten by keeping quiet, but in first grade, when he blurted out an Italian insult at another kid, his teachers caught on. They deepened his misery by holding him back a grade.

He was a marked boy. Bullies pummeled him with rocks, taunted him, punched him, and kicked him. He could have run away, but he refused to bend. "You could beat him to death," said Sylvia, "and he wouldn't say 'ouch' or cry." He just put his hands in front of his face and took it.

———

As Louie neared his teens, he took a hard turn. He pretended to be tough but was secretly tormented. Frustrated by his inability to defend himself, he made a study of it. His father taught him how to punch and made him a barbell from lead-filled coffee cans welded to a pipe. The next time a bully came at Louie, he ducked left and swung his right fist straight into the boy's mouth. The bully shrieked, his tooth broken, and fled. On his walk home, Louie felt light as air.

Louie's temper grew shorter, his skills sharper. He socked a girl. He pushed a teacher. He pelted a policeman with rotten tomatoes. Kids who crossed him wound up with fat lips, and bullies learned to give him a wide berth.

Louie's father, Anthony, was at wits' end, but his forceful spankings did no good. Louie's mother, Louise, took a different tack. Louie was a copy of her, right down to the vivid blue eyes. She loved mischief and understood Louie's restiveness, and when pushed, she shoved. One Halloween, she dressed as a boy and raced around town with Louie and Pete. A gang of kids, thinking she was one of the local toughs, tackled her and tried to steal her pants. Little Louise Zamperini, mother of four, was deep in the melee when the cops picked her up for brawling.

Knowing that punishing Louie would only arouse his defiance, Louise tried bribing a soft boy named Hugh, giving him pie in exchange for information on Louie. Louise suddenly knew everything Louie was up to, and her children thought she was psychic. Sure that Sylvia was snitching, Louie chased her around the block and into their father's shed. When Louie flushed her out by feeding his pet snake into the crawl space, Sylvia locked herself in the car and didn't come out until nightfall.

For all her efforts, Louise couldn't tame Louie. He ran away and wandered for days, sleeping under a highway overpass. Eventually, he limped home with a gashed knee, having tried to ride a steer in a pasture and gotten tossed into a tree. Twenty-seven stitches didn't reform him. He punched a kid so hard he broke his nose. He upended another boy and stuffed paper towels in his mouth. Parents forbade their kids to go near him. A farmer, furious over Louie's robberies, loaded his shotgun with rock salt and blasted him in the tail. Louie beat one boy so badly, leaving him unconscious in a ditch, that he was afraid he'd killed him. When Louise saw the blood on Louie's fists, she burst into tears.

As Louie entered Torrance High, he was looking less like a mischievous kid and more like a dangerous young man. High school would surely be the end of his education. There was no money for college; Anthony's paycheck always ran out before week's end, forcing Louise to improvise meals with eggplant, milk, stale bread, and rabbits Louie and Pete shot. Louie's job prospects were poor. The Depression had come, and nearly a quarter of Americans were unemployed. Louie had no ambitions. If asked what he wanted to do with his life, he would have said, "Be a cowboy."

In the 1930s, a fake science known as eugenics was gaining a mass follow-ing. By preventing "unfit" people from having children, eugenicists believed, the human race would be strengthened. Along with the "feebleminded," in-sane, and criminal, the unfit included orphans, the disabled, and the poor. Some eugenicists advocated killing undesirables, and in mental hospitals, scores of patients were quietly done away with. At one mental hospital, pa-tients were given milk from cows infected with tuberculosis, in the belief that the unfit would perish. Some forty percent of patients died. A more popular tool of eugenics was forced sterilization, a surgical procedure that rendered patients unable to have children. The State of California would ultimately sterilize about twenty thousand people.

When Louie was in his early teens, a local kid was mistakenly deemed feebleminded by state authorities, institutionalized, and barely saved from sterilization by a frantic legal effort by his parents. As a chronic troublemaker, a failing student, and a suspect Italian, Louie knew he was just the sort of rogue eugenicists would want to cull. Suddenly understanding what he was risking, he felt deeply shaken.

He tried to do better. He scrubbed the kitchen floor, but Louise assumed Pete had done it. He baked biscuits and gave them away. He doled out nearly everything he stole.

Each attempt Louie made to right himself ended wrong. At night, he'd lie awake, feeling snared on something, unable to kick free. Far away, he heard the beckoning whistles of trains. Lost in longing, Louie imagined himself on a train, rolling away, growing smaller until he disappeared.

CHAPTER 2

Run Like Mad

The rehabilitation of Louie Zamperini began with a key.

It was 1931, and Louie was fourteen. While in a locksmith's shop, he heard someone say if you put any key in any lock, it has a one in fifty chance of fitting. Inspired, he began collecting keys and trying locks. He had no luck until he tried his house key on the back door of the Torrance High gym. When basketball season began, no one understood why the stands were full when so few tickets had been sold. Finally, someone discovered Louie sneaking kids in the back door. Louie was hauled to the principal, who punished him by barring him from athletic and social activities. Louie, who never joined anything, was indifferent.

Pete headed straight to the principal. Louie craved attention, Pete told him, but had never won it in the form of praise, so he sought it in the form of punishment. If Louie was recognized for doing something right, he'd turn his life around. Pete asked the principal to let Louie join a sport. When the principal refused, Pete asked if he could live with allowing Louie to fail. It was a cheeky thing for a boy to say to his principal, but Pete was the one kid who could get away with such a remark. The principal gave in.

Pete had big plans for Louie. A senior in 1931–32, Pete was a track star,

Louie at the 1933 UCLA two-mile cross-country race. COURTESY OF LOUIS ZAMPERINI

having set the school's mile record of 5:06. Watching Louie, whose getaway speed was his saving grace, Pete thought he saw the same talent. He wanted to make a runner out of him.

In the end, it wasn't Pete who got Louie onto a track. It was Louie's weakness for girls. In February, some girls began assembling a team for an interclass track meet, and long-legged Louie looked like he could run. The girls worked their charms, and Louie found himself on the track, barefoot. When everyone ran, he followed, churning along with jimmying elbows. As he labored home last, he heard tittering. Gasping and humiliated, he ran straight off the track and hid under the bleachers. The coach muttered that that kid belonged anywhere but in a footrace.

From then on, Pete was all over Louie, herding him out to train and riding his bike behind him, whacking him with a stick. Resentful, Louie dragged his feet, bellyached, and quit. Pete made him keep going. He entered Louie in races, and Louie started winning.

Pete was right about Louie's talent, but being forced to run made Louie defiant. At night he listened to the train whistles, and one day in the summer of 1932, he couldn't bear it any longer.

————

It began over a chore Louie's father asked him to do. Louie resisted, a spat ensued, and Louie threw clothes into a bag and stormed toward the front door. His parents ordered him to stay; Louie was beyond persuasion. As he walked out, his mother rushed to the kitchen and emerged with a sandwich. Louie stuffed it in his bag and left. He was on the front walk when he heard his name called. When he turned, there was his father, grim-faced, two dollars in his outstretched hand. It was a lot of money for a man whose pay didn't last the week. Feeling a swell of guilt, Louie took it and walked away.

He rounded up a friend, and together they hitchhiked to Los Angeles, broke into a car, and slept on the seats. The next day, they jumped a train, climbed onto the roof, and rode north.

The trip was a nightmare. The boys got locked in a boxcar so hot they were frantic to escape. Louie found a metal bar, climbed on his friend's shoulders, pried open a roof vent, squirmed out, and helped his friend through. Then they were discovered by the railroad detective, who forced them to jump from the moving train at gunpoint. For several days, they walked. One night as they sat in a rail yard, filthy, sunburned, shivering, and wet, sharing a stolen can of beans, Louie remembered the money in his father's hand, the fear in his mother's eyes as she gave him a sandwich. He stood up and headed home.

When Louie came in the door, Louise threw her arms around him, led him to the kitchen, and gave him a cookie. Anthony came home, saw Louie, and sank into a chair, his face soft with relief. Louie went upstairs, dropped into bed, and whispered his surrender to Pete. He was going to be a runner, and he was going to go all out.

———

In the summer of 1932, Louie did almost nothing but run. On a friend's invitation, he went to a cabin in California's high desert. Each morning, he rose with the sun, picked up his rifle, and jogged into the sagebrush. He ran over hills, over the desert, through gullies. He chased bands of horses, trying in vain to snatch a fistful of mane and swing aboard. On his run back each afternoon, he shot a rabbit for supper. In the morning he rose to run again. For the first time in his life, he wasn't running from something or to something, not for anyone or in spite of anyone; he ran because it was what his body wished to do. All he felt was peace.

He came home with a mania for running. On Pete's orders, he ran everywhere. He ran his entire paper route for the *Torrance Herald*, to and from school, and to the beach and back, veering onto neighbors' lawns to hurdle bushes. He gave up drinking and smoking. To expand his lung capacity, he ran to a public pool, dove to the bottom, grabbed the drain plug, and floated there, hanging on a little longer each time. Eventually, he could stay underwater for three minutes and forty-five seconds. People kept jumping in to save him.

He also found a role model. Track was hugely popular, and its elite performers were household names. Among them was Kansas University miler Glenn Cunningham. As a boy, Cunningham was in a schoolhouse explosion,

Louie with friends at the beach. Courtesy of Virginia Bowersox Weitzel

and his lower body was burned so badly that a month and a half passed before he could sit up. Once he could stand, he pushed himself about by leaning on a chair, his legs floundering. Eventually, hanging off the tail of a horse named Paint, he began to run, a gait that initially caused him excruciating pain. In a few years, he was racing, obliterating his opponents by the length of a homestretch. By 1932, he was a national sensation, soon to be acclaimed the greatest miler in American history. Louie had his hero.

In the fall of 1932, Pete entered Compton, a tuition-free junior college, where he became a star runner. In the afternoons, he commuted home to coach Louie, perfecting his stride and teaching him strategy. Pete thought the sprints Louie had been running were too short. He'd be a miler, just like Cunningham.

In California, winter-born kids started new grades in January. In the first days of 1933, just before he turned sixteen, Louie began tenth grade. When the track season began, he set out to see what training had done for him. Competing in black silk shorts that his mother had made from a skirt, he won an 880-yard race, breaking the school record, co-held by Pete, by more than two seconds. A week later, he ran a field of milers off their feet, stopping the watches in 5:03, three seconds faster than Pete's record. Week after week, he kept winning, and getting faster. By late April, his mile time was down to 4:42. "Boy! oh boy! oh boy!" read a local paper. "Can that guy fly? Yes, this means that Zamperini guy!"

Louie streaked through the season unbeaten and untested. When he ran out of high schoolers to whip, he took on Pete and thirteen other college runners in a two-mile race at Compton. Though he'd never even trained at the distance, he won by fifty yards. Next he tried the two-mile in UCLA's Southern California Cross-Country meet. Running so effortlessly he couldn't feel

Louie wins the 1933 UCLA two-mile cross-country race by more than a quarter of a mile. Pete is running up from behind to greet him. COURTESY OF LOUIS ZAMPERINI

his feet touching the ground, he took the early lead and kept pulling away. At the halfway point, he was an eighth of a mile ahead, and observers began speculating on when the boy in the black shorts would collapse. Louie didn't collapse. After he flew past the finish, rewriting the course record, he looked back. None of the other runners was even in sight. Louie had won by more than a quarter of a mile.

He felt as if he would faint, but it wasn't from exertion. It was from the realization of what he was.

Louie and Pete. Bettmann/Corbis

CHAPTER 3

The Torrance Tornado

It happened every Saturday. Louie went to the track, limbered up, lay in the infield visualizing his coming race, then walked to the line, awaited the pop of the gun, and sprang away. Pete dashed around the infield, yelling instructions. When Pete gave the signal, Louie stretched out his legs and opponents scattered behind him. Louie glided over the line, Pete tackled him, and the kids in the bleachers cheered and stomped. Louie won so many wristwatches, the traditional prize of track, that he handed them out all over town.

Louie's supreme high school moment came in the 1934 Southern California Track and Field Championship. Running in the best field of high school milers ever assembled, he routed them all and smoked the mile in 4:21.3, shattering the national high school record. His main pursuer so exhausted himself that he had to be carried from the track. A reporter predicted that Louie's record would stand for twenty years. It stood for nineteen.

Once his hometown's archvillain, Louie was now a superstar, and Torrance forgave him everything. The *Los Angeles Times* was striped with stories on the "Torrance Tornado." Rumor had it that the *Torrance Herald* insured Louie's legs for $50,000. Torrancers carpooled to his races and

Louie shatters the national high school mile record at the 1934 Southern California Track and Field Championship. COURTESY OF LOUIS ZAMPERINI

crammed the grandstands. Embarrassed, Louie asked his parents not to come. Louise snuck to the track fence anyway but got so nervous she covered her eyes.

Not long ago, Louie's aspirations had been satisfied by robbing kitchens. Now, he latched on to a wildly ambitious goal: qualifying for the 1936 Olympics in Berlin. The Games had no mile race, so milers ran 1,500 meters, a little short of a mile. It was a seasoned man's game; most milers peaked in their mid to late twenties. The 1,500-meter favorite was Glenn Cunningham, who set the mile world record, 4:06.7, just after Louie set the high school record. At the '36 Games, Cunningham would be almost twenty-seven, and wouldn't peak until he was twenty-eight. In 1936, Louie would be only nineteen.

But Louie was improving so quickly, he'd lopped a staggering forty-two seconds off his mile time in two years. Track experts thought he might be the exception to the rule, and after he went undefeated in his senior season, their confidence was strengthened. Louie and Pete believed he could make the team. Louie wanted to run in Berlin more than he'd ever wanted anything.

In December 1935, Louie graduated from high school, and days later rang in 1936 with his thoughts full of Berlin, seven months away. He was buried in college scholarship offers. Pete, now at the University of Southern California, urged Louie to choose USC but delay entry until fall so he could train. Louie moved into Pete's frat house and, with Pete coaching him, trained obsessively for Berlin.

Louie's track shoes. In these shoes, he never lost a race.
PHOTO BY DAVID MACKINTOSH

By spring, he realized he wasn't going to make it. Though he was getting faster every day, he couldn't force his body to improve quickly enough to catch his 1,500 meter rivals by summer. He was simply too young. He was heartbroken.

In May, Louie was leafing through a newspaper when he saw a story on the Compton Open, a prestigious track meet to be held on May 22. The headliner in the 5,000 meters was twenty-six-year-old Norman Bright, America's second-fastest 5,000-meter man, behind Don Lash, a twenty-three-year-old record-smashing machine. America would send three 5,000-meter men to Berlin, and Lash and Bright were considered locks. Pete urged Louie to enter Bright's race. "If you stay with Norman Bright," he said, "you make the Olympic team."

The idea was a stretch. The mile was four laps; the 5,000 was more than twelve—three miles and 188 yards. Louie had only twice raced beyond a mile, and the 5,000, like the mile, was dominated by much older men. He had only two weeks to train, and with the Olympic trials in July, two months to become America's youngest elite 5,000 man. But he had nothing to lose. He trained so hard his foot bled.

The race was a barnburner. Louie and Bright flew off, leaving the field far behind. Lap after lap, they dueled, trading the lead and sending roars through the crowd. They turned into the final homestretch together, and with the crowd screaming, finished almost dead even. In the fastest 5,000 run in America in 1936, Bright had won by a glimmer.

In June, after Louie performed brilliantly in two more 5,000s, an invitation to the Olympic trials arrived. His Berlin dream was on again.

———

On July 3, 1936, residents of Torrance gathered to see Louie off to the Olympic trials in New York. They gave him a wallet and traveling money, a train ticket, and a suitcase emblazoned with the words TORRANCE TORNADO. Fearing the suitcase made him look brash, Louie discreetly stuck adhesive tape over the nickname, then set off. He spent the journey introducing himself to every pretty girl on the train.

The suitcase presented to Louie by the city of Torrance upon his departure for the 1936 Olympics. PHOTO BY DAVID MACKINTOSH

When the train doors opened in New York, Louie felt he was walking into an inferno. It was the hottest summer on record in America, and New York was especially hard hit. In 1936, air-conditioning was a rarity, found only in a few theaters and department stores, so escape was nearly impossible. That week, the heat would kill three thousand Americans, forty of them in New York, where it hit 106 degrees.

In spite of the heat, Louie had to train. Sweating profusely day and night, training in the sun, unable to sleep in the heat, virtually every athlete lost a huge amount of weight. By one estimate, no athlete lost less than ten pounds. One virtually moved into an air-conditioned theater, buying tickets to movies and sleeping through every showing. Louie was as miserable as everyone else. His weight fell precipitously.

The prerace newspaper coverage riled him. Don Lash was considered unbeatable. Bright was pegged for second. Louie wasn't mentioned. He was daunted by Lash, but the first three runners would go to Berlin, and he believed he could be among them. "If I have any strength left from the heat," he wrote to Pete, "I'll beat Bright and give Lash the scare of his life."

The trials were held at a stadium on New York's Randall's Island. It was just short of ninety in the city, but the stadium was much hotter, probably far over a hundred degrees. Everywhere, athletes were keeling over and being carted to hospitals. Louie waited for his race under a scalding sun that, he later said, "made a wreck of me."

At last, the men were told to line up. The gun cracked, and the race was on. Lash bounded to the lead with Bright in pursuit. Louie dropped back.

In the Zamperini house, a throng crouched around the radio. They were in agony. Louie's start time had passed, but the announcer was lingering on the swimming trials. Pete was so frustrated he considered putting his foot through the radio. At last, the announcer listed the positions of the 5,000-meter runners. He didn't mention Louie. Overwhelmed, Louise fled to the kitchen.

Lash and Bright led the runners through laps seven, eight, nine. Louie hovered midpack, waiting to make his move. The heat was suffocating. One runner collapsed, and the others hurdled him. Another dropped, and they jumped him, too. Louie could feel his feet cooking as the spikes on his shoes conducted heat up from the track. Bright's feet were burning particularly badly. In terrible pain, he took a staggering step off the track and twisted his ankle, then lurched back on. Louie passed him, and he had no resistance to offer.

As the runners entered the final lap, Louie accelerated, closing in on Lash. Looking at the bobbing head of the mighty Don Lash, Louie felt intimidated. For several strides, he hesitated. Then he saw the last curve ahead. He opened up as fast as he could go.

Louie and Lash at the finish line at the 1936 Olympic trials. Courtesy of Louis Zamperini

Banking around the turn, Louie drew alongside Lash, and the two ran side by side down the homestretch. Neither man had any more speed to give, and neither could get past the other. Exhausted, straining, with heads thrown back and legs moving in sync, they hit the line together.

The announcer's voice echoed across the living room in Torrance. Zamperini, he said, had won.

In the kitchen, Louise heard the crowd in the next room suddenly shout. Outside, car horns honked; the front door swung open and neighbors gushed in. As a crush of hysterical Torrancers celebrated around her, Louise wept happy tears. Anthony poured wine and sang out toasts. Louie's voice came over the airwaves, calling a greeting to Torrance.

The announcer was mistaken. The judges ruled Lash the winner. The announcer corrected himself, but it hardly dimmed the revelry in Torrance.

A few minutes later, Louie stood under a cold shower. His feet were burned, the marks following the patterns of his spikes. After drying off, he weighed himself. He'd sweated off three pounds.

Norman Bright was slumped on a bench, staring at his foot. It, like the other one, was burned so badly that the skin had peeled off. He'd finished fifth.

By day's end, Louie had received some 125 telegrams. `Torrance Has Gone Nuts`, read one. `Village Has Gone Screwy`, read another. There was even one from the Torrance police, who must have been relieved that someone else was chasing Louie.

Louie pored over photos of his race in the evening papers. In some, he appeared tied with Lash; in others, he appeared to be in front. On the track, he'd felt sure he'd won. The top three finishers would go to Berlin, but Louie felt cheated nonetheless.

As Louie studied the papers, the judges were reviewing photos and a film of the 5,000. Later, Louie telegrammed the news home: `Judges called it a tie. . . . Will run harder in Berlin.`

The Zamperinis' house was packed with well-wishers and newsmen. Anthony drank toasts until four in the morning. Pete walked around to back slaps. "Am I ever happy," he wrote to Louie. "I have to go around with my shirt open so that I have enough room for my chest."

Louie Zamperini was going to compete in the Olympics in an event he'd run only four times. He was the youngest distance runner to ever make the team.

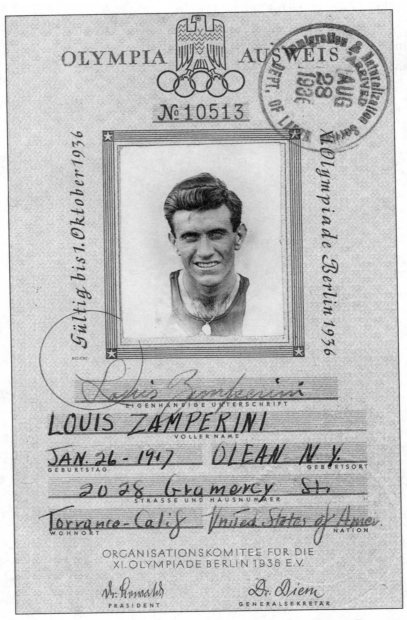

OLYMPIA AUSWEIS

№ 10513

Gültig bis 1. Oktober 1936

XI. Olympiade Berlin 1936

Louis Zamperini
EIGENHÄNDIGE UNTERSCHRIFT

LOUIS ZAMPERINI
VOLLER NAME

JAN. 26 - 1917   OLEAN N.Y.
GEBURTSTAG   GEBURTSORT

2028 Gramercy St.
STRASSE UND HAUSNUMMER

Torrance - Calif.   United States of Amer.
WOHNORT   NATION

ORGANISATIONSKOMITEE FÜR DIE
XI. OLYMPIADE BERLIN 1936 E.V.

Dr. Lewald   *Dr. Diem*
PRÄSIDENT   GENERALSEKRETÄR

COURTESY OF LOUIS ZAMPERINI

CHAPTER 4

Plundering Germany

The ship bearing the Olympic team to Germany wasn't long at sea before Louie began stealing. In his defense, it wasn't he who started it. Self-conscious about being a teenaged upstart, he at first curbed his coltish impulses and began growing a mustache. But he soon noticed that practically everyone was "souvenir collecting." The mustache was abandoned, and Louie joined the other lightfingers in denuding the ship.

On pitching seas, training was chaotic. Basketball players did passing drills on deck, but the wind kept jettisoning the balls into the Atlantic. The water in the ship's pool sloshed back and forth violently, and big swells heaved the water, and everyone in it, onto the deck, so the coaches tied the swimmers to the wall. Gymnasts fell off their apparatuses; fencers lurched all over the ship. Louie and the other runners trotted around, dodging deck chairs. In high seas, they all staggered in one direction, then the other.

For a poor kid accustomed to stale bread and milk for breakfast, the ship was paradise. Food and beverages were everywhere, in amazing abundance. Louie devoured everything. In the dining room, he plowed through anything the seasick athletes couldn't stomach. Discovering a shot-putter with a tiny appetite, he began sitting with him, dropping onto his plate like a vulture the moment the shot-putter was full. On the first-class deck, he found a window in which pints of beer kept magically appearing. He made them magically disappear.

One night, Louie jotted down what he'd just eaten:

> 1 pint of pineapple juice
>
> 2 bowls of beef broth
>
> 2 sardine salads
>
> 5 rolls
>
> 2 tall glasses of milk
>
> 4 small sweet pickles
>
> 2 plates of chicken
>
> 2 helpings of sweet potatoes
>
> 4 pieces of butter
>
> 3 helpings of ice cream with wafers
>
> 3 chunks of angel food cake with white frosting
>
> 1½ pounds of cherries
>
> 1 apple
>
> 1 orange

"Biggest meal I ever ate in my life," he wrote. "Where it all went, I don't know."

He soon found out. When the ship docked, a doctor weighed Louie. In nine days, he'd gained twelve pounds.

———

The Olympic village was breathtaking. Nestled among forests and lakes were 140 beautiful cottages, a shopping mall, a barbershop, a post office, a dentist's office, a sauna, training facilities, and dining halls. A new technology called television was on exhibit. Imported animals bounded over wooded trails. Someone wondered aloud where the storks were. The next day, two hundred storks appeared.

Louie and the other Olympians were driven through Berlin for the opening ceremonies. Adolf Hitler and his militaristic, ferociously anti-Semitic Nazi party were in power, and their presence was everywhere. Swastikas papered the city. Soldiers drilled, and military gliders swooped over oceans of uniformed kids called Hitler Youth. Gypsies and Jewish students had vanished—the Gypsies dumped in camps, the Jews confined to the University of Berlin campus. The only visible sign of discord was the broken glass in the windows of Jewish businesses.

Entering the Olympic stadium, the athletes were treated to a thunderous show culminating in the release of twenty thousand doves. With the birds circling in panicked confusion, cannons fired, prompting the startled birds to relieve themselves in a shower over the athletes. Louie stood at attention, shaking with laughter.

———

As Louie prepared for his race, he knew he had no shot at a medal. It wasn't just that he was almost pudgy from idleness and overeating. Few nations dominated an Olympic event as Finland did the 5,000. Finn Lauri Lehtinen, the 1932 gold medalist, was back, along with his swift teammates Gunnar Höckert and Ilmari Salminen. Louie was too young and green to beat the Finns. His day would come, he believed, in the 1,500 in 1940.

One of two playing cards Pete mailed to Louie at the Olympics. "Let's see you storm through as the best in the deck," it reads. "If the joker does not appeal to you, throw it away and keep this for good luck. Pete." PHOTO BY DAVID MACKINTOSH

An envelope arrived from Pete. Inside were two playing cards, a joker and an ace. On the joker Pete had written, "Which are you going to be, the joker, which is another word for horse's ass, or the TOPS: Ace of spades . . . Take your choice!" On the ace he'd written, "Let's see you storm through as the best in the deck."

On August 7, Louie lay in the Olympic stadium infield, readying himself for his race. One hundred thousand spectators ringed the track. Louie was terrified. He buried his face in the grass, inhaling deeply, trying to settle his nerves. When the time came, he walked to the starting line, bowed forward, and waited.

At the sound of the gun, Louie's body, electric with nervous energy, wanted to bolt, but Louie made a conscious effort to relax. As the pacesetters surged forward, he kept his stride short. Don Lash emerged with the lead, the three Finns behind him. Louie settled into the second tier of runners.

Louie smelled a sickening odor—the hair pomade of a runner ahead. Feeling nauseous, he slowed, letting the pomaded runner pull away. The laps wound by, and Louie kept losing ground. Lash and the Finns were slipping out of reach, and Louie wanted to go with them, but his body felt heavy. He slipped to twelfth.

Louie's Olympic number.
PHOTO BY DAVID MACKINTOSH

Louie, #751, runs in the Olympic 5,000-meter final.

Ahead, the Finns sidled into Lash, roughing him up. On the eighth lap, Salminen rammed his elbow into Lash's chest. Lash folded abruptly, in evident pain. The Finns bounded away. They entered the eleventh lap together, looking to sweep the medals. Then, for an instant, they strayed too close. Their legs tangled, and Salminen fell heavily to the track. His race, like Lash's, was lost.

Louie saw none of it. He passed Lash, but it meant little. He was tired and so far behind. Then he found himself thinking of something Pete once said: *A lifetime of glory is worth a moment of pain*. Louie thought: *Let go*.

With one lap to go, Louie fixed his eyes on the gleaming head of the pomaded runner, far ahead. He began a dramatic acceleration. Around the turn and down the backstretch, Louie kicked, his legs reaching and pushing, his speed dazzling. One by one, runners came up ahead and faded behind.

As Louie flew around the last bend, Höckert had already won. Louie wasn't watching him. He was chasing the glossy head, still distant. He heard a roar and realized the crowd was cheering him on. Even Hitler watched him. Louie ran, Pete's words beating in his head, his whole body burning. The shining hair was distant, then nearer, then so close that Louie again smelled the pomade. With the last of his strength, he threw himself over the line.

Louie had clocked by far the fastest 5,000-meter run by an American in 1936, almost twelve seconds faster than Lash's best for the year. He'd just missed seventh place.

As he bent, gasping, over his spent legs, he marveled at the kick he'd forced from his body. It had felt very, very fast. Two coaches hurried up, gaping at their stopwatches.

In 1930s elite distance running, it was exceptionally rare for a man to run a last lap in 60 seconds, even at a mile. In the 5,000, well over three miles, a final lap in less than 70 seconds was astounding.

Louie had run his last lap in 56 seconds.

———

After cleaning up, Louie climbed into the stands, near Hitler's box. Someone pointed out a ghoulish man and said it was Joseph Goebbels, Hitler's minister of propaganda. Louie, who knew nothing about the Nazis, had never heard of him. He carried his camera to Goebbels and asked if he'd snap Hitler's picture. Goebbels asked his name and event, then took the camera, moved away, snapped a photo, and returned. Hitler, he said, wanted to see him.

Goebbels led Louie to Hitler. The Führer bent from his box, smiled, and offered his hand. Louie had to reach far up. Their fingers barely touched. Hitler spoke. An interpreter translated.

"Ah, you're the boy with the fast finish."

———

Itching to raise hell, Louie donned his Olympic dress uniform and went out with a friend. They prowled bars, sarcastically chirped, *Heil Hitler!* at everyone in uniform, and stole anything they could pry loose. In an automat, they discovered German beer. By the time he finished his second liter, Louie was feeling very brave.

Trolling around Berlin, they stopped at the Chancellery, the building housing Hitler's office. A car pulled up and out stepped Hitler, who walked inside. On the building, Louie spotted a Nazi flag that he thought would make a swell souvenir. The banner didn't yet carry much symbolic meaning for him, or many other Americans, in 1936. Louie just had a hankering to steal in his head and two persuasive liters of beer in his belly.

Watching the guards pacing before the Chancellery, Louie noted that on each pass, there was a point at which both had their backs to the flag. As they turned, Louie ran to the flag and began jumping, trying to grab it. The guards spotted him. Louie took a last leap, snagged the flag's edge, and fell, tearing the banner down with him. He scrambled to his feet and ran like mad.

He heard a *crack!* Looking back, he saw a guard running at him, his gun pointed up, yelling, *"Halten Sie!"* Louie stopped. The guard spun him around, saw his Olympic uniform, hesitated, and asked Louie his name. The one thing Louie knew about Nazis was that they were anti-Semitic, so he gave his name in an exaggeratedly Italian fashion.

The guards summoned an official, who asked Louie why he'd stolen the

Louie in Berlin, 1936. Courtesy of Louis Zamperini

flag. Louie, laying it on thick, said he wanted a souvenir of the happy time he'd had in beautiful Germany. The Germans gave him the flag and let him go.

When the press heard of Louie's adventure, reporters took creative liberties. Louie had "stormed Hitler's palace" to steal the flag in a hail of bullets. Plunging "eighteen feet," he'd raced away, pursued by "two columns" of guards who tackled and beat him. Just as a rifle butt had been about to crush Louie's head, the German army's commander in chief had halted the attack, and Louie had talked the general into sparing his life. In one version, Hitler himself allowed him to keep the flag. Louie had done it all, went the story, to win the heart of a girl.

When Louie arrived in Torrance, he was plunked on a throne and paraded downtown, where four thousand people, whipped up by a band, sirens, and whistles, cheered. Louie shook hands and grinned. "I didn't only start too slow," he joked, "I ran too slow."

As he settled into home, he thought of his future. Running the 1936 Olympic 5,000 at nineteen on four races' experience had been a shot at the moon. Running the 1940 Olympic 1,500 at twenty-three after years of training would be another matter. The same thought was circling Pete's mind: Louie could win gold in 1940.

Officials had just announced which city would host the 1940 Games. Louie shaped his dreams around Tokyo, Japan.

CHAPTER 5

The Red Circle

At USC, Louie spent mornings in class and afternoons training. In the evenings, he and his teammates wedged into his '31 Ford and drove to Torrance for Louise Zamperini's spaghetti. In his spare time, Louie crashed society weddings, worked as a movie extra, and harassed his housemates with practical jokes, replacing their deviled ham with cat food and milk with a laxative. He pursued girls by all means necessary, once landing a date by hurling himself into a girl's car, then pretending to have been struck.

On the track, he was unstoppable. Focused on the 1940 Tokyo Olympics, he smashed record after record. By spring of '38, he'd whittled his mile time down to 4:13.7, some seven seconds off of the world record, which now stood at 4:06.4. "There's the next mile champion," said Glenn Cunningham to reporters one afternoon. "When he concentrates on this distance, he'll be unbeatable." The reporters turned to see who Cunningham was looking at. It was Louie, blushing to the roots of his hair.

In the 1930s, runners were beginning to toss around the idea of a four-minute mile. Most observers, including Cunningham, had long believed it couldn't be done. In 1935, after studying data on human structural limits, Cunningham's legendary coach proclaimed it impossible. The fastest a human could run a mile, he wrote, was 4:01.6.

Pete disagreed. He was certain Louie had a four-minute mile in him. Louie had always laughed this off, but in May of 1938, he reconsidered. His coach forbade him to run hills in the mistaken belief it would damage his heart, but Louie didn't buy the warnings. Every night, he climbed the Los Angeles Coliseum fence and ran the stairs until his legs went numb. By June, his body was humming, capable of speed and stamina beyond anything he'd ever known. He began to think Pete was right, and he wasn't alone. Running experts published articles suggesting Louie could be the first four-minute man. Even Cunningham agreed.

In June, Louie arrived at the National Collegiate Athletic Association (NCAA) Championships in Minneapolis. Gushing with confidence, he babbled to everyone about his training, his strategy, and how he was gunning for four minutes. Word spread that Louie was primed for an epic performance. On the night before the race, a coach visited Louie, his face grim. He said other coaches were ordering their runners to injure Louie. Louie dismissed him, certain no one would do such a thing.

Louie lines up for a start. COURTESY OF LOUIS ZAMPERINI

With a cracked rib and puncture wounds to both legs and one foot, Louie celebrates his record-setting NCAA Championship victory. COURTESY OF LOUIS ZAMPERINI

He was wrong. Halfway through the race, just as Louie was about to take the lead, several runners shouldered in around him, boxing him in. The man beside him swerved and stomped on his foot, impaling Louie's toe with his spike. Then the man in front kicked back, cutting Louie's shins. A third man elbowed Louie's chest so hard, he cracked Louie's rib. The crowd gasped.

Bleeding and in pain, Louie was trapped. For a lap and a half, he ran in the cluster of men, restraining his stride to avoid running into the man ahead. At last, nearing the final turn, he saw a tiny gap. He burst through, sprinted to the lead, and with his shins streaming blood and his chest aching, won easily.

He slowed to a halt, bitter and frustrated. When his coach asked him how fast he thought he'd gone, he said he couldn't have beaten 4:20.

The race time was posted. From the stands came a *wooo!* Louie had run the mile in 4:08.3. It was the fifth fastest outdoor mile ever run, missing the world record by 1.9 seconds. His time would stand as an NCAA record for fifteen years.

Weeks later, Japan withdrew as Olympic host, and the 1940 Games were transferred to Finland. Louie rolled on, winning every race in the 1939 school season. In early 1940, in indoor miles against America's best runners, he was magnificent, twice beating Cunningham and getting progressively faster. In February, he ran a 4:08.2, six-tenths of a second short of the fastest indoor mile ever run. Two weeks later, he scorched a 4:07.9. With the Olympics months away, Louie was peaking at the ideal moment.

———

Far away, history was turning. In Europe, Hitler was preparing to conquer the continent. In Asia, Japan's leaders had designs of equal magnitude. Poor in natural resources, its economy floundering, Japan was struggling to support a growing population. Eyeing their nation's resource-rich neighbors, Japan's leaders saw the prospect of economic independence, and more. Central to the Japanese identity was the belief that the Japanese were mankind's superior race, with the divine right to rule "inferior" Asians. Moved by economic need and a sense of destiny, Japan's leaders planned to conquer the Far East.

For decades, Japan's military-dominated government had been preparing for its quest, crafting a muscular army and navy and, through a military-run school system that violently drilled children on Japan's imperial destiny, shaping its people for war. Most ominously, its army encouraged and celebrated extreme brutality in soldiers.

In the late 1930s, Germany and Japan were ready. In 1937, Japan sent its armies smashing into China. Two years later, Hitler invaded Poland, and war began in Europe. America was pulled into both conflicts: in Europe, its allies lay in Hitler's path; in the Pacific, its ally China was being ravaged by the Japanese, and its territories of Hawaii, Wake, Guam, and Midway, as well as its commonwealth of the Philippines, were threatened. The world was falling into catastrophe.

On a dark day in April 1940, the crisis reached into Louie's life. Hitler and his Soviet allies had unleashed their armies on Europe, and the continent was exploding into total war. Finland was reeling, her Olympic stadium partially collapsed by Soviet bombs. The Olympics had been canceled.

———

Louie spent the summer of 1940 working as an aircraft factory welder and mourning his lost Olympics. America slid toward war. In Europe, Germany was routing America's allies. In the Pacific, Japan was tearing through China and moving into mainland Southeast Asia. To stop Japan, President Franklin Roosevelt declared an embargo—a trade ban—on war-making materials. Soon, he'd declare an oil embargo, freeze Japanese assets in America, and finally ban all trade with Japan. Still Japan stormed onward.

Watching fighter planes soaring over his work hangar, Louie felt a pull. He was still feeling it when Congress passed a bill requiring all young men to

Left: *Louie in military training.* Right: *Louie boarding a training plane in the Army Air Corps.* COURTESY OF LOUIS ZAMPERINI

register for the military draft. Those who enlisted before being drafted could choose their service branch. Louie joined the Army Air Corps. In November 1941, he arrived at a flight school in Houston. The air corps was making him a bombardier.

Early on a Sunday morning a few weeks later, a pilot guided a small plane over the Pacific. Below, a dark sea gave way to a strand of white: waves slapping Hawaii's Oahu Island.

Below, Pearl Harbor, headquarters of the United States Pacific Fleet, was beginning to stir. At Hickam Field, soldiers were washing a car. At the officers' club, men were wrapping up a poker game. In a barracks, two men were having a pillow fight. Outside, a sergeant was peering through a camera lens at his son. Many sailors were sleeping in the warships swaying in the harbor. On the deck of the U.S.S. *Arizona*, men were assembling to raise flags, a Sunday-morning tradition.

Far above them, the pilot sent a flare skidding green across the sky. Behind him, 180 warplanes, emblazoned with Japan's red circle emblem, dove for Pearl Harbor. On the *Arizona*, the men looked up.

In the barracks, one of the men in the pillow fight suddenly collapsed. He was dead, a three-inch hole blown through his neck. His friend ran to a window and saw a building heave upward and crumble down. A dive-bomber had crashed straight into it. There were red circles on its wings.

———

In Texas, Louie was in a theater, watching a matinee. The screen went blank, light flooded the theater, and a man hurried forward. *Is there a fire?* Louie thought.

Servicemen must return to their bases, the man said. Japan has attacked Pearl Harbor.

Louie sat there, eyes wide, mind fumbling. America was at war. He grabbed his hat and ran from the building.

PART

II

B-24 Liberator.

CHAPTER 6

The Flying Coffin

As Japanese planes dove over Oahu, some two thousand miles west, marines were sitting in a tent on Wake Atoll, eating pancakes. The tiny atoll, a strategically critical air base, was home to about five hundred bored American servicemen, mostly marines. Nothing interesting ever happened there. But that morning, as the marines started on their pancakes, a siren began wailing. Soon, the sky was streaked with Japanese bombers, buildings were exploding, and a few startled men found themselves on the front in the Second World War.

All over the Pacific that morning, the story was the same. In less than two hours over Pearl Harbor, Japan mauled America's navy and killed more than 2,400 people. Almost simultaneously, it attacked Thailand, Shanghai, Malaya, the Philippines, Guam, Midway, and Wake. In one day of breathtaking violence, Japan's main onslaught had begun.

In America, invasion was expected at any moment. Less than an hour after Japan bombed Hawaii, mines were laid in San Francisco Bay. In Washington, D.C., the civil defense minister looped around in a police car, sirens blaring, shouting *"Calm!"* into a loudspeaker. At the White House, a butler heard the president speculating on what he'd do if Japanese forces advanced as far as Chicago. First Lady Eleanor Roosevelt wrote to her daughter, urging her to flee the West Coast. In subsequent days, trenches were dug along California beaches, windows across America were draped in blackout curtains, and bridges, tunnels, and factories were put under guard. In Nebraska, citizens were taught to disable firebombs with garden hoses.

Japan galloped over the globe, invading the Philippines, Guam, Burma, Borneo, Rabaul, Hong Kong, Singapore. But Wake wouldn't give in. The Japanese bombed and strafed it for days, then launched a massive invasion attempt. The little group of defenders shoved them back. It wasn't until December 23 that Japan finally captured Wake and the men on it.

For days, the captives were held on the airfield, singing Christmas carols to cheer themselves, as the Japanese made plans to execute them. Then plans were changed. Most captives were forced onto ships, bound for Japan and occupied China as prisoners of war (POWs). Ninety-eight men were kept on Wake. The Japanese enslaved them.

———

In August 1942, Louie graduated from flight school as an officer—a second lieutenant. He drove to Torrance to say goodbye to his family before heading into his final round of training, then to war. Before he left, his family gathered on their front steps for a last photograph. Louie put his arm around his mother, who was fighting back tears. His father rode with him to the train station, crowded with uniformed young men and crying parents. Embracing his father, Louie could feel him shaking.

As his train pulled away, Louie looked back. His father stood with his hand up, a wavering smile on his face. Louie wondered if he'd ever see him again.

———

The train carried him to Ephrata, Washington, where an air base sat in a dry lakebed. The lakebed was determined to bury the base in blowing dirt, and it was succeeding. Men waded through drifts more than a foot deep, all the meals were gritty with sand, and ground crews, which had to replace twenty-four dirt-clogged aircraft engines in twenty-one days, had to spray oil on the taxiways to keep the dust down.

A last family photograph as Louie leaves to go to war. Rear, left to right: *Sylvia's future husband, Harvey Flammer; Virginia, Sylvia, and Anthony Zamperini.* Front: *Pete, Louise, and Louie.* COURTESY OF LOUIS ZAMPERINI

Louie was standing in the dust, sweating, when a man walked up and introduced himself. He was Russell Allen Phillips. He would be Louie's pilot.

The son of an Indiana pastor, Phillips was small, built like a fireplug. A gentle, generous-hearted young man, he was so quiet he could be in a room for hours before anyone noticed him. He had one consuming passion. Back home, where everyone called him Allen, he'd met a girl from the church choir, Cecy Perry. She had a curvy figure, a buoyant disposition, a quick mind, and a

Russell Allen Phillips (Phil). Courtesy of Karen Loomis

Phil's crew. Left to right: Phillips, temporary copilot Gross, Zamperini, Mitchell, Douglas, Pillsbury, and Glassman. Moznette, Lambert, and Brooks are not pictured.

COURTESY OF LOUIS ZAMPERINI

family cat named Chopper. At a prom in Terre Haute, Allen kissed Cecy. He was a goner, and so was she.

On a Saturday night in November 1941, when he left for the air corps, Phillips spent five last minutes with Cecy at the Indianapolis train station. When the fighting was over, he promised, he'd make her his bride.

In Ephrata, Louie and Phillips became best friends. Phillips floated along in Louie's chatty good humor; Louie liked Phillips's quiet, kind steadiness. He called Louie "Zamp"; Louie called him "Phil." They never had an argument and were almost never apart.

The rest of Phil's bomber crew assembled. The top turret gunner and engineer was Stanley Pillsbury. The other engineer was Clarence Douglas, who manned one of the two waist guns behind the wings. The navigator and nose gunner was Robert Mitchell. Frank Glassman was the belly gunner.

The Flying Coffin • 53

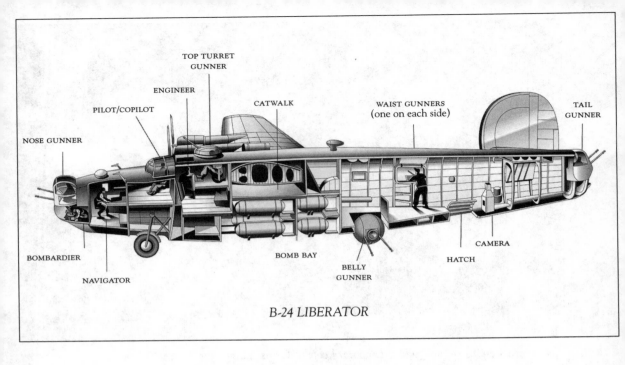

TOP TURRET
GUNNER

ENGINEER

PILOT/COPILOT

CATWALK

WAIST GUNNERS
(one on each side)

TAIL
GUNNER

NOSE GUNNER

BOMBARDIER

NAVIGATOR

BOMB BAY

BELLY
GUNNER

HATCH

CAMERA

B-24 LIBERATOR

Ray Lambert was the tail gunner. The radioman and second waist gunner was Harry Brooks. The copilot was George Moznette, Jr. Together, they'd be crew No. 8 in the nine-crew 372nd Bomb Squadron.

All the men were bachelors, but Harry Brooks, like Phil, had a steady girl back home. Her name was Jeannette, and she and Harry had set their wedding date for May 8, 1943.

All the crew needed was a plane. Everyone was hoping to be assigned to a B-17, a handsome, fiercely armed, practically indestructible bomber. The plane no one wanted was a giant new plane, Consolidated Aircraft Corporation's B-24 Liberator.

On paper, the B-24 was comparable to the B-17 but for one major edge: it could fly literally all day without refueling. To the men, though, it left much to be desired. Flat-faced and rectangular, it had looks only a nearsighted mother could love. Crews called it "the Flying Brick" and "the Constipated Lumberer," a play on Consolidated Liberator. The cockpit was oppressively cramped. Navigating the narrow catwalk could be difficult; one slip and you'd tumble into the bomb bay, which had fragile aluminum doors that would tear away with the weight of a falling man.

The B-24's wheels had no steering, so when taxiing, the pilot had to coax the bomber along by powering one side's engines, then the other, and working the left and right brakes, one of which was usually more sensitive than the other. The taxiways were a pageant of lurching planes, all of which eventually veered into places nowhere near where their pilots intended them to go, and from which they often had to be dug with shovels.

Flying the B-24, one of the world's heaviest planes, was like wrestling a bear. Because pilots strong-armed the yoke—the control lever—with their

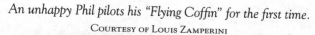

An unhappy Phil pilots his "Flying Coffin" for the first time.
COURTESY OF LOUIS ZAMPERINI

Louie training in the nose gun. All crew members received training in other men's stations.
COURTESY OF LOUIS ZAMPERINI

left hands, they were instantly recognizable when shirtless, because the muscles on their left arms dwarfed those on their right. The plane was so clumsy that it was hard to fly in tight formations without hitting other planes.

It was also plagued with mechanical difficulties. If one of the four engines died, staying airborne was challenging; if two quit, it was an emergency. Early on, there were incidents in which B-24 tails fell off in midair. And the plane had a reputation for frailty, especially in the wings, which could snap off if struck in combat. Some men thought it was a death trap.

When the 372nd squadron's planes flew in, Phil's crew walked out to look. Louie heard someone mutter.

"It's the Flying Coffin."

For the next three months, the crew practically lived in their B-24. They flew in formation, fired at targets, and simulated combat runs. They buzzed so low over Iowa that the propellers kicked up a sandstorm, skinning the paint off the plane's belly and scouring the legs of Pillsbury, sitting by the open tail hatch. Through it all, Louie perched in the glass-windowed "greenhouse" in the nose, bombing with superb proficiency. The squadron's prowess was soon well known. An angry farmer came calling after the 372nd's bombs flattened an outhouse.

Russell Allen Phillips. COURTESY OF LOUIS ZAMPERINI

Phil at the helm of Super Man. COURTESY OF LOUIS ZAMPERINI

Training transformed Louie's crew. They worked together with seamless efficiency, and in the grim business of bombs and bullets, they were the squadron's best crew. The warmest praise would go to Phil. B-24s were built for tall pilots, and though small-statured Phil needed to sit on a cushion to get his feet to the pedals and his eyes over the control panel, he was, in Louie's words, "a damn swell pilot," dealing with adversity with calm, adaptive acceptance.

The surprise of this pliant pilot, Louie would learn, was that in a crisis, Phillips was as brave as they come.

The crew's B-24 had its own personality. It oozed fuel into the bomb bay, inspiring Pillsbury's nervous habit of pacing around, sniffing the air. It loved venting deafening backfires. When nearing empty, the fuel gauges sometimes reported that the plane was magically gaining fuel. But for all its quirks, the plane never failed the men. It was a noble thing, rugged and inexhaustible, and they loved it. They named it *Super Man*.

———

In October 1942, the men packed their bags. Training was over; they were being sent to Oahu, to war. Phil was crestfallen. Cecy was about to come to see him, and they'd spoken of getting married. He'd miss her by three days.

Before he left, Louie sent a package to his mother. In it were airman's wings. Every morning, as she waited for her boy to return, Louise pinned the wings to her dress. Every night, she pinned them to her nightgown.

On November 2, *Super Man* lifted off. Land slid away, and then there was nothing but the Pacific. Its bottom was already littered with downed warplanes and the ghosts of lost airmen. Every day of this long and ferocious war, more would join them.

CHAPTER 7

"This Is It, Boys"

Oahu was still ringing from the Pearl Harbor attack. The roads were pocked with bomb craters. The island was on constant alert for attack or invasion, and so camouflaged, a serviceman wrote, "one sees only about 1/3 of what is actually there." At night, it disappeared; every window had lightproof curtains, every car had covered headlights, and blackout patrols forbade even the striking of a match. Servicemen wore gas masks in hip holsters. Surfers had to worm under barbed wire running along Waikiki Beach.

A dog rides a five-hundred-pound bomb at Hickam Field, Oahu,
site of the Pearl Harbor attack.

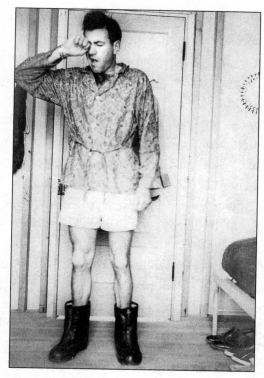

Louie in the Oahu barracks, up late. Courtesy of Louis Zamperini

At Kahuku air base on Oahu's north shore, Louie and Phil were assigned to a barracks with Mitchell, Moznette, twelve other officers, and hordes of mosquitoes. "You kill one," Phil wrote, "and ten more come to the funeral." The barracks, Phil added, looked "like a dozen dirty Missouri pigs have been wallowing on it." The nonstop revelry didn't help. One night, as Louie and Phil wrestled over a beer, they plowed down three wall partitions. When William Matheny, their colonel, saw the wreckage, he grumbled that Zamperini must have been involved.

———

Everyone was eager to fight, but there was no combat. In its place was "sea search"—dull daylong ocean flying patrols overseen by a lieutenant everyone hated. A nitpicker and rank-puller, he was loathed thanks to an incident in which one of *Super Man*'s engines quit in midflight. When Phil returned the plane to base, the furious lieutenant ordered them back up. When Louie offered to fly on three engines if the lieutenant joined them, the lieutenant abruptly changed his mind.

The tedium of sea search made practical joking irresistible. When a ground officer griped about airmen's higher pay, the crew invited him to fly the plane. They sat him in the copilot's seat while Louie hid under the navigator's table, by the yoke control chains. When the officer took the yoke, Louie tugged the chains, making the plane swoop up and down. The officer panicked, Louie smothered laughter, and Phil kept a poker face. The officer quit carping about airmen's pay.

Louie's two most notorious pranks involved Phil, chewing gum, and their new copilot, a massive ex–football player named Charleton Cuppernell, who replaced Moznette when the latter joined another crew. In the first incident, after Cuppernell and Phil swiped his beer, Louie retaliated by jamming gum

Copilot Charleton Hugh Cuppernell.

into the cockpit urine relief tube. On the next flight, the call of nature was followed by an inexplicably brimming urine tube, turbulence, and at least one wet airman. Louie hid in Honolulu to escape punishment.

On another occasion, to get even with Cuppernell and Phil for stealing his gum, Louie replaced it with a laxative variety. Just before a long flight, Cuppernell and Phil each stole three pieces, triple the standard dose. As *Super Man* flew, pilot and copilot, in great distress, made alternating dashes to the back of the plane, yelling for someone to get a toilet bag. When the bags were used up, Cuppernell dropped his pants and hung his enormous rear out the window while four crewmen clung to him to keep him from falling out. When the ground crews saw the results on the plane's tail, they were furious. "It was like an abstract painting," Louie said.

Phil's boredom remedy was hotdogging. Returning from sea search, he'd buzz Oahu so low he could look straight into the first-floor windows of buildings. It was, he said, "kind of daring."

———

On their days off, the crew played poker and divvied up Cecy's care packages, and Louie and Phil tooled around in borrowed cars. Along the way, they came upon several airfields, and were amazed to discover that all the planes and equipment were made of plywood, an elaborate ruse to fool Japanese flying reconnaissance. One day, this information would be very important.

Paradise was the officers' club, where there was beer and pretty girls with ten-thirty curfews. When the crew got the squadron's best gunnery scores, Louie pinned officers' insignia to the enlisted men's uniforms and snuck them in. Just after Louie rose to dance with a girl, Colonel Matheny sat down in his place and began talking to the terrified Clarence Douglas, who was pretending to be a second lieutenant. When Louie ran to Douglas's rescue, the unsuspecting colonel got up and told him what a fine man Douglas was.

On the dance floor, Louie spotted the hated lieutenant who'd ordered them to fly on three engines. He found a bag of flour, recruited a girl, and began dancing near the lieutenant, dropping flour down his collar with each pass. After an hour, the whole club was watching. Louie snagged a glass of water, danced up behind his victim, dumped the water down his shirt, and took off. The lieutenant spun around, his back running with dough. Unable to find the culprit, he stormed out.

Just before Christmas, the crew's hour finally came. Ordered to fly to Midway Island, they were greeted with a case of Budweiser and big news. The Japanese had built a base on Wake Atoll. In the Pacific War's biggest raid yet, America was going to burn it down. It would be a sixteen-hour mission, nonstop, pushing the B-24s as far as they could go. Even with auxiliary fuel tanks, they'd be cutting it extremely close.

Waiting to fly. COURTESY OF LOUIS ZAMPERINI

On December 23, 1942, twenty-six B-24s lifted off of the Midway runway. *Super Man* slipped toward the rear. The planes flew through the afternoon and into night.

At eleven p.m., Phil switched off the outside lights. Clouds closed in. Wake was very close now, but they couldn't see it. In the greenhouse, Louie felt a buzzing in himself, the same sensation he'd felt before races. Ahead, Wake slept.

———

At midnight, Colonel Matheny, piloting the lead plane, broke radio silence.

"This is it, boys."

Matheny sent his bomber plunging out of the clouds, and there was Wake. He barreled toward a string of buildings, hauled the plane's nose up, and yelled to the bombardier.

"When are you going to turn loose those incendiaries?"

"Gone, sir!"

At that instant, the buildings exploded. Behind Matheny, wave after wave of B-24s dove at Wake. The Japanese ran for their guns.

In *Super Man*, well behind and above the leading planes, Louie saw throbs of light in the clouds. As Phil began the plane's dive, Louie opened the bomb bay doors, flipped his bomb switches, and fixed the settings. The orders were to dive to four thousand feet, but when the plane reached that altitude, it was still in clouds. Louie's target was the airstrip, but he couldn't see it. Phil pushed the plane lower, moving at terrific speed. At 2,500 feet, *Super Man* speared through the clouds and Wake stretched out, sudden and brilliant, beneath it.

The islands were a blaze of garish light. Everywhere, bombs were striking targets in mushrooms of fire. Searchlights swung about, their beams reflecting off the clouds and back onto the ground, illuminating scores of Japanese in their sleeping clothes, sprinting in confusion.

To Pillsbury, "every gun in the world" seemed to be firing skyward. Antiaircraft guns lobbed shells over the planes, where they erupted, sending shrapnel showering down. Tracer bullets, emitting color to allow gunners to see where

A bombardier working his bombsight.

they were firing, streaked the air in yellow, red, and green. Watching the clamor of colors, Pillsbury thought of Christmas. Then he remembered: they'd crossed the international date line and passed midnight. It *was* Christmas.

Phil wrestled *Super Man* out of its dive. Louie spotted the taillight of a Japanese Zero fighter plane rolling down the runway. He aimed for it. Very close, something exploded, and *Super Man* rocked. A shell burst by the left wing, another by the tail. Louie loosed a bomb over the Zero, then dropped his five other bombs over bunkers and parked planes.

Relieved of three thousand pounds of bombs, *Super Man* bobbed upward. Louie yelled "Bombs away!" and Phil rolled the plane left, through streams of antiaircraft fire. Louie looked down. His bombs landed in splashes of fire on the bunkers and planes. He missed the Zero but had bull's-eyed the runway. Phil turned *Super Man* back for Midway. Wake was a sea of fire and running men.

As *Super Man* flew for home, Louie realized they had a major problem. The bomb bay doors were stuck open. He climbed back and looked. When

Phil had wrenched the plane out of its dive, the auxiliary fuel tanks had slid into the doors. Nothing could be done. With the open bomb bay dragging against the air, *Super Man* would burn right through its fuel. Given that this mission was stretching the plane's range to the limit, it was sobering news.

They could do nothing but wait. They passed around pineapple juice and sandwiches. Drained, Louie stared at the sky, watching the stars through breaks in the clouds.

Seventy-five miles away from Wake, one of the men looked back. He could see the island burning.

———

As day broke, a general stood by the Midway airstrip, waiting for his bombers, his face furrowed. Fog hung low over the ocean, spilling rain. For the pilots, finding tiny Midway would be difficult, and there was the question of whether their fuel would last long enough.

One plane appeared, then another and another. One by one, they landed, all critically low on fuel. *Super Man* wasn't in sight.

Out in the fog, Phil must have looked at his fuel gauge and known he was in trouble. With his bomb bay open and wind howling through the fuselage, he'd dragged away his fuel. He didn't know if he'd find Midway, and didn't have enough fuel to fly around searching for it. At last, he spotted the island. At that moment, one of *Super Man*'s engines sputtered and died.

Phil nursed the plane along, aiming for the runway. The remaining engines kept turning. At touchdown, a second engine died. Moments later, the other two engines quit. Had the route been only slightly longer, *Super Man* would have hit the ocean. The general came running, smiling. Every plane had made it back.

News of the raid broke, and the airmen were given medals and lauded as heroes. In the *Honolulu Advertiser*, Louie found a cartoon depicting his role in bombing Wake. He clipped it out and tucked it in his wallet.

The men felt cocky. An admiral said Japan might be finished within a year. Phil heard men talking about going home.

"Methinks," he wrote to his mother, "it's a little premature."

The B-24 Stevenovich II *just after being struck by flak. The plane spun several times, then exploded. The radar operator, First Lieutenant Edward Walsh, Jr., was thrown from the plane and managed to open his parachute. He survived. The other crewmen were presumed dead.*

CHAPTER 8

Dying in Droves

Before dawn on January 8, 1943, a B-24 taxied to a beachside runway on Kauai, readying for a training flight. Aboard were *Super Man's* former copilot, George Moznette, and five other officers from Louie and Phil's barracks. The plane lifted off and disappeared in the darkness.

After sunrise, Louie and Phil got the news: the plane was missing. They rushed to Kauai and walked the beach, looking for any sign of their friends. A slip of paper washed ashore. It was a paycheck, made out to Moznette.

Later that morning, the plane was found, lying on the ocean floor just offshore. All ten crewmen were dead.

The plane had barely made it past takeoff, clearing the runway, turning, and slamming into the water. Several men had tried to swim to shore, but sharks had found them. The men were, Louie wrote in his diary, "ripped to pieces."

———

Louie was shaken. He'd been in Hawaii for only two months, yet already several dozen men from his bomb group, including six of the sixteen men in his barracks, were dead.

The first loss came on the flight from the States, when a B-24 vanished.

Then a plane caught fire and crashed, killing four men. Another plane hit a mountain, killing everyone aboard. A bomber crash-landed, killing two. Another exploded in midair. Only three men survived, including one whose hand happened to be resting on a parachute when the blast flung him from the plane. A plane photographing Wake was shot down. Then, Moznette's crash.

These crashes, only one caused by enemy action, weren't unusual. In World War II, some 36,000 Army Air Forces planes were lost in combat and accidents. The surprise is how many were lost in accidents. In 1943 in the region in which Louie served, for every plane lost in combat, some six planes were lost in accidents. In the war, almost 36,000 airmen died in nonbattle situations, the vast majority in accidental crashes.

Often, the culprit was the planes. In January 1943 alone, Louie encountered ten serious mechanical problems in planes in which he flew, including two engine failures and jammed landing gear. Once, *Super Man's* brakes failed on landing. By the time Phil stopped the plane, it was three feet short of the runway's end, which abutted the ocean.

A B-24 that crashed on takeoff.

Many island runways were so short that planes skimmed trees on takeoff.

The tropical weather was another danger. Once, as Phil detoured around a squall, Cuppernell asked if he'd dare fly into it. "I can fly this thing anywhere," Phil said, turning into the storm. It was a near-fatal mistake. *Super Man* was swallowed; wind pivoted it sideways, and it began "porpoising"—swooping up and down like a swimming dolphin—leaving the men clinging to anything bolted down. They'd been at only one thousand feet when they entered the storm. Now, with no visibility and the plane pitching wildly, they didn't know where the ocean was. Each time the plane plunged, the men braced for a crash. Oahu had been in sight a moment before, but now they'd lost all sense of its location. Pillsbury strapped on his parachute.

Radioman Harry Brooks saved them. He found a signal from a Hawaiian station and determined the direction from which it was coming. Phil hauled the plane around and followed the signal home. When they landed, he was exhausted, his shirt wringing wet.

Runways were another problem. Many islands were so small that coral had to be plowed onto one end to create enough length for an airstrip. Even then, runways were often too short. So many planes shot off Funafuti's runway and into the ocean that ground crews kept a bulldozer equipped with a towing cable parked by the water.

For loaded B-24s, which needed well over four thousand feet for takeoff, the cropped island runways, often abutted by towering palm trees, were a challenge. "The takeoff proved exciting," wrote Staff Sergeant Frank Rosynek of one overloaded departure. "The plane lumbered down the runway for an eternity and we could see the hard packed coral through the cracks [in] the bomb bay doors. . . . There was a SWOOSH and pieces of palm fronds suddenly appeared jammed in the cracks, on both sides! . . . Only the laundry knew how scared I was."

Then there was human error. Pilots flew or taxied planes into each other. In B-24s notorious for fuel leaks, airmen lit cigarettes and blew up their planes. Louie was once asked to fill in on a crew, but feeling sick, he declined. On that flight, the tower warned the pilot of a mountain ahead. The pilot said he saw it, then flew right into it. On another flight, when a bomber flew sharply upward, a falling crewman inadvertently grabbed the life raft release handle.

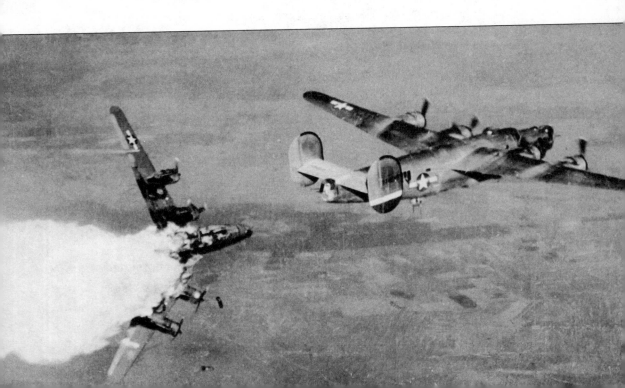

The raft sprang from the roof and wrapped around the plane's tail. Barely able to control the plane, the pilot ordered his men to bail out. Somehow, he landed, and everyone survived.

Finally, there was navigation. Employing a crowd of instruments, navigators groped over thousands of miles of ocean toward tiny islands that were blacked out at night and flat to the horizon. Procedures could be comically primitive: to get sextant readings, one navigator had to stand on a table and dangle out of the roof hatch while a crewman held his legs so he wouldn't be sucked out. Given how difficult navigation was, it's amazing any crews found their destinations. Many didn't.

The risks of flying were compounded in combat, as planes faced enemy fighters and AA (antiaircraft) fire. Bunching together to fend off fighters and hit narrow target islands, planes collided, fired on each other, and worse. In one incident, as three B-24s flew together through a canyon under fire, two of them bumped. The collision sent Lieutenant Robert Strong's bomber under the plane he bumped just as that plane dropped a giant mine. The mine crashed into Strong's plane, tearing an eighteen-square-foot hole in the

A B-24 makes its way through antiaircraft fire.

fuselage, cutting the plane nearly in two. Impossibly, Strong flew the plane eight hundred miles home as a gaping crack advanced up the fuselage and the tail flapped behind. Later, when a pilot pulled on the plane's tail, it nearly came off in his hand.

These combat risks created grim statistics. In World War II, 52,173 airmen were killed in action. A Pacific bomber crewman's tour of duty was just forty missions. His chances of getting killed before he fulfilled it were fifty percent.

———

Stricken Pacific bombers usually came down on water. Every airman had a life vest, called a "Mae West" after the busty movie star. Survivors had to get to rafts immediately, because sharks often arrived in vast numbers almost the moment planes hit. Once, coming upon a crash site, *Super Man*'s crew saw this firsthand. Hundreds of sharks, some of which looked twenty feet long, were swirling around the life rafts, on the verge of overturning them. The survivors were rescued, but the *Super Man* crew was horrified.

In 1943, Louie's USC track teammate, Art Reading, was knocked unconscious as he "ditched" his plane—landed it on water. As the plane sank, Reading's navigator, Everett Almond, pulled Reading out and lashed himself to him. As Reading woke, Almond began towing him toward the nearest island, twenty miles away. Sharks began circling. One swept in, bit Almond's leg, and dove, dragging both men under. Then something gave way and the men surfaced in a pool of blood. Almond's leg had apparently been torn off. He gave his Mae West to Reading, then sank away. For eighteen hours, Reading floated, kicking and hacking at attacking sharks, before a search boat found him.

For good reason, sharks were feared and loathed by airmen. On one island, it was a popular pastime to lure them to jetties with bait tied to long sticks and lob grenades into their mouths. When the sharks snatched the bait, the men would watch them blow up.

———

For downed men, the odds of rescue were very poor. Many crews went down without sending a distress call, so rescuers had no idea where they'd crashed.

Often, the military didn't even learn planes were missing until they failed to land at their destinations, sometimes as long as sixteen hours after the crash. To make things worse, life rafts could drift dozens of miles a day. Because of this, search areas often extended over thousands of square miles.

If searchers did fly near a raft, they likely wouldn't see it. Though search planes generally flew at just one thousand feet, even from that height, rafts could be mistaken for whitecaps. To avoid stalling, many rescue planes had to be flown so fast that crewmen only had a moment to scan each area before it was gone.

The sad truth, known to Louie, Phil, and all other airmen, was that the vast majority of downed men were never found. The improbability of rescue, coupled with the soaring rate of accidental crashes, created a terrible equation. Search planes appear to have been more likely to go down themselves than to find the men they were looking for. It's likely that for every man rescued, several would-be rescuers died.

Hunger, thirst, and exposure depleted raft-bound men with frightening rapidity. Some died in days. Others went insane. In 1942, a bomber crashed in the Pacific, stranding nine men on a raft. Within a few days, one had died, and the rest had gone mad. Two heard music and baying dogs. Two scuffled over an imaginary case of beer. Another shouted curses at a sky he believed was full of bombers. Seeing a boat that wasn't there, he leapt overboard and drowned. When the men were rescued on day seven, they were too weak to wave their arms.

Of all the horrors facing downed men, the one most feared was capture by the Japanese. The roots of this fear lay in an event that occurred in 1937, early in Japan's invasion of China. The Japanese military surrounded the city of Nanking, stranding civilians and 90,000 Chinese soldiers, who surrendered. Japanese officers then issued an order to execute all POWs.

What followed was a six-week frenzy of killing. POWs were beheaded, machine-gunned, bayoneted, and burned alive. The Japanese turned on civilians, staging killing contests, raping tens of thousands of people, mutilating and crucifying them. The Japanese press ran tallies of the killing contests, praising the contestants. Historians estimate that the Japanese murdered between 200,000 and 430,000 Chinese, including the 90,000 POWs, in what became known as the Rape of Nanking.

Every airman knew about Nanking, and since then, Japan had reinforced the precedent. In Louie's squadron, there was a rumor that on a Japanese territory in the Marshall Islands called Kwajalein, POWs were murdered. The men called it "Execution Island." It is testament to the reputation of the Japanese that in one doomed B-24 falling over Japanese forces, only one man bailed out. The rest were so afraid of capture that they chose to die in the crash.

———

For airmen, the risks couldn't be ignored. The dead were their roommates, their friends, the crew flying off their wing ten seconds ago. Men didn't die one by one. A quarter of a barracks perished at once. There were rarely funerals, for there were rarely bodies. Airmen didn't speak of death, but privately, many were tormented by fear.

Before Louie had left the States, he'd been issued a Bible. He tried reading it to soothe his anxiety, but it made no sense to him. He often left Phil sprawled on his bed, penning love letters to Cecy, as he ran off his worries on the mile course he'd measured around the runway. He also tried to prepare for every contingency, even taking an elderly Hawaiian's seminar on fending off sharks. (Open eyes wide, bare teeth, bop shark in nose.)

Phil carried two good-luck charms. One was a bracelet Cecy had given him. Believing it protected him, he wouldn't fly without it. The other was a silver dollar. When he finally ran away with Cecy, he said, he'd use it to tip the bellboy. "When I do get home," he wrote to her, "I'm going to hide with you where no one will find us."

As Oahu's airmen died in droves, a ritual began. When a man was lost, his friends would open his footlocker, take out his liquor, and have a drink in his honor. In a war without funerals, it was the best they could do.

CHAPTER 9

Five Hundred and Ninety-Four Holes

About twenty-five hundred miles southwest of Hawaii sat a lonely little island called Nauru. The world might have left it alone, were it not for what lay under the feet of the grass-skirted natives: phosphate, a central ingredient in armaments. Japan slammed onto Nauru in 1942, violently enslaving the locals to mine phosphate and build a runway. By spring of 1943, the runway was ready, making Nauru an ideal base from which the Japanese could launch air strikes.

On April 17, Louie's crew and twenty-two others were ordered to fly to Funafuti Atoll, the launch point for a strike against Nauru. The pre-mission briefing alarmed Louie: they'd bomb from only eight thousand feet. That week, they'd practiced bombing from that altitude, and the potential of ground fire to butcher them had worried them. Stanley Pillsbury was spooked by another piece of news. There were about a dozen Zero fighter planes defending Nauru. Zeros had a deservedly fearsome reputation. The prospect of twelve of them scared Pillsbury to death.

The next morning, the men walked to *Super Man*. At five a.m., they were airborne.

The planes took six and a half hours to reach Nauru. No one spoke. *Super*

Man led the mass of bombers, flying with a plane on each wing. The sun rose and the planes flew into a clear morning. The Japanese would see them coming.

Navigator Mitchell broke the silence. They'd be over the island in fifteen minutes. In the greenhouse, Louie shivered.

Super Man was the first plane to cross over Nauru. The air was eerily still. Louie's first target, a collection of planes and buildings, appeared below. Louie began lining up on the gleaming planes.

Then, shattering. The sky became a fury of color, sound, and motion as the Japanese gunned skyward. Metal flew everywhere, streaking up from below and raining down from above.

Something struck the bomber to *Super Man*'s left. The plane sank as if drowning. Then the plane to the right fell away. Pillsbury could see the men inside, and his mind briefly registered that they were probably about to die. *Super Man* was alone.

Louie kept his focus below, trying to aim for the parked planes. There was a tremendous *bang!* and a terrific shudder. A dinner table–sized chunk of *Super Man*'s right rudder blew off. Louie lost the target. While he tried to find it, the plane rocked as a shell bit a wide hole in the bomb bay.

At last, Louie had his aim, and the first bombs spun into their targets. Then Louie lined up on a barracks and a gun battery and watched the bombs crunch in. He had one bomb left, to use as he chose. He spotted a shack. The bomb fell, and Louie yelled "Bombs away!" and turned the valve to close the bomb doors. There was a pulse of dazzling light. Louie had made a lucky guess and a perfect drop. The shack was a fuel depot, and he'd struck it dead center. A giant orb of fire billowed upward.

Phil and Cuppernell pushed *Super Man* full-throttle for home. Zeros were suddenly all around, spewing bullets and cannon shells that exploded on contact. They flew at the bombers head-on, cannons firing, slicing between planes, so close Louie could see the pilots' faces. The Zeros were ravaging *Super Man*. In every part of the plane, the sea and sky were visible through gashes in the bomber's skin. Every moment, the holes multiplied. The plane

In the battle of Nauru, a bomb cloud rises over the fuel depot struck by Louie's bombs.

was gravely wounded, trying to fly up and over onto its back. The pilots needed all their strength to hold it level.

In the greenhouse, Louie saw a Zero dive at *Super Man*'s nose. Nose gunner Mitchell and the Zero pilot fired simultaneously. Louie felt bullets slashing around him, one just missing his face. Then, as the planes sped toward a head-on collision, the Zero pilot jerked. Mitchell had hit him. For a moment, the Zero continued directly at *Super Man*. Then the stricken pilot collapsed onto the yoke, forcing the Zero down under the bomber before crashing into the ocean.

Super Man trembled on. There were still two Zeros circling it.

———

In the top turret, facing backward, Pillsbury had twin machine guns that could take down a Zero, but the Zeros were below, where he couldn't hit them. Feeling a Zero's rounds thumping into *Super Man*'s belly, he thought, *If he'd just come up, I could knock him down.*

He waited. The plane groaned and shook, the gunners fired, and still he waited. Then he heard an earsplitting *Ka-bang! Ka-bang! Ka-bang!* and felt a sensation of everything tipping and blowing apart, and excruciating pain.

A Zero had sprayed the entire right side of *Super Man* with cannon shells. The first rounds hit the tail, spinning the plane onto its side. Shrapnel tore into the leg of tail gunner Lambert, who hung on as *Super Man* rolled. The plane's twist saved him; a cannon round struck the spot where his head had been an instant earlier, exploding so close his goggles shattered. Ahead, shrapnel dropped Brooks and Douglas at the waist guns and Glassman in the belly turret. Finally, a shell blew out the wall of the top turret, shooting metal into Pillsbury's leg. *Super Man* reeled crazily on its side and for a moment spiraled out of control. Phil and Cuppernell wrenched it level.

Clinging to his gun as shrapnel struck his leg and the plane spun, Pillsbury shouted the only word that came to mind.

"*Ow!*"

———

Louie heard a scream. When he ran from the nose, the first thing he saw was Harry Brooks, lying on the bomb bay catwalk, his torso bloody. The bomb bay doors were wide open, and Brooks was dangling partway off the catwalk, one hand gripping the catwalk and one leg swinging in the air. He reached toward Louie, a plaintive expression on his face.

Louie grabbed Brooks and pulled him off the catwalk. He could see holes dotting Brooks's jacket. There was blood in his hair.

Louie dragged Brooks into a corner. Brooks passed out. Louie returned to the bomb bay. He remembered turning the valve to close the doors and couldn't understand why they were open. Then he saw it: a slash in the wall, purple liquid splattered everywhere. The hydraulic fluid lines, which controlled the doors, had been severed. With the lines broken, Phil would have no hydraulic control of the landing gear or flaps, which he'd need to slow the plane on landing. And without hydraulics, they had no brakes.

Louie cranked the bomb bay doors shut, then looked to the rear. Douglas and Lambert, both bloody, were pawing along the floor, trying to reach their guns.

Louie shouted to the cockpit for help. Phil yelled back that he was losing control of the plane and needed Cuppernell. Louie said it was an emergency. Phil braced himself at the controls, and Cuppernell got up, saw the men in back, and ran to them.

Louie knelt beside Brooks. Feeling through the gunner's hair, he found two holes in his skull. There were four large wounds in his back. Louie strapped an oxygen mask to Brooks's face and bandaged his head. He thought about the plane. The gunners were wounded, the plane was shot to hell, and there were still two Zeros near. *One more pass*, he thought, *will put us down.*

Louie felt something drip on his shoulder. He glanced up and saw Pillsbury in the top turret, blood streaming from his leg. Looking absolutely livid, he was gripping the gun and sweeping his eyes around the sky. His leg dangled below him, his pants shredded and boot blasted. Next to him was a large, jagged hole in the side of the plane.

Louie tried to doctor Pillsbury's wounds. Pillsbury ignored him. He knew the Zero that had hit them would return to finish the kill, and he had to find it.

Top turret gunner Stanley Pillsbury, shown here at the waist gun. COURTESY OF LOUIS ZAMPERINI

Suddenly, there was a whoosh of upward motion, a gray shining plane, a red circle. Pillsbury shouted something unintelligible, and Louie let go of his foot just as Pillsbury whirled his turret around to face the Zero.

The Zero sped directly toward *Super Man*. Pillsbury was terrified. With a flick of the Zero pilot's finger on his cannon trigger, *Super Man* would carry ten men into the Pacific. Pillsbury could see the pilot who would end his life, the sun illuminating his face, a white scarf coiled about his neck. Pillsbury thought: *I have to kill this man.*

Pillsbury sucked in a sharp breath and fired. He watched the tracers skim away from his gun and punch through the Zero cockpit. The windshield blew apart and the pilot pitched forward. The Zero faltered like a wounded bird and fell from the sky.

The last Zero came up, then dropped. Clarence Douglas, with his thigh, chest, and shoulder torn open, had risen to his gun and brought the plane down.

———

Pillsbury slid into Louie's arms. Louie laid him beside Brooks and eased his boot off. Pillsbury screamed in pain. His left big toe was gone. The toe next to it hung by a string of skin, and portions of his other toes were missing. His lower leg bristled with shrapnel. Louie bandaged Pillsbury, gave him morphine, then hurried away to see if they could save the plane.

Super Man was dying. Its control cables were cut, one rudder was ruined, fuel was trickling onto the floor, and hydraulic fluid was sloshing in the bomb bay. Phil couldn't turn it with the normal controls, and the plane was pulling upward extremely hard, trying to flip. It was on the verge of stalling, and was porpoising up and down.

Phil did what he could. Slowing the engines on one side forced the plane to turn. Pushing the plane to high speed eased the porpoising and reduced the risk of stalling. By putting both feet on the yoke and pushing as hard as he could, he could stop the plane from flipping.

Funafuti was five hours away. If *Super Man* could carry them that far, they'd have to land without hydraulic control of the landing gear, flaps, or

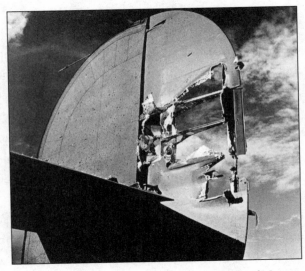

Super Man's destroyed rudder after the battle of Nauru.

brakes. They could work the gear and flaps with hand pumps, but there was no manual alternative to hydraulic brakes. Brakeless, coming in fast, they might need 10,000 feet to stop. Funafuti's runway was 6,660 feet long. At its end were rocks and sea.

Louie had an idea. What if they tied parachutes to the plane, pitched them out the windows at touchdown, and pulled the rip cords? No one had ever tried to stop a bomber this way, but it was all they had. They decided to try.

Hours passed. *Super Man* shook and struggled. Brooks gurgled blood. Pillsbury couldn't bear the sound. Brooks opened his eyes and whispered. Louie put his ear near Brooks's lips but couldn't understand him. Brooks drifted off.

They all knew they'd probably crash on landing, if not before. No one spoke of it.

———

At last, Funafuti appeared. Phil began dropping the plane. They had to slow down. Someone cranked open the bomb bay doors, and the plane, dragging on the air, began to slow. Douglas went to the landing-gear pump. He needed two hands—one to push a valve and one to work the pump—but had only one working arm. Pillsbury couldn't stand, but by stretching, he reached the valve. Together, they got the gear down. Mitchell and Louie pumped the flaps down, and Louie and Douglas placed a parachute in each waist window and tied them to the gun mounts. Louie stood between the windows, holding the rip cords.

Super Man sank toward Funafuti. Pillsbury looked at the airspeed gauge. It read 110 miles per hour. For a plane without brakes, it was much too fast.

———

For a moment, the landing was perfect, the wheels just kissing the runway. Then came a violent gouging sensation. The left tire had been hit and was flat. The plane caught hard and careened left, toward two bombers. More out of habit than hope, Cuppernell stomped on the right brake. There was just enough hydraulic fluid left to save them. *Super Man* spun around and stopped, barely missing the bombers. Louie was still gripping the parachute cords. He hadn't had to use them.

In seconds, the plane was swarming with marines, rushing the injured out. Louie jumped down and surveyed his ruined plane. All the bombers had returned, every one shot up, but none as badly as *Super Man*. Later, ground crewmen would count its holes: 594.

That evening, Pillsbury was lying in a barracks, awaiting treatment, when a doctor came in and asked if he knew Harry Brooks. Pillsbury said yes.

"He didn't make it," the doctor said.

———

Harold Brooks died days before his twenty-third birthday. His fiancée, Jeannette, learned he was gone nine days before the wedding date she and Harry had set before he left for the war.

Harry Brooks.

Funafuti, the morning after.

CHAPTER 10

"The Whole Island Was Blowing Up"

On the night after the Nauru raid, as he lay in a tent in Funafuti's coconut grove, Louie woke to a forlorn droning. It was a small plane, crossing back and forth overhead. Thinking it was a crew lost in the clouds, he lay listening, hoping they'd find home. Eventually, the sound faded away.

Before Louie could fall back asleep, he heard the growl of heavy aircraft engines. Then, from the atoll's north end, came a sudden *BOOM!* Then another and another, each one louder. There was a siren and distant gunfire. Then a marine ran by, screaming, *"Air raid!"* The droning hadn't been a lost American crew. It was probably a scout plane, leading Japanese bombers. Funafuti was under attack.

The airmen, Louie and Phil among them, jammed on their boots, bolted from their tents, and stopped, some spinning in panic. They couldn't see any bomb shelters. The explosions were getting louder and closer. The ground shook.

Men ran for any cover they could find. Pilot Joe Deasy and several other men plowed into a shallow pit around a coconut sapling. Herman Scearce, Deasy's radioman, leapt into a trench next to a truck, joining five crewmates. Pilot Jesse Stay jumped into another hole nearby. Three men crawled under the truck; another ran into a garbage pit. One man ran right into the ocean, even though he didn't know how to swim.

Dozens of natives crowded into a large white church. Realizing it would stand out brilliantly, a marine ran in and ordered the natives out. When they wouldn't move, he drew his sidearm. They scattered.

In the infirmary, Pillsbury lay in startled confusion. One moment he was asleep; the next, the atoll was rocking with explosions, a siren was howling, and people were dragging patients onto stretchers and rushing them out. Then Pillsbury was alone. He'd apparently been forgotten. He sat up, frantic. He couldn't stand.

Louie and Phil ran through the coconut grove. Bombs were overtaking them, making a sound one man likened to a giant's footfalls: *Boom . . . BOOM . . . BOOM!* At last, with the bombs so close they could hear them whistling, they dove under a hut built on flood stilts, landing in a heap of men.

An instant later, everything was scalding white and splintering noise. The ground heaved, the air whooshed, the hut shuddered. Trees blew apart. A bomb struck the tent where Louie and Phil had been seconds before. Another hit the truck, sending it and the remains of the men under it skimming past Jesse Stay's head. Another bomb landed on a gunner in Scearce's trench. It didn't go off but sat there hissing. The gunner shouted, "Jesus!" It took them a moment to realize the bomb was actually a fire extinguisher.

The bombs moved down the atoll. Each sounded farther away; then the explosions stopped. Louie and the others stayed put, knowing the bombers would return. Matches were struck and cigarettes pinched in trembling fingers. If we're hit, a man grumbled, there'll be nothing left of us but gravy. Far away, the bombers turned. The booming began again.

Someone running by the infirmary saw Pillsbury, raced in, and carried him into a tiny cement building where the other wounded had been taken. It was pitch dark, and so crowded that men had been laid on shelves. Pillsbury lay panting, listening to the explosions, feeling claustrophobic, imagining bombs entombing them. The booming was louder, louder, and then it was overhead, tremendous crashing. The ceiling trembled, and cement dust sifted down.

Outside, it was hell on earth. Men moaned and screamed, one calling for his mother. Men's eardrums burst. A man died of a heart attack. Another man's arm was severed. Others sobbed, prayed, and lost control of their bowels. Phil had never known such terror. Louie crouched beside him, seized with fear.

Staff Sergeant Frank Rosynek huddled in a trench, wearing nothing but a helmet, untied shoes, and boxers. "The bombs sounded like someone pushing a piano down a long ramp before they hit and exploded," he wrote. "Big palm trees were shattered and splintered all around us; the ground would rise up in the air when a bomb exploded and there was this terrific flash of super-bright light. . . . At intervals between a bomb falling it sounded like church: voices from nearby slit trenches all chanting the Lord's Prayer together. Louder when the bombs hit closer. I thought I even heard some guys crying. You were afraid to look up because you felt your face might be seen from above."

On the fourth pass, the Japanese hit the jackpot, bull's-eyeing a row of parked B-24s that were gassed up and loaded with bombs. One exploded, and another burst into flames, sending machine gun bullets whizzing everywhere, tracers drawing ribbons in the air. Then the five-hundred-pound bombs on the planes started going off.

Finally, silence. Men began stirring, hesitantly. As they did, a B-24 blew in a gigantic explosion, accelerated by its 2,300 gallons of fuel and 3,000 pounds of bombs. It sounded, wrote one man, "like the whole island was blowing up." With that, it was over.

———

At dawn, men crept from their hiding places. The man who'd run into the ocean waded ashore, having clung to a rock for three hours in rising tide. Louie and Phil joined a procession of stunned, shaking men.

Funafuti was wrecked. A bomb had leveled the church, but thanks to the marine, no one had been inside. Where Louie and Phil's tent had been, there was only a crater. Another tent lay collapsed, a bomb standing on its nose

The remains of a B-24 after the Funafuti bombing.

on top of it. Someone tied the bomb to a truck, dragged it to the beach, and turned sharply, sending the bomb skidding into the ocean.

Where the struck B-24s had been, there were giant holes ringed by decapitated coconut trees. One crater was thirty-five feet deep and sixty feet across. Bits of bomber were everywhere. Landing gear and seats that had seen the sunset from one side of Funafuti greeted the sunrise from the other. All that was left of one bomber was a tail, two wingtips, and propellers. An engine sat alone on the runway; the plane it belonged to was nowhere to be found. Louie saw a journalist staring into a crater, crying. Louie walked to him, bracing to see a dead body. Instead, he saw a typewriter, flat as a pool table.

The wounded and dead were everywhere. Two mechanics who had been caught in the open were bruised all over from the concussive force of explosions. They were so traumatized they couldn't talk. Men stood in a solemn circle around what was left of the truck. The three men who had been under it were beyond recognition. Louie came upon the body of a native, half his head gone. Phil was unscathed; Louie had only a cut arm.

Louie went to the infirmary. Pillsbury lay with his leg hanging in the air, dripping blood on the floor. Cuppernell sat with him, thanking him for shooting down that Zero.

Pillsbury's leg, which a doctor described as "hamburgered," needed immediate surgery. There was no anesthetic. As Pillsbury gripped the bed and Louie lay over his legs to hold them still, the doctor used pliers to tear tissue from Pillsbury's foot, then pulled a long strip of hanging skin over his toe-bone stump and sewed it up.

Louie walked to *Super Man*, which still sat where it had spun to a halt. The Japanese had missed it, but he couldn't tell by looking at it. Its 594 holes covered it: swarms of bullet holes, shrapnel slashes, cannon-fire gashes as large as a man's head, the gaping hole in Pillsbury's turret, and the rudder hole, big as a doorway. Men circled the plane, amazed that Phil had kept it airborne for five hours in that condition.

Louie ran his fingers along the tears in the plane's skin. *Super Man* had saved him and all but one of his crew. He would think of it as a dear friend.

Louie boarded another plane and headed home with Phil, Cuppernell, Mitchell, and Glassman. Pillsbury, Lambert, and Douglas were too badly wounded to rejoin the crew. Brooks was lying in Funafuti's cemetery.

The crew was broken up forever. They'd never see *Super Man* again.

———

Back on Hawaii, Louie and Phil sank into depression. With a gutted crew and no plane, they were grounded. Louie ran obsessively, trying to forget Harry Brooks's stricken face.

On May 24, the *Super Man* survivors were transferred to the 42nd squadron of the 11th Bomb Group. Six new men replaced the lost crewmen. "Don't like the idea a bit," Louie wrote in his diary. "Every time they mix up a crew, they have a crack-up." The only thing noteworthy about the new men was

Left: *Louie at* Super Man *on the day after Nauru.*

Below: *Louie peers through a cannon hole in the side of* Super Man.

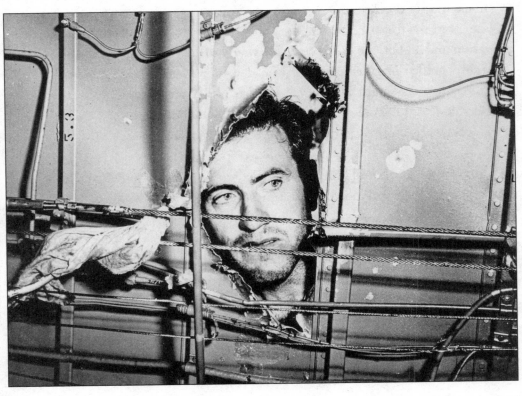

that the tail gunner, Sergeant Francis McNamara, ate practically nothing but dessert. They called him "Mac."

B-24s destined for their squadron began arriving. One, *Green Hornet*, worried everyone. Even with an empty bomb bay and all four engines roaring, it was only just able to stay airborne, flying with its tail far below its nose. It was relegated to errands, and mechanics pried parts off of it for other planes. Louie flew in it briefly, called it "the craziest plane," and hoped he'd never be in it again.

The battered B-24 Green Hornet.

MAY 27

Stayed at the base – Worked on
our beach home.
Got a call from operations that
a B-25 had a forced landing 200
miles north of the Island of Palmyra
We were the only crew on the
base & there was only one ship.
"The Green Hornet" a 'musher' We
were reluctant, but Phillips finally
gave in for rescue mission

Louie's last diary entry, May 27, 1943. He referred to Green Hornet as a "musher,"
meaning a plane that flew with its tail below its nose. COURTESY OF LOUIS ZAMPERINI

CHAPTER 11

"Nobody's Going
to Live Through This"

On Thursday, May 27, 1943, Louie rose at five a.m. He pulled on his workout clothes, hiked to the runway, and began his morning mile run. Four minutes and twelve seconds later, he finished. It was a dazzling time, given that he was running in sand. He was in the best shape of his life.

After breakfast, he climbed into a car with Phil and Cuppernell and headed for Honolulu for their day off. At the base gate, the despised lieutenant who oversaw their flights flagged them down. A B-24 piloted by a Tennes-

Lieutenant Clarence Corpening, pilot of the missing B-24.
COURTESY OF JIM AND CHARLES CORPENING

sean named Clarence Corpening was missing, and they needed volunteers to hunt for it. Phil told him they had no plane. The lieutenant said they could take *Green Hornet*. When Phil said the plane wasn't airworthy, the lieutenant disagreed, saying it had passed inspection. Phil knew that though the word *volunteer* was being used, this was an order. He volunteered. The lieutenant woke pilot Joe Deasy and recruited his crew as well. They'd take the B-24 *Daisy Mae*.

Phil, Louie, and Cuppernell turned back to round up their crew. Stopping at his room, Louie opened his diary. "There was only one ship, the *Green Hornet*," he wrote. "We were very reluctant, but Phillips finally gave in for rescue mission."

Just before he left, Louie laid a note on his footlocker, in which he kept his liquor, hidden in mayonnaise jars. *If we're not back in a week*, it read, *help yourself to the booze.*

————

Meeting the crews at *Green Hornet*, the lieutenant unrolled a map. He believed Corpening had gone down two hundred miles north of Palmyra, an island several hours south of Hawaii. He assigned each crew to a search area.

Green Hornet *being loaded for its final flight.* COURTESY OF LOUIS ZAMPERINI

Preparing for takeoff, everyone worried about *Green Hornet*. Without heavy bombs aboard, Louie told himself, the plane should be able to stay airborne. Phil was concerned that mechanics had removed parts from the plane. He hoped nothing critical was missing.

The crew reviewed crash procedures and checked survival equipment. There was a provisions box containing food, water, and survival supplies, the responsibility of the new tail gunner, Mac. Louie made sure the extra life raft was there. He put on his Mae West. Phil left his off.

At the last moment, a man ran up and asked for a ride to Palmyra. There were no objections, and the man climbed aboard.

———

Daisy Mae and *Green Hornet* flew together toward Palmyra. *Green Hornet* couldn't keep up. After about two hundred miles, Phil radioed to Deasy to go on ahead. The planes parted, and the crews lost sight of each other.

Midafternoon, *Green Hornet* reached its search area. Because of clouds, no one could see the water. Phil dropped the plane under the clouds, to just eight hundred feet. Louie stood just behind Phil and Cuppernell, scanning the ocean.

Cuppernell asked if he could switch seats with Phil, taking over as pilot. Phil agreed. The enormous Cuppernell squeezed around Phil and into the left seat as Phil moved to the right.

A few minutes later, there was a shudder. Louie looked out the window. Engine No. 1, on the far left, was shaking violently. Then it died. The bomber tipped left and began dropping rapidly toward the ocean.

It was a dire emergency. Because *Green Hornet* was already very low, Phil and Cuppernell had only seconds to save the plane. They began working rapidly. To minimize drag from the broken engine, they needed to "feather" it—turn the dead propeller blades parallel to the wind and stop their rotation. Normally, this was Cuppernell's job, but now he was in the pilot's seat. Busy trying to keep the plane airborne, he shouted to the new engineer to come feather the engine.

The new engineer ran forward. There were four feathering buttons, one for each engine. Leaning between Cuppernell and Phil, the engineer banged on a button. *Green Hornet* heaved and lurched left. The engineer had hit the wrong button. Both leftward engines were now dead.

Phil pushed the two working engines full on, trying to keep the plane up long enough to restart the good left engine. The racing right engines rolled the plane halfway onto its left side, sending it into a spiral. The engine wouldn't start. The plane kept dropping.

Green Hornet was doomed. Phil grunted three words:

"Prepare to crash."

Louie ran from the flight deck, yelling for everyone to get to crash positions. As the plane whirled, he grabbed the extra life raft, then clambered toward his crash position by the right waist window. He saw Mac clutching the provisions box. Other men were frantically pulling on Mae Wests. But Mitchell didn't emerge from the nose. As the navigator, it was his duty to gather navigation instruments for use on the life raft and relay the plane's position to the radioman so he could send a distress signal. But with the plane gyrating down nose first and the escape passage narrow, perhaps Mitchell couldn't get out.

As the men behind the cockpit fled toward the comparative safety of the rear, one man, almost certainly the engineer who'd hit the wrong feathering button, apparently stayed in front. It was his duty to pull the raft release handle behind the cockpit. To ensure that rafts would be near survivors, he would have to wait until an instant before the crash to pull the handle. This meant he'd have no chance to get to a crash position, and thus, little chance of survival.

Phil and Cuppernell fought the plane. *Green Hornet* rolled onto its left side, moving faster and faster as the right engines thundered. Phil felt strangely fearless. He watched the ocean rotating up at him and thought: *There's nothing more I can do.*

Louie sat on the floor by the right waist window. There were five men near him. No one said anything. Louie looked out the window. All he saw was the cloudy sky, turning around and around. Sensing the ocean coming up at the plane, he took a last glance at the twisting sky, then pulled the life raft in front of him and pushed his head into his chest.

One terrible, tumbling second passed, then another. An instant before the plane struck the water, Louie's mind throbbed with a single, final thought: *Nobody's going to live through this.*

———

For Louie, there were jagged, soundless sensations: his body catapulted forward, the plane breaking open, something wrapping itself around him, the cold slap of water, and then its weight over him. *Green Hornet* stabbed into the ocean and blew apart.

Louie felt himself being pulled deep underwater. Then, abruptly, the downward motion stopped, and Louie was flung upward. The fuselage, momentarily buoyed by the air trapped inside, leapt to the surface. Louie opened his mouth and gasped. The air hissed from the plane, and water rushed up over Louie again. The plane slipped under and sank toward the ocean floor.

Louie tried to orient himself. The tail was no longer behind him, the wings no longer ahead. The men who'd been around him were gone. The impact had rammed Louie into a machine-gun mount and wedged him under it, facedown. Countless wires were coiled around his body, binding him to the gun mount. He looked at them and thought: *Spaghetti.* He thrashed uselessly against them. He felt frantic to breathe.

In the cockpit, Phil was fighting to get out. When the plane hit, he was thrown forward, his head striking something. A wall of water punched through the cockpit, and the plane carried him under. From the darkness, he knew he was far below the surface, sinking deeper by the second. He apparently saw Cuppernell squeeze his big body out of the plane. Phil found what he thought was the cockpit window frame, its glass missing. He pushed himself through and swam toward the surface.

He emerged in a puzzle of debris, his head gushing blood. He found a hunk of wreckage and clung to it. It began to sink. There were two empty life rafts far away. Cuppernell was nowhere to be seen.

Far below, Louie was writhing in the wires. He saw a body, drifting passively. The plane coursed down, and the world fled away above. Darkness enfolded him, and the water pressure bore in with greater and greater intensity. He struggled helplessly. He thought: *Hopeless.*

He felt a sudden, excruciating bolt of pain in his head. There was an oncoming stupor as he tore at the wires and clenched his throat against the need to breathe. With a soft realization that this was the last of life, he passed out.

He woke in total darkness. He thought: *This is death.* Then he felt the water still on him, the weight of the plane around him. Inexplicably, the wires were gone. He was floating inside the fuselage, which was bearing him downward. The air was gone from his lungs, and he was gulping reflexively, swallowing water. He tasted oil, fuel, and blood. He was drowning.

Louie flung out his arms, trying to find a way out. His right hand struck something, and his college ring snagged on it. His hand was caught. He reached toward it with his left hand and felt a smooth length of metal: he was at the open right waist window. He put his feet on the frame and pushed off, wrenching his right hand free and cutting his finger and scraping his back on the fuselage. He kicked clear. The plane sank away.

Louie yanked the inflation cords on his Mae West. He was suddenly light, the vest pulling him urgently upward.

He burst into dazzling daylight. He gasped in a breath and immediately vomited up the salt water and fuel he'd swallowed.

He had survived.

PART

III

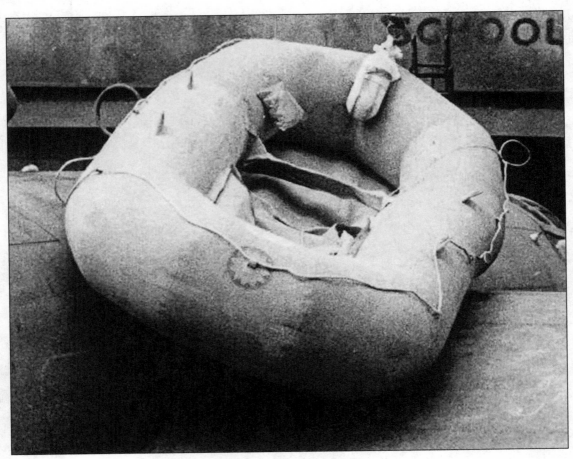

A typical World War II bomber life raft.

CHAPTER 12

Downed

The ocean was a jumble of bomber remains. The plane's lifeblood—oil, hydraulic fluid, and some one thousand gallons of fuel—slopped on the surface.

Louie heard a voice. He turned and saw Phil and Mac, far away, clinging to debris. Blood spouted in arcs from Phil's head and streamed down his face. No one else had surfaced.

Louie saw two rafts. The engineer, in the heroic last act of his life, had apparently yanked the release handle just before he was killed. The rafts had inflated themselves and were drifting away rapidly.

Louie knew he had to stop Phil's bleeding, but if he lost the rafts, they'd all perish. He swam for one of the rafts. His clothes weighed him down, and the current and wind carried the raft faster than he could swim. As the raft slid hopelessly out of reach, Louie looked back at Phil and Mac, sharing the recognition that their chance was lost. Then he saw a cord trailing behind the raft. He snatched it, reeled the raft to him, and climbed aboard. He grabbed the oars, rowed to the second raft, and tied the two together.

He rowed to Phil and Mac and pulled Phil aboard. Mac, uninjured, climbed up on his own. Both men, like Louie, were filmy with fuel and oil. With all three in one raft, it was cramped; the raft interior was only about six feet long and a little more than two feet wide.

There were two gashes on Phil's forehead, spurting blood. Louie ran his fingers down Phil's throat until he felt a pulse, the carotid artery, then put Mac's hand on it and told him to press down. He pulled off his top shirt and T-shirt and pulled Phil's shirts off as well. He asked Mac to do the same. He folded Phil's shirt, pressed it to the wounds, then tied the other T-shirts around his head. He slid Phil into the second raft.

Phil felt woozy. As the pilot, he was in charge, but knew he was in no condition to make decisions. He asked Louie to take command.

"I'm glad it was you, Zamp," he said softly.

From the water came a small sound: a moan, trailing off into a gargle, then silence. Louie grabbed an oar and circled, searching for the drowning man, but whoever had made the sound had slipped under. He didn't come up again.

Eleven men had gone up on *Green Hornet*. All but three were dead.

———

With Phil stable, Louie turned his attention to the rafts. They were made of rubber-coated canvas divided into two air pockets. The critical issue was provisions. The provisions box, which Mac had been holding as the plane went down, was gone, ripped from his hands in the crash or lost in his escape from the wreckage. In their pockets, the men had only wallets and coins. Their watches were still on their wrists, but the hands had stopped when the plane hit. Cecy's bracelet wasn't on Phil's wrist, and his lucky silver dollar wasn't in his pocket. Maybe he'd forgotten them, or maybe they'd been lost in the crash.

Whatever was in the raft pockets was all they'd have. In them, Louie found several chocolate bars, several half-pint tins of water, a brass mirror, a flare gun, sea dye, fishhooks, fishing line, a leak patching kit, and two air pumps in canvas cases. There was also a set of pliers with a screwdriver in the handle. Louie pondered it, wondering why anyone would need a screwdriver or pliers on a raft. That was all there was. No knife, nothing for shelter, no fishnet, no radio.

Most worrisome was the water situation. A few half pints wouldn't last long. Because sea water is so salty it's poisonous, they couldn't drink it.

Adrift near the equator with little water, Phil, Louie, and Mac would soon be in dire trouble.

———

Since the crash, Mac hadn't said a single word. He'd done everything Louie asked of him, but his face had never lost its glazed, startled expression.

Louie was assessing the rafts when Mac suddenly began wailing, "We're going to die!" Louie tried to reassure him, but Mac kept shouting. Exasperated, Louie threatened to report Mac when they returned. It had no effect. At wits' end, Louie whacked Mac's face with the back of his hand. Mac thumped back and fell silent.

Louie established rules. Each man would eat one square of chocolate in the morning, one in the evening. Louie allotted one water tin per man, with

Francis McNamara on May 26, 1943, the day before the crash of Green Hornet.
COURTESY OF LOUIS ZAMPERINI

each man allowed two or three sips a day. Eating and drinking at this rate, they could stretch the supplies for a few days.

There was nothing to do but wait. Louie's back hurt. The skin down the length of it had been scraped off as he escaped the wreckage, and he assumed that this was the source of his pain. He had no idea that he was hurt much worse than that. When he'd been thrown into the gun mount as the plane struck the ocean, every one of his ribs had broken.

Pushing away thoughts about the men who'd died, Louie pondered his escape from the wreckage. If he'd passed out from the water pressure, and the plane had continued to sink and the pressure build, why had he woken again? And how had he been loosed from the wires while unconscious?

The men watched the sky. Louie kept his hand on Phil's head, stanching the bleeding. The last trace of *Green Hornet*, a shimmer of gas, hydraulic fluid, and oil, faded away. In its place, rising from below, came massive blue shapes, gliding in lithe arcs around the rafts. Sharks had found them.

The sharks, which Louie thought were of the mako and reef species, were so close that the men could touch them. The smallest were about six feet long; some were twelve feet. They bent around the rafts, testing the fabric, but not trying to get at the men. They seemed to be waiting for the men to come to them.

The sun sank, and it became sharply cold. The men used their hands to bail a few inches of water into each raft. Once their bodies warmed the water, they felt less chilled. They fought the urge to sleep, afraid a ship or submarine would pass and they'd miss it. Phil was so cold he shook.

It was absolutely dark and absolutely silent, save the chattering of Phil's teeth. The ocean was a flat calm. A rough, rasping tremor ran through the men. The sharks were rubbing their backs along the rafts.

Louie's arm was still draped over the side of his raft, his hand resting on Phil's forehead. Phil drifted to sleep, feeling the sharks scraping down his back. In the next raft, Louie, too, fell asleep.

Mac lay awake, his mind spinning with fear. Grasping at a panicked resolution, he began to stir.

CHAPTER 13

Missing at Sea

Joe Deasy landed *Daisy Mae* on Palmyra late that afternoon, having seen no trace of Corpening's plane. That night, he received stunning news: *Green Hornet* had never landed. "Holy smoke!" he said. Two planes were now down, taking twenty-one men with them.

A rescue effort was organized. Because *Daisy Mae* and *Green Hornet* had flown together at first, the organizers knew *Green Hornet* had gone down after *Daisy Mae* left it but before it reached Palmyra. That was a stretch of eight hundred miles. In the whorl of currents in that area, survivors could be drifting in any direction. The search area would have to be enormous.

At dawn, the search planes took off.

Louie woke with the sun. Mac lay beside him. Phil lay in his raft, his mind still fumbling. Only the sharks stirred.

Louie decided to divvy up breakfast. He reached in the raft pocket. The chocolate was gone. He looked at Mac. Mac looked back at him with wide, guilty eyes.

The realization that Mac had eaten their only food rolled hard over Louie. He knew they could die without it, but he quelled the thought. They'd be rescued today, perhaps tomorrow, he told himself, and the chocolate wouldn't matter. Curbing his anger, he told Mac he was disappointed in him, but understanding that Mac had acted in panic, he reassured him they would soon be rescued. Mac said nothing.

The night chill gave way to a sweltering day. The men were hungry, but they could do nothing about it. The fishing gear was useless. There was no bait.

As they lay in silence, a purring sound drifted between their thoughts. Searching the sky, they saw a bomber, well to the east. Flying much too high to be a search plane, it was probably headed to Palmyra.

Louie lunged for the flare gun, loaded it, aimed high, and squeezed the trigger. The gun bucked in his hand, and the flare streaked up. As it shot overhead, Louie shook a sea dye pack into the water. A pool of vivid yellow bloomed over the ocean.

Louie, Phil, and Mac watched the bomber, hoping, hoping. Slowly, the flare sputtered out. The bomber kept going, then was gone.

The sighting gave the castaways a distressing piece of information. They hadn't known in which direction they were drifting. Since the Hawaii–Palmyra flight lane ran near *Green Hornet*'s crash site, the appearance of a bomber far to the east meant the rafts were drifting west, away from the view of friendly planes. Their chances of rescue were already dimming.

That evening, the search planes returned to their bases. No one had seen anything. They'd be back up at first light.

———

Phil slept for most of the following day. Louie thought about food. Mac hunkered down. For another day, rescue didn't come.

On the third morning, they again heard engines. Then there it was, a B-24, low and right overhead, plowing through the clouds. A search plane.

Louie fired the flare gun. The flare shot at the bomber, and for a moment, the men thought it would hit the plane. It missed, passing alongside and making a fountain of red. Louie reloaded and fired three more flares.

The plane was *Daisy Mae*. Its crewmen were straining their eyes at the

Daisy Mae, *shown after a forced landing.*

ocean, passing binoculars between them. But with clouds closing and parting, searching was extremely difficult.

The flares died, and *Daisy Mae* flew on. No one aboard saw anything.

The castaways' best chance of rescue was lost. Every hour, they were farther west. If they weren't found, their only hope would be to find land. Ahead, there wasn't a single island for some two thousand miles. If by some miracle they made it that far alive, they might reach the Marshall or Gilbert Islands. Then they'd have another problem. Both sets of islands belonged to the Japanese. Watching *Daisy Mae* fly away, Louie had a dark feeling.

———

The castaways' bodies were declining. They drank the last of their water and were intensely thirsty and hungry. They spent another frigid night, then a long fourth day. They knew if the search hadn't been called off, it soon would be.

On the fifth day, Mac snapped. After having said almost nothing for days, he suddenly began screaming that they were doomed. Wild-eyed and raving, he couldn't stop shouting. Louie slapped him. Mac went silent.

As the lost men drifted into oblivion, their last letters reached their loved ones, who had not yet been informed of what had happened; to avoid needlessly alarming family members, military policy was to search for a week before officially declaring men missing. In his last note to Cecy, Phil wrote of the moon over Hawaii and how it reminded him of the last time he saw her. "I'm waiting for the day when we can begin doing things together again as we used to do," he wrote. "I love you, I love you, I love you."

On the weekend after the crash, the Zamperinis had a merry visit with Cuppernell's parents, who lived in Long Beach. Pete, now a navy officer stationed in San Diego, wrote Louie about it, asking him to tell Cuppernell his parents were doing great. He tucked a photo of himself in the envelope. On the back, he wrote, "Don't let 'em clip your wings."

As his brother's letter made its way toward Hawaii, Louie was on a raft far out in the Pacific. For the first time since he was a little boy, he prayed, speaking the words only in his mind.

———

A week after *Green Hornet* vanished, the search was abandoned. Phil's crew was officially declared missing, and the process of informing family members began.

On Oahu, an officer walked into the quarters that Louie, Phil, Mitchell, and Cuppernell had shared. He was there to catalog the men's belongings and send them home. Louie's room was mostly as it had been when he'd left that Thursday morning: a footlocker, a diary that ended with words about a rescue mission, a pinup of actress Esther Williams on the wall. The note Louie had left on the locker was gone, as was the liquor.

In Princeton, Indiana, on Friday, June 4, 1943, Kelsey Phillips, Phil's mother, received a telegram.

I REGRET TO INFORM YOU THAT THE COMMANDING GENERAL PACIFIC AREA REPORTS YOUR SON—FIRST LIEUTENANT RUSSELL A PHILLIPS—MISSING SINCE MAY TWENTY-SEVEN. IF FURTHER DETAILS OR OTHER INFORMATION OF HIS STATUS ARE RECEIVED YOU WILL BE PROMPTLY NOTIFIED.

At Camp Pickett in Virginia, the same news reached Phil's father, who was serving as an army chaplain. He took leave and rushed for home.

The telegram reached the Zamperinis that same evening. Louie's mother, Louise, called Sylvia, who was living in a nearby suburb with her new husband. Sylvia became so hysterical that a neighbor ran to her, but Sylvia was crying too hard to speak. Sobbing, she got in her car and drove to Torrance. Pulling up at her parents' house, she put on a brave face.

Her father was quiet; her mother was consumed with anguish. Sylvia, who like everyone else assumed Louie had crashed in the ocean, told her mother not to worry. "With all those islands," Sylvia said, "he's teaching someone hula." Pete arrived. "If he has a toothbrush and a pocket knife and he hits land," he said, "he'll make it."

Louise found the snapshot taken the day Louie left, when he'd stood beside her on her front steps, his arm around her waist. On the back, she wrote, *Louis Reported missing—May 27, 1943.*

———

Stanley Pillsbury and Clarence Douglas were in a hospital, trying to recover from the wounds incurred over Nauru. Douglas's shoulder was ravaged, and he seemed emotionally gutted. Pillsbury still couldn't walk. In his dreams, planes dove at him, endlessly.

Pillsbury was in his bed when Douglas came in.

"The crew went down," he said.

Pillsbury could barely speak. His first emotion was overwhelming guilt. "If I had only been there," he said later, "I could have saved it."

On Oahu, Louie's friends hung a small flag in his memory. It would hang there as Louie, Phil, and Mac drifted west and the Allies carried the war across the Pacific and into the throat of Japan.

———

In Torrance, Louise Zamperini's hands broke out in weeping sores, a consequence of her emotional trauma. Somewhere in those jagged first days, a fierce conviction came over her. Her son, she was absolutely certain, was alive.

CHAPTER 14

Thirst

Phil felt as if he were on fire. The men's scalded skin cracked and their lips ballooned, bulging against their nostrils and chins. Their feet were cratered with quarter-sized salt sores. The water cans were empty. The rafts baked, emitting a bitter smell. The sharks circled.

At last, on the third day without water, down came rain. The men spilled their bodies back, spread their arms, and opened their mouths as the water drummed over them. It was a sensory explosion.

They had to find a way to save the water. The water tins, opened to the downpour, caught virtually nothing. Louie grabbed the air pump cases, tore the seams, spread the fabric into bowls, and let the rain pool, sucking it up and spitting it in the cans. Once the cans were full, he kept harvesting the rain, giving each man a drink every thirty seconds or so.

———

For the moment, they had water, but they still had no food. They were ravenous. They stared into the ocean, crowded with fish, but they had no bait. They studied their shoes and wondered if they could eat the leather. They decided they couldn't.

Days passed. They grew weaker. Louie resented Mac for eating the chocolate, and Mac seemed to know it. Louie sensed he was consumed by guilt.

Nine or ten days after the crash, Louie was lying back, wearing the air pump case as a hat, when he felt something alight on his head. It was an albatross. Slowly, slowly, Louie raised his hand, fingers open, then clamped down on the bird's legs. The bird pecked frantically, slashing Louie's knuckles. Louie grabbed its head and broke its neck.

Louie used the pliers to tear the bird open. The men recoiled: the bird reeked. They tried to eat it but gagged from the stench. Eventually, they gave up.

At least they finally had bait. Louie tied a small hook to a fishing line, baited it with albatross meat, and fed it into the water. A shark bit down on the hook and severed the line. Twice more, Louie tried, and twice more, sharks stole the hook. Finally, the sharks let a hook hang. Louie felt a tug and pulled up the line. On it hung a slender fish.

It was their first food in well over a week. Between three men, a small fish didn't go far, but it gave them a push of energy. Louie had demonstrated that if they were persistent and resourceful, they could catch food, and he and Phil felt inspired. Mac remained unchanged.

Phil reminded Louie that according to lore, killing an albatross was bad luck. After a plane crash, Louie replied, what more bad luck could they have?

———

Several days passed. Louie caught nothing, and his hook supply dwindled. Periodically, rain replenished the water tins, but only partway.

Phil began thinking about a magazine article he'd read, written by World War I ace pilot Eddie Rickenbacker. The previous fall, Rickenbacker's bomber had ditched in the Pacific. The raftbound crew drifted for weeks, surviving on their two rafts' provisions, rainwater, fish, and bird meat. One man died, and the rest hallucinated, babbling at invisible people, arguing about their imaginary car, one man speaking to a specter that tried to lure him into the ocean. Finally, the rafts split up, and one reached an island. Natives radioed for help, and the other men were rescued.

Rickenbacker wrote that he'd drifted for twenty-one days (he'd actually drifted for twenty-four), and Phil, Louie, and Mac believed this was a record. In fact, the record for inflated raft survival appears to have been set in 1942, when three crash victims survived for thirty-four days.

To Louie, the most important aspect of Rickenbacker's story was how quickly the survivors had gone insane. He remembered a college instructor telling him to think of the brain as a muscle, needing exercise to stay in shape. Louie was determined to keep himself and the others lucid.

Soon after the crash, Louie began peppering Phil and Mac with questions on every conceivable subject. They shared their histories, from first memories onward. They reminisced about the best dates they'd ever had. Phil sang church hymns; Louie taught the other two the lyrics to "White Christmas." They sang it over the ocean, a Christmas carol in June, heard only by circling sharks.

Every conversation meandered back to food. Louie boasted about his mother's cooking, so Phil asked him how she made a meal. Louie began describing the preparation of a dish, and all three men found it satisfying, so Louie began a daily ritual, detailing breakfasts, lunches, and dinners. Devouring each imaginary meal, the men would describe every mouthful. They conjured up the scene so vividly that their stomachs were fooled, if only briefly.

Once the food was eaten and the past exhausted, they moved to the future. Louie laid plans to open a restaurant. Phil spoke of seeing the Indy 500, maybe teaching school. And he talked about Cecy. In his mind, she never left him.

For Louie and Phil, the conversations kept their minds sharp, pulled them out of their suffering, and set the future before them as something to live for. But Mac usually sat in silence. Though the others encouraged him, he couldn't see a future. The world was too far gone.

The one thing they never discussed was the crash. Louie wanted to, but something about Phil stopped him. At times, Phil seemed lost in troubled thoughts, and Louie guessed he was reliving the crash, perhaps feeling responsible for his men's deaths. Louie wanted to reassure Phil he'd done nothing wrong but feared raising the issue would be painful to him. So he said nothing.

———

Two weeks had passed. The rafts were decomposing, bleeding vivid yellow dye onto the men. They looked grotesque. Salt sores were marching up their legs and backs. Their flesh had evaporated.

They were reaching a stage of their ordeal that, for other castaways, had been a gruesome turning point. In the history of seafaring, incidents of cannibalism among starving castaways weren't uncommon. But for all three *Green Hornet* survivors, the idea was unthinkable. Cannibalism wouldn't be considered, then or ever.

The two-week mark was a different turning point for Louie. He began praying aloud. He had no idea how to speak to God, so he recited snippets of prayers he'd seen in movies. Phil bowed his head as Louie spoke, offering "Amen" at the end. Mac only listened.

The second albatross fluttered onto Louie's head around the fourteenth day. Again Louie caught and killed it. When Louie opened it, they were relieved to find it didn't smell bad. They ate all of it. Because Mac was fading fastest, they gave him all the blood.

Time spun out endlessly. Baiting his hooks with albatross meat and tiny fish from the bird's stomach, Louie caught a few fish, once parlaying a little one, thrown into the raft by a whitecap, into bait that yielded a bigger fish. Rains came intermittently, leaving the men sucking up every drop. Louie and Phil took turns leading prayers. Mac remained in his own world.

Then the rains stopped and the water tins dried up. They reached day twenty-one. They caught a fish and celebrated passing what they thought was Rickenbacker's mark.

———

Louie was out of bait. Other than sharks, the only sea creatures that ventured within arm's reach were the small pilot fish that always swam alongside the sharks, but when Louie tried to grab them, they squirted away. With no more small hooks, Louie tried albatross bones, but the fish spat them out.

He had an idea. He used fishing line to tie large hooks to his pinky, middle finger, and thumb, orienting them like claws. He held his hand over the water and waited.

Sergeant James Reynolds, a survivor of World War I pilot Eddie Rickenbacker's crash, after drifting for twenty-four days at sea in 1943. Though this photo was taken a month after Reynolds's rescue, he remained shockingly emaciated. GETTY IMAGES

A shark, attended by a pilot fish, swam by. Once its head had passed, Louie sank his hand into the water. When the pilot fish moved under his hand, he snapped his fingers shut around it and yanked it from the water, jubilant.

Sometime that week, a tern landed on the raft, and Phil clapped down on it. It was tiny and offered little meat, but not long after, another tern arrived. This time, Mac caught it. Using his teeth to rip the feathers out, Louie soon felt a tickle on his chin. The tern was teeming with lice.

Louie rubbed his face, but the lice burrowed into his beard and hair. Frantic, he pitched his upper body into the water. Realizing Louie was going to get his head ripped off, Phil and Mac grabbed the oars and bumped the sharks away while Louie splashed. Finally, the tickle was gone.

As the days passed, the men caught a few more birds. One kept dipping low over the raft, then soaring off again. Mac suddenly shot his hand up and snagged the bird by the leg, then handed it to Louie, who was amazed. The men ate every morsel.

———

For days, Louie lay over the side of the raft, fishhooks on his fingers, trying in vain to catch another fish. Day after day passed with no rain, and the thirst was agonizing. Twice, they rowed toward squalls, but each time, the rain died out as they reached it. When the next squall passed, they were too weak to chase it.

On the sixth day without water, the men knew they weren't going to last much longer. Mac was failing especially quickly.

They bowed their heads together as Louie prayed. If God would quench their thirst, he vowed, he'd dedicate his life to him.

The next day, the sky broke open and rain poured down. It gave them just enough water to last a short while longer. If only a plane would come.

CHAPTER 15

Sharks and Bullets

On the twenty-seventh day, a plane came.

It began with a distant rumble, then a spot in the sky. It was a bomber, moving briskly west. It was so far away that expending the flares and dye was questionable. The men decided to try.

Louie fired two flares, drawing vivid lines across the sky. He spilled dye into the ocean, then used the mirror to angle light toward the bomber.

The men waited. The plane faded away.

As the castaways slumped in disappointment, there was a glimmer on the horizon. The bomber was coming back. Crying with joy, Louie, Phil, and Mac waved and called out. The plane dropped, skimming the water. Louie squinted at the cockpit. He saw two silhouettes, a pilot and copilot.

All at once, the ocean erupted. There was a deafening noise, and the rafts began hopping and shuddering. The plane's gunners were shooting at them.

Louie, Phil, and Mac clawed for the raft walls and threw themselves overboard. They swam under the rafts and huddled there, wincing, watching bullets cut bright slits in the water around them. Then the firing stopped.

The men surfaced. The bomber had overshot them. Two sharks were nosing around. The men had to get out of the water immediately.

A Japanese "Nell" bomber, the type that strafed Louie's raft.

Trying to get onto Louie and Mac's raft, Phil floundered. Louie gave him a push, and Phil slopped on board. Mac, too, needed help. Louie dragged himself up, and the three sat, stunned but uninjured. They couldn't believe the airmen, mistaking them for Japanese, would strafe unarmed castaways. Beneath them, the raft felt doughy. Bullets had struck it. It was leaking air.

The bomber turned and flew toward the rafts again. Louie hoped the crew had realized their mistake and was returning to help. As the plane closed in, its side passed into view.

All three men saw it at once. Behind the plane's wing, painted on the fuselage, was a red circle. The bomber was Japanese.

As Louie turned to dive in the water, Phil and Mac didn't move. They were too weak to go back in the ocean. As the bomber flew toward them, they lay down. Phil pulled his knees to his chest and covered his head with his hands. Mac balled himself up beside him. Louie took a last glance at them, then dove under the rafts.

The bullets showered the ocean in a glittering downpour. Louie saw them pop through the canvas, shooting beams of sunlight through the raft's shadow. After a few feet, they spent their force and fluttered down, fizzing. Louie pushed against the bottom of the raft, trying to get below the bullets' lethal range. Above, he could see the depressions of Mac's and Phil's bodies. Both were still.

As the bullets raked overhead, the current began dragging Louie away. He knew if he lost touch with the rafts, he wouldn't be able to swim hard enough against the current to get back. As he was pulled loose, he saw a raft tether, grabbed it, and tied it around his waist.

As he lay underwater, his legs tugged in front of him, Louie looked at his feet, watching his sock flap in the current. Then, in the murky blur beyond it, he saw the huge, gaping mouth of a shark, emerging out of the darkness and rushing straight at his legs.

Louie recoiled, swinging his legs to the side, but the shark kept coming, directly at his head. He remembered the advice of the old man in Honolulu: make a threatening expression, then stiff-arm the shark's snout. As the shark lunged, Louie bared his teeth, widened his eyes, and rammed his palm into the shark's nose. The shark flinched, circled away, then charged back. Louie waited until the shark was inches from him, then struck it again. Again, the shark peeled away.

Above, the shooting had stopped. Louie pulled himself along the tether, grabbed the raft wall, and scrambled aboard.

Mac and Phil were still, bullet holes all around them. Louie shook Mac. Mac made a sound. Louie asked if he'd been hit. Mac said no. Louie spoke to Phil. Phil said he was okay.

The bomber circled back. Phil and Mac played dead, and Louie tipped back into the ocean. As bullets knifed the water around him, the shark came at him, and again Louie bumped its snout and repelled it. Then a second shark attacked. Louie hung there, flailing his arms and legs, as the sharks snapped and the bullets shot past. The moment the bomber sped away, he clambered onto the raft again. Phil and Mac were still unhit.

Four more times the Japanese strafed them, sending Louie into the water to kick and punch at the sharks. Each time he emerged, he was certain Phil and Mac would be dead. Impossibly, though there were bullet holes around the men, even in tiny spaces between them, not one bullet had hit either man.

The plane returned, and Louie dove again. The bomb bay doors opened, and a depth charge—an underwater bomb—rolled out. The men braced for an explosion, but none came. Either the charge was a dud, or the bombardier had forgotten to arm it.

Louie heaved back onto the raft and collapsed. When the bomber passed again, he was too tired to move. The gunners didn't fire. The bomber flew west and disappeared.

————

Phil's raft was slashed in two. Shrunken and formless, it lapped on the ocean surface. The men were sardined on Mac and Louie's raft, its canvas speckled with dozens of tiny bullet holes. Both of its air chambers were punctured. Each time someone moved, air sighed out, and the raft sat lower in the water. The sharks whipped around it, wildly excited.

As the men sat, exhausted and in shock, a shark lunged onto the raft, mouth open, trying to drag a man off. Someone grabbed an oar and hit it, and it slid away. Then another shark jumped on, and after it, another. The men wheeled about, frantically swinging at the sharks. As they swung and the sharks flopped up, air was forced out of the bullet holes, and the raft sank deeper. Soon, the men's legs were underwater.

If the men couldn't reinflate the raft immediately, the sharks would take them. One pump had been lost; only one remained. The men hooked it to a valve and took turns pumping. Air flowed into the chamber and seeped out through the bullet holes, but if the men pumped very quickly, just enough air passed through the raft to lift it. The sharks kept coming, and the men beat them away.

Louie groped for the patching kit, and as Phil and Mac pumped and fought sharks, he began the laborious task of gluing patches on the bullet holes. Sharks kept snapping at him. They began stalking about, waiting for a moment when an oar was down or a back turned before bulling their way aboard. Over and over, they lunged at Louie from behind. Mac and Phil smacked them away.

Hour after hour, the men worked, clumsy with fatigue. All three were indispensable. Had there been only two, they couldn't have pumped, patched, and hit sharks. For the first time, Mac was truly helpful.

Night fell. In the dark, patching was impossible, but the pumping couldn't be stopped. They pumped all night, so drained their arms went numb. In the morning the patching resumed. The rate of air loss gradually lessened.

Once the top was patched, they had to patch the bottom. All three squeezed onto one side of the raft. They deflated the other side, lifted it up, turned it over, and let it dry. Then Louie patched as the other two pumped and struck sharks. When that half was patched, they reinflated it, crawled onto the repaired side, deflated the other side, and began again.

Finally, they could find no more holes. Because bubbles kept coming up from below, they knew there were holes they couldn't reach. They had to live with them. The patches had slowed the air loss dramatically. They cut back on pumping to once every fifteen minutes or so by day, and none at night. With the raft reinflated, the sharks stopped attacking.

———

The crisis over, Louie and Phil thought about the bomber. They thought it must have come from the Marshall or Gilbert Islands, which were probably roughly equidistant from them. It had probably been on sea search, and likely took off at around seven a.m., a few hours before it reached the rafts.

Estimating the bomber's cruising speed and range, they made rough calculations to arrive at how many hours the bomber could remain airborne after it left them, and thus how far they were from its base. Crunching these numbers, they guessed that they were some 850 miles from the base. If this was correct, given they'd crashed about two thousand miles east of the Marshalls and Gilberts, they'd already traveled more than half the distance to them, covering more than forty miles per day. They'd had no idea they were so far west.

Using these figures, they made educated guesses of when they'd reach the islands. Phil guessed the forty-sixth day; Louie guessed the forty-seventh. This would mean surviving on the raft for almost three more weeks.

As frightening as it was to imagine what might await them on those islands, it was good to know land lay somewhere ahead. The bomber had given them something on which to ground their hope.

Mac didn't join in the conversation. He was slipping away.

After the strafing destroyed their second raft, Louie, Phil, and Mac had to crowd together in their remaining two-man raft. This World War II demonstration of the use of a bomber raft shows how tight a fit it was for three men. GETTY IMAGES

CHAPTER 16

Singing in the Clouds

Louie sat awake, looking into the sea. Phil slept. Mac was in a reverie.

Two sharks, about eight feet long, were circling placidly. Louie had banged sharks on the nose but had never really felt their skin. Curious, he dropped a hand in the water and laid it lightly on a shark, feeling its back and dorsal fin. It felt like sandpaper. The second shark passed, and Louie let his hand follow its body. *Beautiful,* he thought.

Soon after, Louie noticed something odd. Both sharks were gone. Never had the sharks left. Louie leaned over the water, looking down, puzzled.

Without warning, one of the sharks Louie had touched leapt up at terrific speed, mouth wide open, lunging at Louie's head. Louie threw both hands in front of his face. The shark struck him head-on, trying to get its mouth around him. Louie shoved, and the shark splashed back into the water. A moment later, the second shark jumped up. Louie grabbed an oar and struck the shark in the nose, and it jerked back and slid away. Then the first shark lunged for him again. Louie saw an oar swing past, sending the animal backward into the ocean. To Louie's surprise, it wasn't Phil who'd saved him. It was Mac.

Louie had no time to thank him. One of the sharks jumped up again, then the other. Louie and Mac clubbed at them. A moment before, Mac had seemed almost comatose. Now he was infused with energy.

For several minutes, the sharks took turns bellying onto the raft. Finally, they gave up. Louie and Mac collapsed.

Louie beamed at Mac, telling him how grateful and proud of him he was. Mac, crumpled on the floor, smiled back. He'd pushed himself beyond his body's capacities, but his frightened expression was gone. Mac had reclaimed himself.

———

Louie was furious at the sharks. He stewed all night, scowled hatefully at them all day, and decided that if the sharks were going to try to eat him, he'd try to eat them. He and Phil made a plan.

Spotting a shark about five feet long, Phil hung bait from one end of the raft. Louie knelt at the other end, facing the water. As the shark swam to Phil, Louie plunged his hands in the water and grabbed its tail. The shark took off, yanking Louie into the ocean and flinging him off. Louie bolted back onto the raft.

Soaked and embarrassed, Louie rethought his plan. His first error was to underestimate the strength of sharks. His second was to fail to brace himself. His third was to allow the shark's tail to stay in the water, giving it water to push against.

A small shark, perhaps four feet long, arrived. Louie knelt at the raft's side, tipping his weight back and spacing his knees. Phil dangled the bait.

The shark swam for the bait. Louie clapped his hands around the tail and heaved it out of the water. The shark thrashed but couldn't get free. Louie dragged it onto the raft. As the shark twisted and snapped, Phil grabbed a flare cartridge and jammed it in the shark's mouth. Pinning the shark down, Louie stabbed the pliers through the animal's eye. The shark died instantly.

Louie had been told the liver was the only edible part of a shark. After much sawing with the mirror edge, Louie found it, and it was sizeable. They ate it with relish. Soon after, they caught a second small shark and ate its liver, too.

Among the sharks, word got around: no more small sharks came near. The men's stomachs were soon empty again.

Mac was in a sharp downward spiral. He rarely moved. His eyes, sunken in their sockets, stared out lifelessly.

———

It was night, around the thirtieth day. The moon shone. The men slept.

Louie woke to a tremendous crash and the sensation of weightlessness. His eyes snapped open and he realized that he, Mac, and Phil were airborne. They flopped down together and twisted in confusion. Something had struck the bottom of the raft with awesome power.

Then they saw it. Swelling up from the sea came a vast white mouth, a broad back, a tall dorsal fin. The animal was gigantic, some twenty feet long. It was a great white shark.

As the castaways watched in terrified silence, the shark swam around the raft, exploring it. It paused, swished its tail away, then slapped it hard into the raft, splashing a wave of water into the men and sending the raft skidding sideways. Louie, Mac, and Phil clung to each other. The shark swam to the

Mac survived for thirty-three days on the raft. COURTESY OF LOUIS ZAMPERINI

other side. Louie whispered, *"Don't make a noise!"* Again came the mighty swing, the shower of water, the jolt.

As the men huddled, around and around the shark went, playing with the raft, drenching it with each pass. Finally, the great back slid under and the sea smoothed behind it.

———

In the morning, Mac couldn't sit up. Louie caught an albatross, wrenched its head off, and handed it to Phil, who let the blood flow into Mac's mouth. They ate the bird eagerly, Louie and Phil dipping the meat in the ocean to give it flavor. They fed bites to Mac, but it didn't revive him.

On the evening of the thirty-third day, Mac turned his face to Louie.

"Am I going to die?"

Louie looked at Mac. He didn't want to lie to him, in case he had something he needed to say or do before life left him. Louie said he thought he'd die that night. Mac had no reaction. Phil and Louie lay down, put their arms around Mac, and fell asleep.

Sometime that night, Louie was lifted from sleep by a breathy sound, a deep outrushing of air, slow and final. He knew what it was.

———

Francis McNamara had begun his last journey with a panicked, disastrous act, consuming the only food they had. But in his last days, in the struggle against the deflating raft and jumping sharks, he'd given all he had left. It probably hastened his death, but it may have saved Phil and Louie. At the end of his brief life, Mac had redeemed himself.

In the morning, Phil and Louie knelt over the body. Louie wanted to give him a religious eulogy, but didn't know how, so he recited passages from movies. And he prayed for himself and Phil. If God would save them, he vowed, he'd serve heaven forever.

Louie cradled Mac's body. It felt as if it weighed no more than forty pounds. He slid Mac gently into the water. Mac sank away. The sharks let him be.

The next night, Louie and Phil completed their thirty-fourth day on the raft. Though they didn't know it, they'd passed what was almost certainly the record for survival adrift on an inflated raft. If anyone had survived longer, they hadn't lived to tell about it.

———

The raft bobbed west. Storms came now and then, replenishing the water. Louie made a hook out of his lieutenant's pin and caught one fish before the pin broke.

Phil and Louie could see the bend of their thighbones under their skin, their bellies hollow, their ribs stark. Their skin glowed yellow from raft dye. Their hunger dimmed, an ominous sign. They'd reached the last stage of starvation.

One morning, they woke to a strange stillness. The raft sat motionless. The ocean stretched out glossy smooth, reflecting the sky in crystalline perfection. They had found the doldrums, the eerie pause of wind and water that lingers around the equator.

Phil watched the sky, whispering that it looked like the surface of a pearl. The water looked so solid it seemed they could walk upon it. When a fish broke the surface far away, the sound carried to them with absolute clarity. Pristine ringlets of water circled outward around the place where the fish had passed, then faded.

They fell into reverent silence. Their suffering was suspended. They weren't hungry or thirsty. Such extraordinary beauty, Louie thought, was too perfect to have come by chance. That day was, to him, a gift crafted deliberately, compassionately, for him and Phil.

Joyful and grateful as they were dying, Louie and Phil bathed in that day until sunset brought it to an end.

———

On the fortieth day, Louie was lying beside Phil under the remains of Phil's ruined raft, which Louie had made into a canopy. Suddenly, he sat up. He heard singing. He nudged Phil and asked if he heard anything. Phil said no. Louie slid the canopy off and squinted into the daylight.

Above him, floating in a bright cloud, he saw the silhouettes of twenty-one human figures. They were singing the sweetest song he'd ever heard.

Louie stared up, awestruck. What he was seeing was impossible, yet he felt absolutely lucid. This was, he felt certain, no hallucination. He sat under the singers, memorizing the melody, until they disappeared.

Phil had heard and seen nothing. Whatever this was, it belonged to Louie alone.

———

A week passed with no food and no rain. The raft was a gooey mess, its patches bubbling outward, about to pop. It wouldn't bear the men much longer.

Phil noticed that there were more birds. Then they began to hear planes. Sometimes they'd see a tiny speck in the sky, always much too distant to be signaled, and surely Japanese. As days passed, more planes appeared.

On the morning of the forty-sixth day, no sunrise came. There was only a gloomy illumination of an ominous sky. Phil and Louie looked up apprehensively. The wind caught them sharply. The sea churned and arched its back, sending the raft up to dizzying heights.

To the west, something appeared, so distant it could only be glimpsed from the tops of the swells. The moment the sea tossed them up and their eyes grasped it, Phil and Louie knew what it was.

It was an island.

The waterlogged wallet Louie carried throughout his raft journey. Photo by David Mackintosh

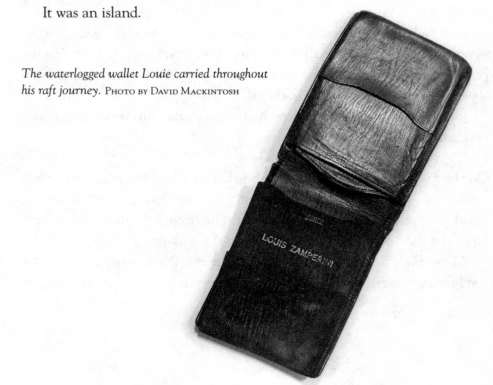

CHAPTER 17

Typhoon

All day, under a gyrating sky, Louie and Phil rode the swells, feeling a weary thrill as the island peeked into view. Slowly, it became distinct. They saw a bright white line where waves dashed against a beach or reef. That afternoon, one island became two, then many. Overhead, a colossal storm was gathering. The men rowed landward.

The sky broke. A slashing rain came down, and the islands vanished. The ocean began heaving and thrashing. The wind sent the raft spinning up swells, perhaps forty feet, then careening down into troughs as deep as canyons. Phil and Louie were in a typhoon.

Wave after wave slammed into the raft, tipping it sideways and peeling it upward. To stop it from flipping, Louie and Phil bailed in water to weigh it down, sat on opposite sides to balance their weight, and lay down to keep the center of gravity low. They held on.

Night fell, and the storm pounded. The raft raced over hundreds of mountains of water. At times, the men felt themselves flying in the darkness as the raft was swept in the air. Louie felt even more intensely afraid than he'd felt as *Green Hornet* was falling. They thought of the land they could no longer see, fearing that any second, they'd be flung into a reef.

Sometime in the night, the storm died away. In its wake came the sweetest scent: soil, greenness, rain washing over living things—the scent of land. As dawn neared, the men heard the hiss of water scouring a reef. Exhausted, they took turns napping, with one man on the lookout for land. Somewhere along the way, they both fell asleep.

———

They woke in a new universe. After weeks in open ocean, they were surrounded by islands. On one, they saw a deserted native village. They'd heard of the Japanese capturing and shipping out natives as slaves and wondered if that had happened here. They began rowing for shore.

Louie had predicted they'd find land on the forty-seventh day. Phil had chosen the forty-sixth. Because they'd spotted land on the forty-sixth and were reaching it on the forty-seventh, they decided they'd both been right.

Louie gazed at a tiny island with one tree on it. A strange thing happened. The tree became two trees. After a moment's confusion, he suddenly understood. It wasn't an island, and those weren't trees. It was a boat. It had been perpendicular to them, leaving only one mast visible, and then it turned, bringing the rearward mast into view.

Louie and Phil ducked and rowed as fast as they could, trying to get ashore before they were spotted. They were too late. The boat sped toward them. Louie and Phil rowed hard, but the boat caught them and drew alongside the raft. Along the deck stood a line of Japanese men, aiming guns at Louie and Phil.

A sailor threw a rope, and Louie caught it. He and Phil tried to climb up to the boat, but their legs were too weak. The sailors tied them to a rope ladder and dragged them up.

On the deck, Louie and Phil tried to rise, but their legs buckled. With the sailors herding them, they crawled to the mast. The sailors lashed them to it and bound their hands behind them. A sailor spoke to them in Japanese, apparently asking questions. Another waved a bayonet past Louie's face, trying to hack off his beard. One cracked a pistol into Phil's jaw, then moved to do the same to Louie. Louie tipped his head forward, then, when the sailor swung, jerked his head back. He made the man miss, but smacked his head against the mast.

The captain approached and chastised the crewmen. The mood changed, Louie's and Phil's hands were untied, and they were given water and two biscuits. Louie ate slowly, savoring each crumb. It was his first food in eight days.

———

Louie and Phil were transferred to a second boat, where a crewman fed them more biscuits and some coconut. A man approached, Japanese-English dictionary in hand, and asked questions. Phil and Louie told of their journey.

The boat drew up to an island. Louie and Phil were blindfolded, and men half carried them off the boat. After a few minutes, Louie felt himself being laid down on something soft. His blindfold was removed.

He and Phil were in an infirmary, lying on beds. Through a window, he saw Japanese soldiers thrusting bayonets into dummies. An officer spoke to the Japanese surrounding the castaways, then spoke in English, apparently repeating himself so Louie and Phil would understand.

"These are American fliers," he said. "Treat them gently."

A doctor came in, smiled, examined Phil and Louie, and smoothed ointment on their salt sores. Louie and Phil took turns standing on a scale, each with a man ready to catch him if his legs failed.

Phil, who'd weighed about 150 pounds when he'd stepped aboard *Green Hornet*, now weighed about eighty pounds. By different accounts, five-foot ten-inch Louie, who'd weighed about 160 before the crash, weighed sixty-seven pounds, seventy-nine and one-half pounds, or eighty-seven pounds.

The doctor had cognac, eggs, ham, milk, fresh bread, and fruit salad brought in. Louie and Phil feasted. When they were done, they were seated before Japanese officers, who gaped at the shrunken, yellow men. An officer asked how they'd ended up there. Louie told the story as the officers listened, fascinated.

Louie and Phil knew where their journey had begun, but didn't know where it had ended. The officers told them. They were in the Marshall Islands. They'd drifted two thousand miles.

Two beds were made up, and the castaways were invited to rest. Slipping between cool, clean sheets, their stomachs full, their sores soothed, they were deeply grateful. Phil had a relieved thought: *They are our friends.*

Louie and Phil stayed in the infirmary for two days, attended by kind Japanese. On the third day, an officer came, bearing beef, chocolate, coconuts, and news. They were being taken to another atoll. The name he gave sent a tremor through Louie: Kwajalein. It was the place known as Execution Island.

"After you leave here," the officer said, "we cannot guarantee your life."

Aboard the freighter, Louie and Phil were treated well. But as they drew up to Kwajalein, the Japanese suddenly became harsh. On came the blindfolds, and Louie and Phil were carried ashore and dumped on a hard surface. When Louie said something to Phil, a boot kicked him as a voice shouted, "No!"

An engine started, and they were moving. They were on a truck. In a few minutes, the truck stopped, and Louie was tugged out and carried again. There was walking, a darkening, and the feeling of being thrown backward. Louie's back struck a wall and he fell to a floor. Someone yanked off his blindfold. A door slammed, a lock turned.

At first, Louie could barely see. His eyes darted about uncontrollably. His mind raced, flitting wildly from thought to thought. After weeks of endless openness, he was disoriented by the compression of space around him.

Slowly, his thoughts quieted and his eyes settled. He was in a cell, about the length of his body and little wider than his shoulders. There was a small window in the door. The floor was strewn with gravel, dirt, and maggots, and the room hummed with flies and mosquitoes, already swarming on him. There was a hole in the floor with a latrine bucket below it. The air hung scorching hot and still, heavy with the stench of human waste.

Louie looked up. In the dimness, he saw words carved in the wall: NINE MARINES MAROONED ON MAKIN ISLAND, AUGUST 12, 1942. Below were nine names.

In August 1942, after an American raid on a Japanese base at Makin in the Marshall Islands, nine marines had been mistakenly left behind. Captured by the Japanese, they'd disappeared. Louie was almost certainly the first

American to learn they'd been taken to Kwajalein. But they weren't here now. Louie felt a wave of foreboding.

He called to Phil. Phil's voice answered, distant and small. He was down the hall in a squalid hole just like Louie's. Each asked the other if he was okay. They knew it was likely the last time they'd talk, but if they wished to say goodbye, neither had the chance. There was shuffling in the corridor as a guard took up his station. Louie and Phil went quiet.

Louie looked down at his body. Legs that had sprung through a 4:12 mile on that last Hawaiian morning were now useless. His vibrant body had shrunken until only the bones remained, draped in yellow skin, crawling with parasites.

All I see, he thought, *is a dead body breathing.*

He dissolved into hard, racking weeping. He muffled his sobs so the guard wouldn't hear him.

PART
IV

PART

IV

CHAPTER 18

A Dead Body Breathing

A biscuit was tossed into Louie's cell, breaking into bits on the floor. A tiny cup of weak tea was set on the windowsill. Louie gulped the tea and crawled around, picking up crumbs and putting them in his mouth.

There was a rustle outside, and a Kwajalein native appeared. He greeted Louie cheerfully, in English, by name. Louie stared at him in confusion.

The man said the castaways were the talk of the island. He was an ardent track fan, and when he'd heard Louie's name, he'd come to meet the great runner. As Louie listened, bewildered, the man chattered about sports, indifferent to Louie's plight. When he glanced at his watch and said he had to go, Louie stopped him. What happened to the marines held there?

They're all dead, the man said. All POWs held on Kwajalein were executed.

As the man left, the guard looked challengingly at Louie, lifted a flattened hand to his throat, and made a slashing gesture. He pointed to the names on the wall, then to Louie.

The second day began. Phil and Louie lay in sweltering silence, expecting to be dragged out and beheaded. Louie developed explosive diarrhea, and cramps doubled him over. Flies, lice, and mosquitoes teemed on him. The heat was smothering. Down the hall, rats wallowed in Phil's waste bucket and skittered over his face. Guards stalked past, snarling and drawing the sides of their hands across their necks with cruel smiles.

Days passed, each bringing two or three rice balls tossed to the floor and a few tiny cups of tea. Louie's diarrhea became bloody. He begged for water. The guard brought a cup. Louie, grateful, drew close to the door to drink. The guard threw scalding water in his face. Desperately dehydrated, Louie kept begging. Each time, the response was the same, leaving Louie's face blistered. He knew dehydration might kill him, and part of him hoped it would.

As he lay in misery, he heard again the singers from the raft. He let their voices wash over him, finding reason to hope. He held the song in his mind, praying intensely. He stared at the marines' names, wondering who they were, how the end had come. He pulled off his belt, bent the buckle up, and carved his name beside theirs.

The guards were in a fixed state of fury at the captives. Nearly every day, they flew into rages that usually ended with Phil and Louie being spat upon and bombarded with rocks and lit cigarettes. Every day, at gunpoint, Louie was forced to dance while his guards roared with laughter. They stabbed him with sticks and taunted him as he crawled around picking up bits of rice. Once, driven to his breaking point by a guard jabbing him, Louie yanked the stick away. He knew he might be killed for it, but under ceaseless humiliation, something was happening to him. He was losing his will to live.

The crash of *Green Hornet* had left Louie and Phil in the most desperate physical hardship, without food, water, or shelter. But on Kwajalein, the guards deprived them of something deeper: dignity. This self-respect and sense of self-worth, the innermost armament of the soul, lies at the heart of humanness. To be deprived of it is to be dehumanized, leaving victims in a state of profound wretchedness and loneliness, unable to hang on to hope.

Few societies treasured dignity, and feared humiliation, as did the Japanese, for whom loss of honor could merit suicide. This is probably one of the reasons why Japanese soldiers in World War II debased their prisoners with such zeal, seeking to take from them that which was most painful and destructive to lose. On Kwajalein, Louie and Phil learned a dark truth known to the doomed in Hitler's death camps, the slaves of the American South, and a hundred other generations of betrayed people: dignity is as essential to human life as water, food, and oxygen. The stubborn retention of it, even in the face of extreme physical hardship, can keep a man alive long past the point when he should have died. The loss of it can carry a man off as surely as thirst, hunger, exposure, and asphyxiation, and with greater cruelty. In places like Kwajalein, degradation could be as lethal as a bullet.

Louie had been on Kwajalein for about a week when his cell door was thrown open and guards pulled him out. Terrified, thinking he was about to be beheaded, he was marched into a building. Before him were Japanese officers, sitting by a table heaped with food meant to entice him. Louie wasn't going to be executed. He was going to be interrogated.

The ranking officer stared coolly at Louie. Which model of B-24 did he crash in? Louie replied, truthfully, that it was a D-model. The officer handed him a pencil and paper and told him to draw the plane. On Oahu, Louie had heard that a crashed D-model had been captured by the Japanese. Knowing that they already knew the plane in detail, he drew it accurately. His interrogators held up a photo of a D-model. They'd been testing his truthfulness.

What did he know about the E-model? Nothing, he replied. It was a lie; D-model *Super Man* had undergone upgrades that effectively made it an E. How do you operate the radar? Louie knew the answer, but replied that as a bombardier, he wouldn't know. Told to draw the radar system, Louie drew an imaginary system so elaborate, it was later written, it resembled "a ruptured octopus." The interrogators nodded.

They moved on to his bombsight, which was top-secret. How do you work it? You twist two knobs, Louie said. The officers knew he was lying and sent him to his cell without giving him any food.

Suspecting he'd be brought back, Louie tried to anticipate questions. He thought of the things he could tell and those he had to keep secret. He invented lies and practiced telling them. Because he'd been partially truthful in the first session, he knew his captors would be more likely to trust his answers.

One day, a new guard appeared at the door. Louie felt an upswell of dread. "You Christian?" the guard asked. Louie said yes. The guard smiled. "Me Christian."

The guard reached into the cell and slipped two pieces of candy into Louie's hand, then gave two pieces to Phil. A friendship was born.

The guard's name was Kawamura, and he spoke almost no English. Each day, he walked between the cells, drawing pictures of things and saying and writing their Japanese names. Louie and Phil would write and say the English names. They understood almost nothing Kawamura said, but his gentle smile and goodwill needed no translation. It was lifesaving.

When Kawamura was off duty, another guard came. He launched himself at Louie, ramming a stick into his face as if trying to put out his eyes. When Kawamura saw Louie's bloody face, he asked who'd done it, then sped away, furious. Later, he returned, opened Louie's cell door a crack, and proudly pointed outside. There stood the guard who'd abused Louie, his forehead and mouth heavily bandaged. He never guarded the cell again.

———

One day Louie and Phil looked up to see angry faces pressed into their cell windows, shouting. Rocks flew in. More men came, screaming, spitting on the captives, hurling sticks. Louie balled up on the floor. On and on it went, some ninety men taking turns attacking the captives. At last, it ended. Louie lay in pools of spit and jumbled rocks and sticks, bleeding.

Kawamura was distraught over what had been done to his friends. He told them the culprits were a submarine crew, stopping over on the island, who had learned Americans were being held there. During interrogation, Louie complained about the attack. It's what you should expect, the officers replied.

The interrogators asked Louie the numbers of aircraft, ships, and servicemen in Hawaii. Louie said he'd left Hawaii in May. Now it was August. He had no current information. He was sent back to his cell.

———

Some three weeks after arriving at Kwajalein, Louie and Phil were suddenly dragged outside. They were taken to the front porch of the interrogation building, where men in medical coats awaited them. Japanese gathered to watch.

Louie and Phil were ordered to lie down. The doctors pulled out two long hypodermic syringes and filled each with a murky solution. Louie and Phil realized they were about to be used for an experiment.

The doctors slid the needles into the captives' forearms and pushed the plungers. Within a few seconds, the porch started gyrating around Louie. The doctor pushed more solution in, and the spinning worsened. Louie felt as if pins were being jabbed all over his body. Then he felt light-headed. His skin burned, itched, and stung. Nearby, Phil endured the same ordeal. The doctors questioned the captives on their symptoms. Louie cried out that he was going to faint. The doctor withdrew the needle.

The captives were returned to their cells. Louie's entire body was covered in a rash. For days, he was maddened by itching and burning. When the symptoms subsided, he and Phil were again injected, this time with more solution. Again they rolled through dizziness and burned with rashes. Then came a third experiment, then a fourth. In the last, a full pint of fluid was pumped into their veins.

They were lucky to survive. In their captured territories, the Japanese were using at least ten thousand POWs and civilians, including infants, as test subjects for unimaginably hellish experiments in medicine and biological and chemical warfare. Thousands died.

———

Battered, emaciated, and sick, Louie was brought to interrogation for the final time. The officers pushed a map of Hawaii in front of him and told him to mark the air bases.

Louie resisted, but the interrogators leaned hard on him. At last, Louie broke. He dropped his head and told them everything—the exact location of the bases, the numbers of planes. The Japanese were jubilant. They opened a bottle of cola and gave it to Louie, along with a biscuit and a pastry.

It was all a lie. The "bases" Louie identified were the fake airfields he'd seen when tooling around Hawaii with Phil. If the Japanese bombed there, the only planes they'd hit would be made of plywood.

———

The captives' usefulness had been exhausted. At headquarters, the decision was made. Louie and Phil would be executed.

On August 24, men gathered before Louie's cell, and once more he was pulled out. *Is this it?* he thought. Expecting to hear he was doomed, he was astonished to be told something else: he and Phil were being sent by ship to Japan, where they'd be placed in a POW camp.

At the last minute, the officers had decided not to kill them. It would be a long time before Louie learned why.

On August 26, 1943, forty-two days after arriving at Execution Island, Louie and Phil were led from their cells for the last time. Louie looked back, searching for Kawamura. He couldn't find him.

CHAPTER 19

"No One Knows You're Alive"

There was something eerie about this place.

It was a cold day in September 1943. Louie stood on Japanese soil for the first time, his eyes adjusting to light after his blindfold was removed. His head and beard had been shorn, and his body bathed in disinfectant.

His nose was a bloody mess. On the voyage to Japan, he and Phil had been confronted by drunken sailors. One of them asked if Japan would win the war.

"No," said Phil.

A fist caught Phil in the face. Louie was asked who'd win the war.

"America."

The sailors tackled the captives. A fist connected with Louie's nose, and he felt a crunch. An officer ran in and stopped the beating. In choppy English, he said that in the captives' confiscated wallets, the sailors had found the clipping Louie had cut from a Hawaiian newspaper, describing his role in the Wake raid. The sailors had been on Wake that night.

Louie's nose was badly broken. He'd pushed the bones back in place with his fingers on the journey, but upon arriving in Japan, an officer had struck his face with a flashlight, breaking his nose again.

After Kwajalein, Louie had been relieved to be going to a POW camp,

American prisoners of war held by the Japanese. The average army or army air forces POW lost a staggering sixty-one pounds in captivity. Many starved to death. GETTY IMAGES

where he thought he'd have the rights international law guaranteed prisoners of war: he'd be well fed, sheltered, given medical treatment, allowed to write home, and tended to by the Red Cross. Now, looking around, he was spooked. It wasn't the barbed wire that unnerved him. Nor was it the tumbledown barracks or the guards, clutching bayoneted rifles, clubs, and baseball bats. It was the prisoners.

Gathered in drifts against the barracks were hundreds of Allied servicemen. They were ghastly thin. Every one of them had his eyes fixed on the ground. They were as silent as snow.

———

Another captive approached Louie, and he seemed to have permission to speak. This isn't a POW camp, he said. It was a secret interrogation camp called Ofuna, where "high-value" captives were held in solitary confinement, starved, and tortured so they'd give up military secrets.

Louie was forbidden to speak to anyone but the guards, to put his hands in his pockets, or to make eye contact with other captives. His gaze was to be directed down at all times. He had to learn Japanese numbers, because every morning there was a roll call in which men had to count off. There were rules about everything, from folding sheets to buttoning clothes, each reinforcing total obedience. The slightest violation would bring a beating.

In this secret place, the Japanese could, and did, do anything they wanted to captives. "They can kill you here," Louie was told. "No one knows you're alive."

Louie was led to a cell. His bed was a straw mat with three paper sheets. The window had no glass, the walls were particleboard, the ceiling made of tar paper. With winter approaching, Louie would be living in a building that was barely a windbreak.

Louie curled up on his mat. There were dozens of men in cells near him, but there was no sound. In this warren of captives, Louie was alone.

———

Ofuna was a place dedicated to breaking men's souls, and Louie soon learned what a hell it was.

This newspaper clipping, which Louie put in his wallet after the Wake raid, remained in his wallet throughout his raft journey, turning purple from the leached dye of the leather. When it was discovered by the Japanese, Louie and Phil were beaten. COURTESY OF LOUIS ZAMPERINI

Each day began at six: a clanging bell, a shouting guard, captives running outside for inspection. Louie would fall into a line of haggard men. Guards stalked them, yelling unintelligibly. The men were made to count off, bow toward the palace of Japan's Emperor Hirohito, then run to the *benjo*—latrine. Breakfast was a bowl of watery, foul slop, which each man ate alone in his cell. Then they were given knots of wet rope and forced to bend double, put the rope on the floor, and wash the barracks aisle at a run, or sometimes waddling duck-style, while the guards swatted them.

Outside again, the guards forced the captives to run or perform calisthenics, often until they collapsed. When the exercise was over, the men had to stand outside, regardless of the weather. The only breaks in the silence were the screams in the interrogation room.

Beatings were almost constant. Men were beaten for virtually anything: folding their arms, cleaning their teeth, talking in their sleep, and most often, for not understanding orders issued in Japanese. Dozens of men were clubbed in the knees for one man's alleged infraction. Any attempt they made to protect themselves—ducking, shielding their faces—provoked more violence. The beatings, wrote a captive, "were of such intensity that many of us wondered if we'd ever live to see the end of the war."

The captives weren't just beaten, they were starved. Meals usually consisted of a bowl of broth with a bit of vegetable and a bowl or half bowl of rancid rice, sometimes mixed with a little barley. The food was infested with rat droppings, maggots, and so much sand and gravel that Louie's teeth were soon pitted, chipped, and cracked.

The extremely low caloric intake and foul food put men's lives in jeopardy. Parasites and intestinal infections made diarrhea universal. Malnourishment-related diseases were epidemic. Most feared was beriberi, caused by vitamin B1 deficiency. One form of it caused grotesque swelling of the extremities; testicles could swell to the size of bread loaves. Untreated, beriberi was often fatal.

———

The ringmasters of the violence were the guards. At Ofuna, as at the scores of POW camps in Japan and its conquests, the guards were the dregs of the military. Some were too incompetent for any other duty. Others were deranged. Among nearly all Ofuna guards, there were two common characteristics. One was marked stupidity. The other was murderous cruelty.

The cruelty was a product of Japan's military culture. All Japanese soldiers were regularly beaten by their superiors, in the belief it would strengthen them. Guards, occupying the lowest station in a military that applauded brutal domination of underlings, vented their frustrations on the helpless prisoners under their authority.

Louie's barracks at Ofuna. His window was the third from right. Courtesy of Frank Tinker

This tendency was powerfully reinforced by two opinions then common in Japan. Just as Allied soldiers, like the cultures they came from, often held venomously racist views of the Japanese, Japanese soldiers and civilians usually carried caustic prejudices about their enemies, seeing them as brutish beasts or fearsome devils. This racism, and the hatred and fear it generated, further inspired abuse of Allied prisoners.

From earliest childhood, Japanese citizens were taught that to surrender or be captured was intolerably shameful. The Japanese Military Field Code made clear what was expected of men facing capture: "Rather than live and bear the shame of imprisonment, the soldier must die and avoid leaving a dishonorable name." In many hopeless battles, virtually every Japanese soldier fought to the death. At times, soldiers committed mass suicide to avoid surrender. The revulsion most Japanese felt for those who were captured extended to

Allied servicemen. To abuse, enslave, and even murder a prisoner was acceptable, even desirable.

Though under great pressure to conform to a culture of brutality, a few guards refused to join the violence. Such humane behavior took nerve. Everywhere in Japan, demonstrating sympathy for captives or POWs was taboo. Guards caught trying to help prisoners, or even voicing compassion for them, were beaten. At Ofuna, one guard who was kind to captives endured nightly gang attacks from his fellow guards.

———

Deaths from beating and malnourishment were common in Ofuna. For captives, the only hope lay in rescue by the Allies, but this prospect carried tremendous danger.

In 1942, when America attacked Japanese ships near Tarawa Atoll, the Japanese beheaded twenty-two POWs held there. In 1943, when the Americans bombed Japanese-held Ballale, the Japanese executed some seventy to one hundred POWs they'd enslaved on the island. Then, shortly after Louie arrived at Ofuna, American ships attacked Wake, where the ninety-eight captured Americans were still being used as slaves. The Japanese promptly shot all the prisoners.

These mass murders were the first applications of Japan's "kill-all" rule: if Allied advances made the rescue of POWs possible, POWs must be executed. A message sent to all POW camp commanders stated:

> Whether they are destroyed individually or in groups, or however it is done, with mass bombing, poisonous smoke, poisons, drowning, decapitation, or what, dispose of them as the situation dictates. . . . It is the aim not to allow the escape of a single one, to annihilate them all, and not to leave any traces.

As the Allies fought their way toward Japan, the kill-all order loomed over the Ofuna captives. Like every other captive, Louie knew the guards were eagerly awaiting the chance to carry it out.

CHAPTER 20

Farting for Hirohito

At first, there was silence and isolation. At night, no one spoke. Come daylight, Louie was suddenly in a crowd, hustled outside and herded in crazy circles, but with eyes obediently down, mouth obediently closed, he was no less alone. The only break in the gloom came from a guard who would saunter down the barracks aisle, pause before each cell, raise one leg, and fart at each captive. He never quite succeeded in farting his way down the entire cell block.

In stolen glances, nods, and hushed words, Louie sorted out Ofuna. Most men in his barracks were Americans, survivors of sunken ships or crashed planes. Down the hall lived an American navy officer, Commander John Fitzgerald, captured after he scuttled his burning submarine. The Japanese had tried to torture information out of Fitzgerald, clubbing him, jamming knives under his fingernails, tearing his fingernails off, and pouring water up his nose until he passed out. Fitzgerald had never broken, and as one of the highest-ranking captives, did his best to protect the men.

During forced exercise, Louie fell into step with a young marine named William Harris. Captured in the Philippines in 1942, Harris had escaped, diving into Manila Bay and embarking on an eight-and-a-half-hour swim. Wad-

Lieutenant William Harris, who escaped his initial capture by swimming across Manila Bay and fleeing through the jungle, surviving in part by eating ants.

ing ashore on the Japanese-occupied Bataan Peninsula, he'd hiked through jungles and over mountains, sailed in borrowed boats, and hitched rides on burros, surviving in part by eating ants. He'd nearly made it to Australia by boat when civilians turned him in to the Japanese.

Each day, Louie and Harris hung together, laboring through forced exercise, bearing the guards' blows, and whispering. The curious thing about Harris was that while he was tall—six two or three—virtually everyone, including Louie, would remember him as a giant, as tall as six ten. In a sense, Louie and the others were right. Harris was a genius. Highly educated, conversant in several languages, he had a perfect photographic memory. A captive once found him with hands parted as if holding a book. Asked what he was doing, Harris said he was reading a text he'd studied in school. In Ofuna, his astounding memory would be a blessing and a terrible curse.

Ofuna had one other notable resident. Gaga was a duck who limped around on a broken leg that a captive had fitted with a splint. Everywhere the captives went, Gaga peg-legged with them. A captive would later swear that when the men bowed toward the emperor, Gaga bowed in imitation. In so dark a place, this cheerful bird became especially beloved.

Louie rarely saw Phil, who was housed down the hall. The pilot was frail, his eyes haunted. Once, when Louie shuffled up next to him outside, Phil finally spoke of the crash. He said he felt responsible for his men's deaths. Louie tried to reassure him that the crash wasn't his fault. Phil was unswayed.

"I'll never fly again," he said.

As Louie adjusted to Ofuna, he noticed something strange. Every other captive was relentlessly interrogated, but he was never questioned. Clearly, the Japanese had no interest in what he knew. They had some reason for subjecting him to the misery of Ofuna, but he had no idea what it was.

———

Louie soon discovered that Ofuna's submissive silence was an illusion. Beneath the hush was a humming underground of defiance.

It began with sidelong whispers. Men scribbled notes on toilet paper and hid them for each other in the *benjo*. Exploiting the silence rule's loophole—captives were permitted to speak to guards—they'd approach the guards in groups and speak English, using a querying tone. The confused guards thought they were being asked questions, but the men were really speaking to each other.

At night, if the guards stepped away from the cells, the whole barracks would start tapping out Morse code. Outside in daytime, Louie and the others whispered in code—"tit" for "dot" and "da" for "dash," words that could be spoken without moving the lips. Others hid their hands and gestured—a fist was a dot, a flat hand a dash.

Because guards who caught captives speaking about them often responded with savage beatings, the men gave them nicknames, including Turdbird, Flange Face, the Weasel, Liver Lip, and Termite. One guard was especially feared. He was the medical officer, a sadist who tortured and beat captives for pleasure. A massive man, he punched like a heavyweight. They called him the Quack.

The defiance took on a life of its own. Men smiled and addressed guards in friendly tones, cooing out filthy insults. One captive convinced a particularly daft guard that a sundial would work at night if he used a match. A favorite pastime involved saving up intestinal gasses, explosively abundant thanks to dysentery, before roll call. Ordered to bow toward Emperor Hirohito, the captives would pitch forward and fart in unison.

Louie had another private act of rebellion. A captive gave him a tiny book he'd made from rice paste flattened into pages. On the central pages, Louie made it seem a harmless address book. In faint script upside down in the back,

Louie's secret POW diary, made from rice paste pressed into sheets of paper.
PHOTO BY DAVID MACKINTOSH

he kept a diary, forbidden at Ofuna. He hid the diary under a loose board in his cell. With daily cell inspections, discovery was likely and would surely bring a clubbing. But the diary was precious to Louie. He knew he might die here. He wanted to leave a record of what he had endured and who he had been.

After food, what the men wanted most was war news. The Japanese sealed the camps from war information and told the captives preposterous stories of Allied losses, even announcing that their military had shot Abraham Lincoln and torpedoed Washington, D.C. "They couldn't understand why we laughed," said a prisoner.

Ofuna officials had no idea the captives were following the war in spite of them. New captives were questioned by fellow captives, the news tapping through camp in minutes. The Japanese rarely brought newspapers in, but when one did, stealing it was a campwide obsession. Stolen papers were passed to Harris and Fitzgerald, who spoke Japanese. As translations were done, lookouts stood by. When guards neared, the papers vanished, soon to be put to their final use. In a camp with a lot of diarrhea and little toilet paper, newspapers were priceless.

Knowing the Allies were winning was immensely inspiring, enabling men to hang on a little longer. But that wasn't the only benefit of the stealing and defiance. Through acts of resistance, dignity was preserved, and through dignity, life itself. Everyone knew what the consequences would be if anyone was caught stealing papers. At the time, it seemed worth the risk.

———

In the fall, snow came, gliding through gaps in the barracks walls. Wearing the summer clothes he'd crashed in, Louie shivered. Shut outside all day, he and the others huddled, mixing slowly to give each man time in the warmer middle.

The rations dwindled. Unloading ration trucks, captives saw nutritious fare, but it was never served to them, because the Japanese were stealing it. The most flagrant thief was the cook, who packed the food on his bicycle and pedaled off to sell it. He reportedly bought and furnished a house with his profits.

The stealing left Ofuna in famine. Most captives were emaciated, but

Louie was the thinnest. The rations weren't nearly enough, and he was plagued by diarrhea. He teetered through the forced exercise. Once, he collapsed. Sprawled on the ground, he heard laughter.

Learning that Louie was a former Olympian, the guards brought in a Japanese runner for a match race. Forced to run, Louie was trounced, and the guards mocked him. He was angry and shaken, and his growing weakness scared him. Prisoners were dying by the thousands in Japan's camps, and winter was coming.

Captives stepped in to save Louie. A Norwegian gave him a coat, and each day, at enormous risk to themselves, the captive kitchen workers snuck him an extra handful of food, which Louie split with Phil. Grateful, Louie hung on.

———

At the end of 1943, the captives had a taste of liberation. Veteran captives, Louie included, were allowed to speak outside. When new captives arrived, they were whisked into solitary confinement until initial interrogation was over.

In early 1944, Louie was tracked down by a new captive just out of solitary. He was an amputee, one leg gone. His name was Fred Garrett, and he'd been a B-24 pilot. Amazed to see Louie, he told a remarkable story.

In December, America had bombed Japanese bases in the Marshall Islands. Garrett was shot down, incurring a gaping ankle fracture. Captured, he was thrown into a cell block with nineteen other Americans. His ankle became severely infected, maggots hatched in it, and Garrett began running a high fever. He was told he'd be given medical care only if he divulged military secrets. If not, he'd be killed. Garrett lied in interrogation, and the Japanese knew it.

Garrett was tied down, given a spinal anesthetic, and forced to watch as a Japanese corpsman sawed his leg off. Though the infection was limited to the ankle, the corpsman cut Garrett's entire leg off so he could never fly a plane again. Delirious, Garrett was shipped to Ofuna with two other captives. The seventeen Americans left behind were never seen again.

As he'd lain in agony in his cell, Garrett had seen ten names scratched into the wall. He was told the first nine had been executed. No one told him the fate of the tenth man. Garrett had long thought about the last man. When he'd arrived at Ofuna, he'd asked if anyone knew that man. His name was Louis Zamperini. Garrett and Louie, both Los Angeles–area natives, had been imprisoned in the same tiny Kwajalein cell almost five thousand miles from home.

———

Plodding around the compound that winter, Louie and Harris befriended Frank Tinker, a pilot who'd been brought from Kwajalein with Garrett. The three stuck together, distracting each other from the cold with mind exercises. Louie strengthened his legs, lifting his knees high as he walked. The guards began goading him into running.

In spring, the guards brought in another Japanese runner and ordered Louie to race him, warning that if he refused, all captives would be punished. Louie lagged behind, with no intention of winning, but his body was so light that running was surprisingly easy. He saw captives watching him, breathless. As the finish approached, they started cheering.

Louie knew what would happen if he won, but the cheering aroused his defiance. He lengthened his stride, seized the lead, and crossed the line. The captives whooped.

Louie didn't see the guard's club coming at his skull. He just felt the world tip and go away. His eyes opened to the sight of the sky, ringed in his friends' faces. It had been worth it.

———

In March, Phil was taken away, bound for what officials called a "plush" POW camp. He and Louie had a brief goodbye. They spoke of finding each other again someday, when the war was over. Phil was led away.

Phil's new camp, Ashio, was far from plush. Ashio's POWs were enslaved in a copper mine, in horrendous conditions. But there, Phil was told he could write home. He hadn't seen Cecy or his family in well over two years and knew they probably thought he was dead. He wrote about the raft, his capture, and yearning for home. "The first night home will hear some interesting tales," he wrote. "Much love til we're together again."

The Japanese never mailed his letter. It was found in the garbage, partially burned. Phil reclaimed it. If he lived through this war, he'd deliver it in person.

CHAPTER 21

Belief

Behind Torrance High stood a huddle of trees. On many evenings after her brother disappeared, Louie's sister Sylvia would drive to the school, turn her car under the trees, and park. As the car cooled, tears would stream down Sylvia's cheeks. Sometimes she'd let herself sob, knowing no one would hear. Then she'd dry her face, straighten herself, and start the car again.

On the drive home, she'd think of a lie to explain why she'd been gone so long. She never told anyone how frightened she was.

In Torrance, the June 1943 telegram announcing Louie's disappearance was followed by weeks of excruciating silence. In town, hope dissolved. In the Zamperini house, the mood was different. In the first days after the telegram arrived, Louise Zamperini had been seized with the conviction that her son was alive. Her husband and children had felt the same. Weeks passed, but the family's confidence was unshaken.

On July 13, Louise felt a wave of urgency. She wrote to the Seventh Air Force commander and begged him to keep searching; her son, she said, was alive. Unbeknownst to Louise, on that very day, Louie was captured.

Weeks later, a reply came from the commander's office. Given the failure of the search, the letter said, the military had been forced to accept that Louis was dead, and they hoped Louise would accept this also. Louise ripped up the letter.

Pete was still in San Diego, training navy recruits. The stress over Louie wore on him. When he visited home, everyone worried about how thin he was. In September, his last letter to Louie, mailed hours before he learned of Louie's disappearance, came back to him. Scribbled on it were the words *Missing at sea.*

That month, Sylvia's husband left to serve as a tank gunner in Europe. He'd be gone for two years. Living alone, Sylvia was racked with anxiety for her brother and her husband. Like Pete, she was barely able to eat. Yearning to connect with someone, she moved back in with her parents.

She found her father with chin up, smiling bravely. Her little sister Virginia, still living at home, was distraught. At first, Louise cried often. Then she went quiet. The rash on her hands raged so badly that her hands were almost useless. When Louie's footlocker was delivered, Louise couldn't bear to open it. She had it dragged to the basement and covered with a blanket. She would never look inside.

Everyone in the family was suffering, but they never cried together, instead making up stories of Louie's adventures on a tropical island. They never discussed the possibility that he was dead. When they walked in town, passersby glanced at them sadly, as if they pitied the family for being unable to accept the truth.

What the Zamperinis were experiencing wasn't denial, and it wasn't hope. It was belief. They could still *feel* Louie. Their distress came not from grief, but from the certainty that Louie was in trouble and they couldn't reach him.

Every week, Sylvia wrote to Louie, sharing trivial news, writing as if everything were normal. With no idea where he was, she sent his letters to the Red Cross. She'd drive out to mail them, then drive to Torrance High, park under the trees, and cry.

At night, alone in her childhood bed, Sylvia often broke down. When sleep came, it was haunted. Because she knew nothing of her brother's fate, her mind dwelt on an image she'd seen in the newspaper after Nauru: Louie peering through a cannon hole in *Super Man*. This was the focus of her nightmares: Louie being shot in his plane.

In December 1943, the family spent their first Christmas without Louie. The tree was strung with popcorn and cranberries, and beneath it sat a collection of gifts for Louie. In a card for her son, Louise wrote a message.

Christmas 25–43

Dear Louis
Where ever you are, I know you want us to think of you as well and safe. May God be with you, guide you. Love from all Mother Dad Pete Sylvia & Virginia

———

Two months later, after a massive bombing campaign, America seized Kwajalein. Landing troops waded onto a wasteland, bombed flat. In the remains of a building, someone found documents. Outside, a soldier climbing through rubble found a long splinter of wood. Etched along it was the name LOUIS ZAMPERINI.

Joe Deasy, the *Daisy Mae* pilot who had searched for Phil's lost crew, was on Oahu when he was summoned to headquarters and handed translations of the documents found on Kwajalein. Two American airmen, the documents said, had been found on a raft and brought to Kwajalein. The unnamed men were described as a pilot and a bombardier. They'd been in a crash—the date was apparently provided—and had drifted for forty-seven days. With the papers were drawings of B-24s made by the captives. The report said the men had been beaten, then sent to Japan by boat.

The moment Deasy read the report, he knew: Phillips and Zamperini had survived their crash. His elation was tailed by guilt: in their ocean search, they'd overlooked the lost men, but the enemy had not.

"I was happy to have found them," Deasy recalled, "but the next thing is, where the hell are they?" Had they reached Japan alive? Had they survived whatever lay in store for them there?

The military now knew with a fair amount of certainty that everyone who'd gone up on *Green Hornet*, other than Zamperini and Phillips, was dead. But apparently because of the sketchiness of the reports and the fact that Louie's and Phil's fates were still unknown, the families of the dead and the two missing weren't notified.

———

Like the Zamperinis, the Phillips family had been in the dark since Allen had disappeared. They, too, refused to conclude that their boy was dead. Allen's father wrote of "a feeling of confidence that will not be shaken. Some day we are all going to have that reunion we are hoping and waiting for."

Allen's fiancée, Cecy, was desperate for information, and felt isolated in Indiana. She traveled to a Washington, D.C., suburb and moved into a friend's apartment, decorating it with pictures of Allen. She got a job with an airline, hoping that through them, she might learn more about Allen, but she learned nothing. In her anguish, she did something completely out of character. She went to a fortune-teller.

Allen isn't dead, the fortune-teller said. He's injured, but alive. He'll be found before Christmas. Cecy latched on to those words and believed them.

———

On June 27, 1944, exactly thirteen months after *Green Hornet* crashed, telegrams were typed up at the War Department and sent to the mothers of the plane's crewmen. When Louise Zamperini opened hers, she burst into tears. The military had officially declared Louie, and all his crewmates, dead.

Allen's mother, Kelsey, wasn't persuaded. She contacted a newspaper and asked the editors not to print the death notice; her son, she told them, was not gone. The editors honored her request.

When the shock from the death notice faded, the Zamperinis realized it changed nothing. It had been generated as a bureaucratic matter of course, an automatic designation made for all missing servicemen after thirteen months. "None of us believed it," Sylvia said. "None of us."

During family dinners, Pete and his father made plans to hunt for Louie. When the war was over, they'd rent a boat and sail from island to island until they found him. They'd go on for as long as it took.

IN GRATEFUL MEMORY OF

First Lieutenant Louis S. Zamperini, A.S.No. 0-663341,

WHO DIED IN THE SERVICE OF HIS COUNTRY AT

in the Central Pacific Area, May 28, 1944.

HE STANDS IN THE UNBROKEN LINE OF PATRIOTS WHO HAVE DARED TO DIE

THAT FREEDOM MIGHT LIVE, AND GROW, AND INCREASE ITS BLESSINGS.

FREEDOM LIVES, AND THROUGH IT, HE LIVES—

IN A WAY THAT HUMBLES THE UNDERTAKINGS OF MOST MEN

Franklin D Roosevelt

PRESIDENT OF THE UNITED STATES OF AMERICA

CHAPTER 22

Plots Afoot

The plot began with a question. It was the summer of 1944, and Louie and Frank Tinker were walking in Ofuna. Louie could hear planes coming and going from an airstrip nearby, and it got him thinking.

"Could you fly a Japanese plane?" he asked.

"If it has wings," Tinker, replied.

An idea took root. Louie, Tinker, and Harris were going to escape.

―――――

They'd been driven to this point by a desperate spring and summer. They lived in squalor, crawling with fleas and lice and so swarmed by flies that the guards offered a rice ball to the man who could kill the most, inspiring a cutthroat swatting competition. Rations were slashed. Ravenous, Louie made reckless efforts to find food. He stole concentrated miso paste—a fermented Japanese seasoning meant to be diluted in water—swallowed it in one gulp and ended up heaving his guts out. He volunteered to starch the guards' shirts with rice water, exposing himself to the guards' volatility just so he could scavenge flecks of rice from the water. Eventually, he was so frantic to eat that he broke into the kitchen and stole chestnuts reserved for the guards, an act that could've gotten him killed.

When officials asked for a volunteer to barber the guards, offering one rice ball per shave, Louie was desperate enough to step forward. To his surprise, the guards expected him to shave not only their faces, but their foreheads, a standard Japanese barbering practice.

A notoriously cruel guard called the Weasel came to Louie for shaves but never paid him the rice ball. Louie couldn't resist evening the score. Shaving the Weasel's forehead, he thinned his eyebrows to a girlish line. The Weasel left and entered the guardhouse. A moment later, Louie heard a shout.

"Marlene Dietrich!" It was the name of a movie star with famously slender, feminine eyebrows.

Louie backed away, waiting for the Weasel to burst out. Guards crowded in and began laughing. The Weasel never punished Louie, but he stopped coming to Louie for his shaves.

———

In the Pacific, the war raged. The Japanese were increasingly agitated. An Ofuna official told Commander Fitzgerald that if the Allies won, the captives would be executed. The quest for war news took on special urgency.

One morning, Louie was outside, under orders to sweep the compound. He saw the Japanese camp commander sitting nearby, holding a newspaper and nodding off. Louie waited, watching. The commander's head tipped, his fingers parted, and the paper fluttered to the ground. Louie used the broom to slide the newspaper to himself.

There was a war map on the paper. Louie ran to the barracks, found Harris, held the map up while he memorized it, then ran the paper to the trash. Harris drew the map, and captives came to look: America was closing in on Japan.

In July, it was rumored that America was attacking Saipan, tantalizingly close to Japan's home islands. When a new captive arrived, everyone eyed him as a source of information, but the guards isolated him. When the captive was led to the bathhouse, Louie saw his chance. He snuck behind the building and looked in an open window. The captive was holding a pan of water and washing. When the guard stepped away, Louie whispered.

"If we've taken Saipan, drop the pan."

The pan clattered to the floor. The man picked it up, dropped it again, then dropped it once more.

At night, lying in their cells, the captives began hearing a distant wailing sound: air-raid sirens. They listened for American bombers, but for now, no bombers came.

Life in Ofuna grew grimmer. Every day, the men were slapped, kicked, beaten, and humiliated. The Quack was especially ferocious, unleashing explosions of violence that left captives spilled over the ground. Camp officials stole the rations, and the captives wasted away. The little food they were given was inedible.

One day, when Louie saw fish, writhing with maggots, sitting in the captives' foot-washing trough, he recoiled. The Quack saw him, charged at him, and beat him. Later, the fish was ladled into Louie's bowl. Louie wouldn't touch it. A guard jabbed him behind the ear with a bayonet and made him eat it.

Sueharu Kitamura, "The Quack."

Living in vile degradation and suffering, sure they were doomed, Louie, Harris, and Tinker listened to the nearby planes and wondered if there could be a way out. They decided to make a run for it, commandeer a plane, and get out of Japan.

———

At first, they hit a dead end. They didn't know where the airport was or how they'd steal a plane. Then they got hold of a Japanese almanac. Filled with detailed information on Japan's ports, its ships and their fuels, and the distances between cities, it was all they needed to craft an escape.

They discarded the plane idea in favor of escape by boat. Harris plotted a path west, about 150 miles. At a western port, they'd steal a boat, cross the Sea of Japan, and flee into China.

There was one especially worrisome problem. Hiking in Japan, they'd stand out, and not just because of their race. In a land in which the average soldier was five foot three, they were giants. If caught, they'd surely be killed, either by civilians—who often attacked POWs—or by authorities. They decided to move only at night and hope for the best.

As the plan took shape, they walked as much as possible, strengthening their legs. They studied guard shifts, discovering a patch of time at night when only one guard watched the fence. Louie stole supplies—a knife, rice, string, and loose paper to serve as toilet paper. He stashed it under his floorboard.

For weeks, they prepared. The plan was potentially suicidal, but the prospect of taking control of their fates was thrilling. Louie was filled with what he called "a fearful joy."

Just before the escape date, everything changed. A prisoner escaped from another camp, and in response, Ofuna officials issued a decree: all escapees would be executed, and for every escapee, several captive officers would be shot. Louie, Tinker, and Harris were prepared to die, but they couldn't risk other men's lives. They abandoned their plan.

With the escape off, they focused on insurgency. In early September, a captive saw a newspaper with a war map on it on the Quack's desk. Few things were riskier than stealing from the Quack, but with the kill-all order looming, the men were desperate for news. Only one man had the thieving experience to attempt a heist so dangerous.

For several days, Louie staked out the Quack's office, watching him and the guards. At the same time each day, they took a cigarette break of roughly three minutes. It would be Louie's only chance, and it would be a very close call.

On the chosen day, the Quack and guards stepped out. Dropping to all fours so he wouldn't be seen through the windows, Louie clambered into the office, snatched the newspaper, stuck it under his shirt, crawled out, and walked to Harris's cell, striding as quickly as he could without attracting attention. He held the paper up before Harris, then crammed it under his shirt

Lieutenant William Harris. COURTESY OF KATHERINE H. MEARES

again, sped back to the office, crawled in, threw the paper on the desk, and fled.

At the barracks, Harris drew the map on a strip of toilet paper. The Americans were coming closer and closer to Japan.

A few days later, Harris was sitting in a cell when the Quack swept in. Seeing something in Harris's hand, he snatched it. It was the map.

The Quack, his face crimson, called all captives outside. He told Harris to step forward. Louie heard the marine whisper, "Oh my God."

The men who witnessed what followed would never blot it from memory. Screeching and shrieking, the Quack attacked Harris, punching him and clubbing him with a wooden crutch. When Harris collapsed, the Quack kicked him repeatedly in the face, then had other captives hold him up for more clubbing. On and on the beating went, long past when Harris fell unconscious. Two captives fainted.

At last, raindrops began to patter over the dirt. The Quack dropped the crutch, walked to a building, and slid to the ground, panting.

Dragged to his cell, Harris slumped, eyes wide open but blank as stones. It was two hours before he moved.

In coming days, he began to revive. Louie sat with him, helping him eat, but Harris could barely communicate. He wandered about, his face disfigured, eyes glassy. When friends greeted him, he didn't know who they were.

————

Three weeks later, on September 30, 1944, the guards called Louie, Tinker, and several other men out. They were told they were going to a POW camp called Omori, just outside Tokyo.

Louie hurried to his cell, hid his diary in his clothing, said goodbye to Harris, and climbed on the transport truck. As it rattled away, he was euphoric. Ahead lay a POW camp, a promised land.

CHAPTER 23

Monster

It was the last day of September 1944. Louie, Frank Tinker, and a few other Ofuna veterans stood by the gate of Omori POW camp, which sat on a man-made island in Tokyo Bay. The island was nothing more than a sandy spit, connected to shore by a long bridge. Across the water was Tokyo, still virtually untouched by the war.

Before the prisoners stood a Japanese corporal. He was leering at them.

He was a beautifully crafted man, in his midtwenties. His face was handsome, his form trim. A sword angled off of his hip, and circling his waist was a belt with an enormous metal buckle. The only incongruities on this striking corporal were his hands—brutish things that one man would liken to paws.

As the prisoners stood at attention, the corporal stared. Minutes passed. Then, abruptly, the corporal swept forward, walking with chin high, chest puffed. He looked the men over, Louie thought, as if he were God himself.

Down the line the corporal strode, pausing before each man and barking, "Name!" When Louie gave his name, the corporal's eyes narrowed. Decades later, men who'd looked into those eyes would be unable to forget what they saw in them. A wrongness elicited a twist in the gut and sent a prickle up the

Mutsuhiro Watanabe, "The Bird." NATIONAL ARCHIVES

back of the neck. Louie dropped his eyes. There was a rush in the air: the corporal's fist ramming into Louie's head. Louie staggered.

"Why you no look in my eye?" the corporal hissed. The prisoners went rigid.

Louie raised his eyes to the corporal's face. Again came the whirling arm, the blow to the skull, the stumbling legs.

"You no look at me!"

This man, thought Tinker, *is a psychopath.*

———

The corporal marched the men to a quarantine area, ordered them to stand there, and left. The men stood, growing colder. Hours passed. The corporal didn't return. The men sat down, shivering.

Louie saw a discarded apple box nearby. Remembering his Boy Scout training, he pried a slat from it, fit a stick into a hole in the slat, wound a bootlace around the stick, and began alternately pulling the ends, turning the stick until it began to smoke. He picked up bits of a straw mat and laid them on the smoking area. The mat whooshed into flames. The men gathered to warm themselves.

The corporal suddenly reappeared, demanding to know how they'd gotten matches. Louie explained how he'd built the fire. The corporal's face clouded over. Without warning, he slugged Louie in the head again. He barked at Louie to put the fire out, then walked away.

The corporal's name was Mutsuhiro Watanabe. Louie had met the man who would dedicate himself to shattering him.

———

Watanabe had begun life with everything. Born into a fabulously wealthy family, he grew up in luxury's lap, living in beautiful homes, waited on by servants. He attended Tokyo's prestigious Waseda University, studying French literature. In 1942, he graduated, then enlisted in the army.

With prominent military officers in his family, Watanabe had lofty expectations for himself as a soldier. But when he applied to become an officer, he was rejected; he'd be a lowly corporal. His failure derailed him, leaving him feeling disgraced, infuriated, and bitterly jealous of officers. He was exiled to the military's lowest station, POW camp. Assigned to Omori and named disciplinarian of prisoners, he arrived seething with resentment.

He became a monster. He beat POWs every day, fracturing their windpipes, rupturing their eardrums, shattering their teeth, tearing one man's ear half off, tying another to a tree for days. In the ecstasy of an assault, he wailed, drooling and frothing, sometimes sobbing. In the words of one POW, he was "the most vicious guard in any prison camp on the main island of Japan."

Both Watanabe's victims and his fellow Japanese would wonder at the source of his behavior. To some, it was madness. Others saw something calculating. When Watanabe beat men, POW officers looked at him with terror. Brutality gave him power that his rank did not. "He suddenly saw after he hit a few men that he was feared and respected for that," said British POW Tom Wade. "And so that became his style of behavior."

Two things separated Watanabe from other war criminals. One was his love of emotional torture. He forced men to stand for hours bowing at pumpkins. He ordered a chaplain to stand all night saluting a flagpole, shouting the Japanese word for "Salute!"—*Keirei!*—leaving the man weeping and out of his mind. He destroyed POWs' family photographs and burned unopened letters from home in front of them. He ordered men to violate camp policies, then attacked them for breaking the rules. He was, said one POW, "absolutely the most sadistic man I ever met."

The other attribute unique to Watanabe was his inconsistency. He spun from serenity to rage in an instant. One POW recalled seeing him gently praise a POW, fly into a fury and beat him unconscious, then quietly eat his lunch. After beatings, he sometimes apologized, in tears. His regret usually lasted only moments.

When Watanabe wasn't thrashing POWs, he was forcing them to be his buddies, inviting them to his room for tea parties. He expected men to respond as if they adored him. Maybe he held these gatherings because they left POWs feeling more stressed than if he were consistently hostile. Or maybe he was just lonely. Among the Japanese, Watanabe was despised for his haughtiness and boasts about his wealth and education. He had no friends.

One POW compared the tea parties to "sitting on the edge of a volcano." Any misstep, any misunderstood word, might set Watanabe off, leaving him smashing china, flipping tables, and pounding his guests. Even when the gatherings were peaceful, Watanabe seemed to feel humiliated by having had to force friendship from POWs. The next day he'd often attack the previous night's buddies.

He favored a particular type of victim. Enlisted men usually received only the occasional slapped face. But thanks to Watanabe's intense jealousy of officers, high-ranking POWs were in for unrelenting cruelty. A few officers were especially provocative. Some had elevated status, such as physicians, chaplains, and those who'd been prominent in civilian life. Others he resented because they wouldn't crawl before him. These he hunted with inexhaustible hatred.

From the moment Watanabe locked eyes with Louie Zamperini—an officer, a famous Olympian, and an inherently defiant man—no one obsessed him more.

CHAPTER 24

Hunted

After freezing in quarantine all night, Louie was led into a vast compound. As he entered his barracks, a POW slipped a cup of hot tea into his chilled hands. Another ladled in two heaping teaspoons of sugar from a sock. To POWs, sugar was a priceless treasure. Louie was amazed that this man had a sock full of it.

As he sipped his tea, two officers, Englishman Tom Wade and American Bob Martindale, told him about Omori. In the year he'd spent in Ofuna interrogation camp, Louie had longed to be sent to POW camp, where, he believed, he'd be well treated. That morning, he learned the truth. Omori, like most Japanese POW camps, was a slave camp.

The 1929 Geneva Convention, an international agreement concerning POWs, allowed detaining countries to use prisoners for labor. But the workers had to be healthy, they were to be paid, and the work couldn't be dangerous, unreasonably difficult, or connected to war operations. To ensure that POW officers retained authority over their men, they couldn't be forced to work. Japan signed the agreement, but their government never ratified it.

Japan mocked the Geneva Convention, enslaving POWs to support its war effort, forcing them into labor so harsh they died by the thousands. For some eleven hours a day, seven days a week, Omori's POWs slaved at docks, rail yards, warehouses, and a coal yard. Each rail yard slave lifted as much as thirty *tons* of goods a day. The only aspect of the Geneva Convention that the Japanese sometimes heeded was the prohibition on forcing POW officers to work.

Compounding the hardship was the diet. Rations were meager and of terrible quality and nutritive value. About once a week, a wheelbarrow arrived, bearing "meat." Spread over some nine hundred men, servings were thimble-sized, consisting of things like horse intestines and dog parts. Malnutrition-related diseases were epidemic, as was explosive diarrhea—"the *benjo* [latrine] boogie"—which led men to swallow lumps of coal to slow the digestive waterfall. For unenslaved officers and men too sick to work, rations were halved. Ailing, overworked, and malnourished, many men weighed less than ninety pounds.

The saving grace of Omori was the guards. There were a few rogues, but several were kind. The rest were indifferent, enforcing the rules with blows but behaving predictably. There was one enormous exception: Corporal Watanabe.

———

Martindale and Wade were quick to warn Louie about the corporal. He was, they said, a tyrant. He loved to send guards bursting into a barracks ahead of him, screaming *"Keirei!"* then race in to choose a man to beat. Sometimes he leapt through open windows. Because Watanabe eavesdropped on the men and beat those who mentioned him, Louie was told to speak of him in whispers and refer to him by his nickname: "the Bird."

To get almost anywhere in camp, POWs had to walk within view of the Bird's office. The Bird demanded that men salute the office, even if he wasn't there. He often hid nearby, baseball bat in hand, ready to club men who didn't salute. The POWs devised an elaborate sentry system to monitor his movements, with code phrases like "the animal is on the prowl." Men were so attuned to him that they instantly recognized the clopping of his clogs, a sound that usually triggered a stampede to the *benjos*, where the Bird seldom went.

Omori POW camp, on an artificial island in Tokyo Bay.

When prisoners arrived at a POW camp, they were registered with the Red Cross, which forwarded news of their whereabouts to their governments. But Omori officials didn't register Louie. They had special plans for him and wanted to keep his presence secret. The American government was told nothing, and because the Bird burned the letters POWs wrote, Louie couldn't tell his family he was alive.

The warnings about the Bird did no good. When Louie stepped outside, the Bird found him, accused him of an imaginary infraction, and attacked him in a wild fury. The next day came another beating, and the next, another. The corporal was fixated on Louie, hunting the man he would call "number one prisoner."

———

When Louie woke each morning, his first thought was of the Bird. He looked for the corporal through morning roll call, farting at the emperor, and forcing down rations. When the slaves were marched away, Louie had no crowds to hide in. The Bird was on him immediately.

The one good thing about being an officer in Omori was the exemption from slave labor, though at the painful cost of half the ration. But after Louie's arrival, the Bird lined the officers up and announced he was sending them into slavery at the worksites. When the first officer said this violated the Geneva Convention, the Bird swung his kendo stick into the man's head. The next man also refused; he, too, was clubbed. Louie was the third man. Trying to avoid getting his head cracked open, he blurted out an idea. They'd love to work within the camp, he said, making it a better place.

The Bird paused, considering. Then he marched them to the eight *benjo* pits, oozing over with the waste of nine hundred men with diarrhea. From now on, he said, they'd be *benjo* slaves, scooping the waste and carrying it to a cesspit. Louie and the others were horrified, but they had no choice. Every day, they labored in the waste, sickened and degraded, while the Bird stood by. To deprive him of the pleasure of seeing them miserable, they made a point of being jolly.

———

Each evening, the enlisted slaves trudged back to camp. The first time Louie saw them return, he learned where that sock of sugar had come from.

Omori's POW slaves were waging a guerrilla war against Japan. At rail yards, they switched mailing labels, sending tons of goods to the wrong destinations. They threw dirt into gas tanks. Finding the suitcases of the Nazi envoy, they shredded the clothes, soaked them in mud and oil, and repacked them with notes signed "Winston Churchill." They peed on nearly every bag of rice they loaded. In one incident, POWs loading heavy goods onto a barge hurled the material down with such force that they sank the barge, blocking a canal. After an epic effort was put into clearing the sunken barge and bringing in a new one, the POWs sank it, too.

When the rail yard foreman became absorbed in wooing a pretty girl, the POWs dashed to the track, wrenched the pins and bolts out, and rushed back to their work. A train chugged onto the sabotaged strip, the rails shot out from under it, and the entire train tipped over. No one was hurt, but the Japanese were frantic. They looked to the POWs, who kept working, faces blank. The Japanese screamed accusations at each other.

What the POWs couldn't sabotage, they stole. They broke into boxes, lifted warehouse doors off their hinges, raided galleys, and crawled up factory chutes. Scottish POWs who worked in a sugar warehouse ran the most sophisticated operation. They knitted four-foot-long socks and hoarded hollow reeds, and when the Japanese took shoe sizes for work boots, ordered giant boots. At the warehouse, they stabbed one end of each reed into a sugar sack, then ran the other end into their huge socks, allowing sugar to pour through until the socks were full. Others tied up their pant cuffs, stuck the reeds in their waistbands, and filled their pants with sugar.

Each evening, Louie saw the slaves walking in, clothes packed with booty. During inspection, while the guards' backs were turned, men would deftly pass stolen food, or the men bearing it, around. The biggest trick was hiding the POWs who arrived staggering drunk after chugging down stolen alcohol. The drunks were shuffled to the center and braced between sober men so they wouldn't pitch face-first into the guards.

In the barracks, Louie watched the men unpack. Sugar-filled socks hung from necks, under armpits, down pant legs. Salmon emerged from sleeves; oyster cans from boots. Legs were swaddled in tobacco leaves, which Louie helped hide in secret wall compartments, then, once dried, shred into smokable bits. One American built a secret compartment in his canteen, filling the bottom with stolen alcohol while the top, upon inspection, yielded water. One group stole the makings of a cake, only to discover, upon baking it, that the "flour" was cement.

Thieves were often caught, and when they were, all slaves were beaten with fists, bats, and rifle butts. But the men were fed so little and worked so hard that they had to steal to survive. They set up a "University of Thievery" in which "professors"—the best thieves—taught the art of stealing. When the Japanese caught thieves, POW officers suggested that the culprits be transferred to worksites where there was nothing stealable. The Japanese agreed, and the inept thieves were replaced with University of Thievery alumni.

A black market of stolen goods flourished in camp. With so many men, there wasn't a lot to go around, but everyone benefited. Stolen food, especially the Scots' sugar, was the camp currency. The "Sugar Barons" became the rich men of Omori, even hiring assistants to do their laundry, but they donated a fourth of their loot to sick and starving POWs, including Louie. Deaths from illness and malnutrition were once commonplace, but after the stealing school was created, only two POWs died, one from a burst appendix. And in so degrading a place, stealing won back the men's dignity.

———

Weeks passed; the Bird attacked Louie relentlessly. Unable to escape, Louie became increasingly angry. His experience in childhood, when bullies bloodied him, was repeating itself. He lit up with rage.

When the Bird lunged for Louie, Louie imagined strangling him, and his hands drew into fists. He saw the corporal looking furiously at his hands, but refused to unclench them. The Bird demanded that Louie look him in the eyes; Louie wouldn't do it. The Bird tried to knock Louie down; Louie wouldn't fall. Other prisoners told him to give in or the Bird would beat him to death. Louie couldn't do it. When he raised his eyes, all that shone in them was hate. A battle of wills had begun.

All that fall, the POWs could hear air-raid sirens over Tokyo. They were false alarms, but something was coming. Louie watched the sky and hoped the Americans would come before the Bird killed him.

B-29 Superfortress.

CHAPTER 25

"He's Alive!"

On a late October day in 1944, Louie pushed a wheelbarrow into Tokyo, joining a guard to pick up rations. It was the first time he'd passed, unblindfolded, into the society that held him captive.

Tokyo was bled dry. The war had caused massive food shortages, and markets were shuttered. Civilians were slipshod and dirty. Children were digging trenches. The Americans were coming, and the city was holding its breath.

On a wall, Louie saw a scrawl of graffiti: *B Niju Ku*. Louie knew *niju* meant "twenty" and *ku* meant "nine." He walked back to Omori, wondering what "B twenty-nine" meant, and why someone would write it on a wall.

———

On November 1, a wondrous new American plane lifted off a Saipan runway. A gigantic craft, it could rocket across the sky at more than 350 miles per hour and carry giant bomb loads over distances no other bomber could traverse. It was the B-29 Superfortress, and it would bring down Japan.

All morning, the plane flew, splitting the air nearly six miles up. Above was a sky of intense blue; below came Tokyo.

B-29s had been used a few times over Japan, launching from a remote area in China that had not been occupied by Japan. Largely because of the difficulty of flying from Chinese bases, the raids failed, but the swift, huge planes terrified the Japanese, inspiring the graffiti Louie saw. Weeks after the first China-based raid, Americans captured the island of Saipan, only 1,450 miles from Tokyo. The B-24 couldn't make it from Saipan to Tokyo and back, but the B-29 could. The November 1 flight was the first run. The plane carried not bombs, but cameras: it was mapping the path of B-29s that would follow.

Louie was outside when sirens sounded. Sirens were routine now, so they caused no concern. The guards shooed the POWs into the barracks.

Outside, something was different. The guards were gaping at the sky as if, wrote Bob Martindale, "they were looking for the Messiah." Then there was a glint above, a finger pointing urgently, and POWs bolting for the door. Running out, Louie saw a sliver of light over Tokyo, contrails curling behind it like twisting spines. "Oh God, God, an American plane!" someone shouted. In Tokyo, civilians stood in the streets, their frightened shouts carrying over the water.

Louie had never seen a plane like this. Then a new prisoner said it was an American bomber called a B-29. A cheer rang out. Men shouted, "B-29! B-29!" It was the most beautiful thing Louie had ever seen.

As the POWs ran and cheered, Louie glanced to the end of camp. The Bird was standing motionless and expressionless, watching the plane.

"It was not their Messiah," Martindale wrote, "but ours."

———

The B-29 flew at perfect liberty. The guards pursued the elated POWs, trying to force them into the barracks. The men shushed each other, fearing they'd be beaten for celebrating. The clamor quieted. Louie watched the bomber, occasionally darting between barracks to avoid the guards. The plane criss-crossed overhead for more than an hour, then flew off.

The bomber had simply passed over Tokyo, but everyone knew what it meant. Every morning at roll call, the twenty-ninth man sang out *"Niju ku!"* at the top of his lungs. "Not even bayonet prods," wrote Wade, "could wipe the smiles from the POW faces now."

The Bird wasn't smiling.

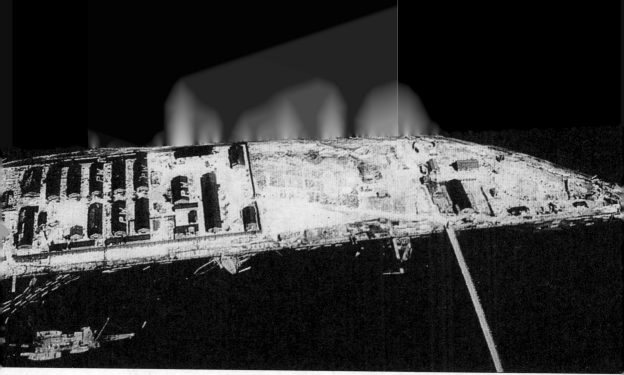

A B-29 over the Omori POW camp. COURTESY OF RAYMOND HALLORAN

———

It was an ordinary day. Louie was in his barracks, sitting with friends. Suddenly, two guards crashed in, screaming *"Keirei!"* Louie leapt up with the other men. In bounded the Bird.

Looking around, the Bird spotted Louie and charged at him. He wore the belt he'd worn on Louie's first day in Omori. The buckle was several inches square, made of heavy brass.

"You come to attention last!"

The Bird jerked his belt off. Grasping the end with both hands, he swung it back, then whipped it forward like a baseball bat, straight into Louie's temple.

Louie felt as if he'd been shot in the head. His legs seemed to liquefy, and he collapsed. The room spun.

When he gathered his wits, he was on the floor, bleeding. The Bird was crouched over him, making a motherly sound, a sort of "*Awwww.*" He pulled a fold of toilet paper from his pocket and pressed it into Louie's hand. Louie held it to his temple.

"Oh, it stop, eh?" the Bird said, his voice soft.

Louie pulled himself upright. The Bird waited for him to steady himself. The corporal seemed compassionate and regretful, and Louie felt grateful. The relief was just entering his mind when the buckle, whirling around from the Bird's swinging arms, struck his head again. Louie felt pain bursting through his skull, his body going liquid again. He smacked into the floor.

––––––

For weeks, Louie was deaf in one ear. The Bird beat him daily. Louie bore it with clenched fists, eyes blazing, but the assaults were wearing him down. The corporal began lording over his dreams, his features alight in vicious rapture. Louie spent hours in prayer, begging God to save him, and lost himself in fantasies of running in the Olympics. He thought of home, tormented by thoughts of what his disappearance must have done to his mother.

One day in mid-November, two Japanese civilians found Louie in his barracks. Friendly and respectful, they said they were producers from Radio Tokyo. They handed Louie a piece of paper. It was a transcript of an American radio broadcast announcing his death. The news that Louie had been declared dead, privately delivered to his family in June, had become public that week.

The producers said they were distressed that Louie's family had been told he was dead. They invited him to write a message to his family and read it on a program called *Postman Calls*.

Louie didn't trust them. *Postman Calls* was a propaganda show, performed in English and broadcast to Allied troops to demoralize them. The broadcasters were POWs known as "propaganda prisoners," usually working under threat of execution or beating. Wary of being made into a propaganda prisoner, Louie wouldn't commit. The producers told him to think about it. Louie asked Martindale what to do. Martindale said as long as Louie wrote his own message, there was no harm in accepting.

Louie set to work. Knowing his family might not believe it was he, he added details he hoped would convince them. To ensure his message aired, he decided to speak positively about his captors.

He was driven to Radio Tokyo. The producers gave his message a hearty approval. It would be taped for later broadcast. The Japanese planned to use that day's broadcast to tease the audience, then wait two days before airing his voice, proof they were telling the truth. Louie taped his message, then returned to Omori.

In San Francisco at 2:30 a.m. on November 18, a young woman named Lynn Moody was working the graveyard shift in the Office of War Information. A colleague was listening to Japanese broadcasts and typing them up for review by propaganda analysts. The colleague asked Moody to fill in during her break.

Moody slipped on the earphones. She was startled to hear a name she knew: Louis Zamperini. Moody was a USC graduate, and Louie was an old friend. Moody began typing.

> Recently a news report . . . stated that First Lieutenant Louis Zamperini is listed as dead by the United States War Department. . . . Louis Zamperini is alive and well as a prisoner of war here in Tokyo.
>
> This is one of the many examples of the men missing in action erroneously reported and later being established as a lie. . . . Much suffering and heartaches could have been avoided by the transmittal of reliable information to the parties concerned regarding the whereabouts of men. . . .
>
> So chin up, Mrs. Louis Zamperini. . . . Louis is neither missing nor dead. . . . Keep on listening, Mrs. Zamperini, and don't mention it; the pleasure is all ours.

Later, Moody wrote that when her colleague returned, "I practically danced around the room telling her about it."

Two nights later, Moody was back on the night shift when a transcriber yelled to her. Moody ran in and put on the earphones.

"Hello, America," the announcer began, "this is the postman calling and bringing a special message . . . to Mrs. Louis Zamperini. . . . Her son has come down to the studio especially to send her this message of reassurance after the erroneous report of a few days ago by the United States War Department that he was officially given up as dead and missing."

A young man began speaking. Moody knew in an instant: it was Louie.

> Hello, Mother and Father, relatives, and friends. This is your Louie talking. Through the courtesy of the authorities here I am broadcasting this personal message to you.
>
> This will be the first time in two and one half years that you will have heard my voice. . . . I am uninjured and in good health and can hardly wait until the day we are together again. . . . I am now interned in the Tokyo prisoners' camp and am being treated as well as can be expected under wartime conditions. The camp authorities are kind to me. . . .
>
> Before I forget it, Dad, I would be very pleased if you would keep my guns in good condition so we might do some good hunting when I return home. Mother, Sylvia, and Virginia, I hope you will keep up your wonderful talents in the kitchen. I often visualize those wonderful pies and cakes you make. Is Pete still able to pay you his weekly visits from San Diego? I hope he is still near home. . . . Merry Christmas and a happy New Year.—Your loving son, Louie

At the Zamperini house, a military telegram arrived, and on it were Louie's words. The telegram stressed that officials couldn't confirm Louie was really the speaker or a POW. But the Zamperinis focused on one sentence: Keep my guns in good condition. Growing up shooting rabbits, Louie was fastidious about his guns. To the Zamperinis, this was the fingerprint, the detail only Louie would have thought to include. Louise and Sylvia began sobbing and shouting with joy.

Pete picked up the phone, called a friend, and shouted two words.

"He's alive!"

CHAPTER 26

Madness

The Radio Tokyo men were back at Omori, gushing compliments. Would Louie broadcast another message to his family? Louie accepted. But when he arrived in Tokyo, the producers announced a change of plans. They didn't need the message he'd written. They had one ready:

> Here's me, Louis Zamperini. . . . I was reported to have died in combat. . . . Boy . . . that's rich. . . . Here I am just as alive as I could be. . . . This reminds me of another fellow. . . . He told me that he was officially reported as killed in action but in reality was a prisoner of war. . . . After several months he received a letter from his wife in which she told him that she had married again since she thought he was dead. . . . Boy, I really feel sorry for a fellow like that. And the blame lies with the officials who allow such unreliable reports. . . . The least they can do is to let the folks back home know just where their boys are. . . . It's certainly a sad world when a fellow . . . is killed off by a so-called official report.

Louie was aghast. This message wasn't meant for his family; it was meant to discourage American troops. He refused to make the broadcast. Undeterred, the producers took him on a tour. They took him to a cafeteria and served him a delicious American meal, then showed him a comfortable bedroom. If Louie would do the broadcast, they said, he could live here. They introduced him to three propaganda prisoners. As Louie offered his hand, the men dropped their eyes. Louie knew they were telling him not to accept.

Louie suddenly understood why he'd been spared execution on Kwajalein. A famous Olympian, criticizing America, would be a priceless propaganda tool. He'd been sent to the hell of Ofuna, then to Omori and the Bird, to make his life in camp unbearable so he'd be willing to betray his country to escape it.

Smiling, the producers invited Louie to accept this easy new life. Louie refused. The smiles evaporated. They ordered him to do it. He said no. The producers left to confer, then returned.

"I think you go to punishment camp," one said. They waited for Louie to change his mind. He didn't.

Louie was dumped at Omori. The Bird was waiting for him, glowing with fresh hatred. His beatings resumed, with intensified vigor. Louie stood his ground with rebellion boiling in him, praying the Americans would come.

———

In the afternoon of November 24, 1944, the Tokyo sirens began to howl. From above came an immense roar. The men looked up to an astounding sight: acres and acres of B-29s, 111 of them, so high they looked like gleaming slits in the sky. The Americans had arrived.

The POWs cheered, calling out to the bombers. The guards stared up, so awed by the planes that they didn't seem to hear the men shouting.

As the POWs watched, a lone Japanese fighter raced up, then abruptly, startlingly, flew straight into a bomber, shattering and raining down on Tokyo Bay. The bomber fell, white smoke twirling from it. A single parachute puffed from its side. The bomber hit the water. The lone survivor, under his parachute, wafted into Tokyo. The other bombers flew on. There was distant booming.

It was only the beginning. B-29s passed over Omori nearly every day, sometimes lone planes, sometimes continents of aircraft. Sometimes the men saw licks of flame far away, Tokyo's war industries burning. Civilians streamed over the Omori bridge and camped by the walls in hopes of escaping the bombs.

One day, Louie stood outside, watching Japanese fighters circling a crowd of B-29s. The battle was so high that only the giant bombers were consistently visible; the tiny fighters flickered in and out of view as sunlight caught them. Every little while, there was a sharp, brief burst of light. It was the fighters, gunned by the B-29s, blowing up. On the bombers went, imperious. The Bird watched, stricken. *"Hikoki dame,"* he said. *"Hikoki dame."* Japan's planes, he was lamenting, were no good.

Every B-29 that crossed over Tokyo wound the Bird tighter. He slapped an officer repeatedly for five minutes. He pawed through the men's belongings, destroying family photographs. He was seized with paranoia. "You win war," he screamed, "and you make all Japanese like black slaves!" He hauled Bob Martindale to his office, accused him of plotting arson, and beat him so wildly that he overturned all his furniture.

One night, during a sleet storm, the POWs were jarred awake by the Bird charging through camp, ordering a fire drill. When the designated firefighters assembled, the Bird punched them, ran through the barracks shouting and hitting men, ordered all POWs outside, then drew his sword, swung it around, and screamed orders. For two hours, as sleet drummed on the shivering men, he forced them to pump water on imaginary fires, beat phantom blazes with brooms, and run through buildings "rescuing" food and documents.

As December progressed and the bombers kept coming, the Bird's mania deepened. He marched the officers into Tokyo, leapt on a water trough, drew his sword, and screamed *"Keirei!"* As the men saluted, the Bird stood in an exaggerated troop-reviewing pose, lost in a fantasy of military glory. After the POWs had passed, he jumped down, ran ahead, and hopped on another trough, shouting, striking his pose, and demanding salutes. Over and over he repeated the farce, driving the men on for miles.

When the bombs were falling, the Bird would snap, running with sword in the air, wailing, foam flying from his mouth, face purple. During one bombing, he ran the POWs outside, stood them at attention, and ordered the guards to aim rifles at them while he raced among them, swinging his sword over their heads.

No one felt the Bird's wrath as did Louie. Every day, the Bird sped around in search of the American. Louie hid, but the Bird always found him, launching himself at him in what Tinker called his "death lunge." Dazed and bleeding, Louie was sure Watanabe wouldn't stop until he was dead.

Under the onslaught, Louie began to come apart. The Bird stalked his dreams, screeching, whipping him with his belt. In the dreams, Louie's rage would overwhelm him, and he'd leap on his monster, his hands on the corporal's neck, strangling the life from him.

———

Some three hundred miles away, Phil was wasting away in Zentsuji POW camp. He'd been transferred there in August, joining one-legged Fred Garrett.

The Zentsuji diet was so poor that men wandered about, ravenous, pulling up weeds and eating them. Their drinking water was runoff from rice paddies fertilized with human excrement, which left all POWs afflicted with severe diarrhea. In one barracks, men lost an average of fifty-four pounds over eighteen months. Some twenty men fainted each day. Others went blind from malnutrition. In November, they buried an American who'd starved to death.

On a Friday night in December 1944, the telephone rang in the home of Phil's mother, Kelsey. The War Department had received news from Zentsuji: Allen was alive. Jubilant, Kelsey asked the department to cable her husband and her son's fiancée.

Phil's fiancée, Cecy Perry. COURTESY OF KAREN LOOMIS

In Washington, Cecy got the news she'd awaited for so long. The fortune-teller had said Allen would be found before Christmas. It was December 8. Cecy shouted with joy, quit her job, dashed through her apartment throwing clothes and pictures of Allen into a suitcase, and hopped a plane for Indiana to wait for her fiancé to come home.

In letters sent to the Zamperinis and Phillipses, the War Department asked family members not to speak publicly about the fact that Louie and Allen were alive. The department probably didn't want it known that it had mistakenly declared two men dead, especially as the Japanese were publicizing this fact in order to demoralize Allied troops. Both families honored this request, and the public went on believing that both Louie and Phil were dead.

As relieved as Kelsey was, she couldn't forget that others were so much less fortunate. Of the *Green Hornet* men, only Louie and Allen had been found.

"It is difficult to rejoice outwardly . . . when I think of the other mothers," Kelsey wrote to Louise. "How my heart goes out to them."

———

As Christmas neared, Louie faltered. Starvation was consuming him. The Red Cross sent relief packages, but the Japanese stole them. "We could see them throwing away unmistakable wrappers, carrying bowls of bulk cocoa and sugar between huts and even trying to wash clothes with cakes of American cheese," wrote Tom Wade. Out of 240 relief boxes, the Bird stole forty-eight, more than five hundred pounds of goods.

One day, the Bird ordered all POWs outside, where they found a truck brimming with apples and oranges. As the famished men grabbed the fruit, photographers snapped photos. Just as the men were ready to eat, the order came to put it all back. The entire thing had been staged for propaganda.

On Christmas Eve came a small, sweet respite from the suffering. Among the POWs was a chronically filthy, ingenious kleptomaniac named Mansfield. Shortly before Christmas, Mansfield broke into the storehouse—slipping past seven guards—and made off with several Red Cross packages, which he buried under his barracks. Discovering his cache, guards locked him in a punishment cell. Mansfield broke out, stole sixteen more parcels, and snuck back to the cell. He built a secret compartment and hid the loot inside, marking the door with a message for other imprisoned POWs: *Food, help yourself, lift here.* Caught again, he was tied to a tree for days.

In conversations with other POWs, Mansfield mentioned that in the storehouse, he'd found a Red Cross theatrical trunk. This gave the POWs the idea of staging a Christmas play. They secured the Bird's approval by naming him "master of ceremonies" and giving him a throne at the front of the "theater"—the bathhouse—with planks perched on washtubs to serve as a stage.

The men put on a production of *Cinderella*, written with hilarious creative liberties. Frank Tinker was Prince Leander of Pantoland. The fairy godmother was a gigantic Brit in a tutu and tights. Characters included Lady Dia Ria and Lady Gonna Ria. The guards laughed and clapped, and Louie thought it was the funniest thing he'd ever seen. The Bird gloried in the limelight, and for that night, he let Louie and the others be.

———

After Christmas, the Bird stopped attacking the POWs, even Louie. He paced, brooding. The men watched him and wondered what was going on. They soon learned: he'd been promoted to sergeant and transferred to another camp. Someone told Louie the Bird was leaving. Louie was overwhelmed with joy and relief.

The Bird threw himself a goodbye party. The officers dashed around camp gathering stool samples from dysentery patients, slathered the "gravy" over rice cakes, and presented them to him as a gift. As the men spoke of how they'd miss him, the Bird ate heartily.

If the rice cakes performed as intended, they didn't do so quickly. As Louie watched, the Bird left, looking perfectly well. The reign of terror was over.

CHAPTER 27

Falling Down

At Omori, life became immeasurably better. Humane, fair-minded Japanese took over. The Bird's rules were abolished. In the Bird's office, they found a pile of old letters sent to POWs by their families but kept from the prisoners. The letters were distributed, and the POWs were allowed to write home. "Trust you're all in good health and in the highest of spirits, not the kind that comes in bottles," Louie wrote in one letter. "Tell Pete," he wrote in another, "that when I'm 50, I'll have more hair on my head than he had at 20."

Two weeks into 1945, a group of battered men trudged into Omori. Louie knew their faces: these were Ofuna men, among them Commander Fitzgerald. Louie spotted Bill Harris, and his heart fell. Harris was a wreck. When Louie greeted him, his old friend looked at him vaguely. After Louie had left Ofuna, the Quack had twice more clubbed Harris into unconsciousness, once for speaking aloud, and once for stealing nails to repair his tattered shoes. Harris was hazy and distant, his mind struggling.

One of the Omori POWs was a physician, and he examined Harris gravely. He told Louie he thought the marine was dying.

That day, the new commander had Red Cross boxes handed out. Louie gave his box to Harris. It was, he said, the hardest and easiest thing he ever did. Harris rallied.

The B-29s kept coming. Louie was worried. The guards were increasingly jumpy and angry. As the assaults on Japan intensified and the probability of invasion rose, they seemed to view the POWs as threatening.

Among American forces, horrifying news had just surfaced. On Palawan Island in the Philippines, 150 American POWs had long been held as slaves by the Japanese. When an American convoy passed nearby, a Japanese commander was apparently sure the Americans would invade, the scenario for which the kill-all order had been written. He radioed to Palawan: "Annihilate the 150 prisoners."

The next day, the Palawan guards suddenly began screaming that enemy planes were coming. The POWs crawled into air-raid shelters and waited, hearing no planes. Then liquid rained onto them: gasoline. The guards tossed in torches, then hand grenades. The shelters, and the men inside, erupted in flames.

As the guards cheered, the POWs fought to escape, some clawing their fingertips off. Those who broke out were bayoneted, machine-gunned, or beaten to death. Only eleven escaped, swimming across a bay and making it to safety.

That night, the Japanese threw a party to celebrate the massacre. The anticipation of an American landing turned out to be mistaken.

———

Sleet was falling over Omori as February 16 dawned. Louie had just finished breakfast when the sirens piped up and the room began shaking.

He ran out into a crashing, tumbling world. The entire sky was swarming with hundreds of fighters, American and Japanese, streaming bullets at each other. Over Tokyo, dive-bombers bellied down, slamming bombs into the aircraft factories and airport. As they rose, quills of fire came up under them. It was the largest air battle yet fought over Japan, and Louie was directly underneath it.

The guards fixed bayonets and forced the POWs inside. Louie and the others waited for the guards to leave, then stole out. They ran behind a building and climbed the camp fence. The view was electrifying. Planes were sweeping over every part of the sky, and all around, fighters were plunging into the water.

One dogfight riveted Louie's attention. An American Hellcat fighter hooked up with a Japanese fighter and began chasing it. The Japanese fighter turned toward the city and dove low over the bay, the Hellcat right behind it. The two planes streaked past the camp, the Japanese fighter flat out, the Hellcat's guns firing. Several hundred POWs watched from the camp fence, their faces pressed to knotholes or their heads poking over the top, hearts leaping, ears roaring. The fighters were so close that Louie could see both pilots' faces. The Japanese fighter crossed over the coast, and the Hellcat broke away.

All told, fifteen hundred American planes, and several hundred Japanese planes, flew over the POWs that day. That night, Tokyo was bathed in fire. The following day, back the planes came. By the end of February 17, more than five hundred Japanese planes, on the ground and in the air, had been lost, and Japan's aircraft works were badly hit. The Americans lost eighty planes.

Seven days later, the hammer fell. At seven a.m., during a heavy snowstorm, sixteen hundred carrier-based planes screamed past Omori and bombed Tokyo. Then came B-29s, two hundred and twenty-nine of them, carrying firebombs. Encountering almost no resistance, they sped for the industrial district and let their bombs fall. The POWs saw fire dancing over the skyline. Twenty-six million square feet of the city was burning.

———

On the last day of February, fifteen POW officers were called out, among them Zamperini, Wade, Tinker, and Fitzgerald. They were told they were being transferred to a camp called Naoetsu. Perhaps this was the promised punishment camp, but Louie greeted the news with bright spirits. Whatever Naoetsu was, he'd be with almost all of his friends.

The following evening, the chosen men gathered their belongings. Louie said goodbye to Harris, then climbed aboard a truck with the other men and rode into Tokyo. They were shocked at the sight. Whole neighborhoods had been reduced to charred ruins, row after row of homes now nothing but black bones.

Transferred to a train, the POWs rode all night, moving west, into a snowy landscape. In early morning, the train drew up to Naoetsu, a seaside village in western Japan. The POWs stared in amazement; the snow rose some fourteen feet around the station. Climbing a stairway cut in the drifts, they found themselves in a blinding white world, standing atop a snow mountain that buried the entire village. It was so deep that residents had dug vertical tunnels to get out of their homes.

Pulling their baggage on sleighs, the POWs began the long walk to camp. It was windy and bitterly cold. Fitzgerald, who had a badly infected foot, struggled. His crutches poked deep in the snow and wouldn't hold his weight.

The prisoners crossed a bridge and saw the Sea of Japan. Just short of it, cornered against two rivers, was Naoetsu POW camp, almost entirely obscured by snow. Louie and the others trudged in and stopped before a shack, where they were told to stand at attention. They waited, the wind frisking their clothes.

A door thumped open. A man rushed out and snapped to a halt, screaming *"Keirei!"*

It was the Bird.

Louie's legs folded, the snow reared up at him, and down he went.

POWs at Naoetsu. AUSTRALIAN WAR MEMORIAL, NEGATIVE NUMBER 6033201

CHAPTER 28

Enslaved

It was the darkest moment of Louie's life. The Bird stood over him, triumphant. *I am in command*, he said. *You will obey.*

Commander Fitzgerald forked forward on his crutches and assumed the duties of senior POW. Ringing with shock, Louie picked himself up and hiked to the barracks, a tumbledown warehouse on the edge of a cliff over the Hokura River. Wind whistled through the walls, snow fell through holes in the roof, and rats trotted along the baseboards. The beds were planks; the bedding was loose straw. To survive subzero temperatures, the POWs had pried up and burned the floorboards, leaving gaping holes. The three hundred residents, mostly Australians, were stick figures, wearing the ragged summer uniforms in which they'd been captured years before.

Stacked against a wall were dozens of boxes, some of which had spilled gray ash to the floor. These were the cremated remains of sixty POWs—one in every five—who'd died here, most from relentless physical abuse. Of the many hells Louie had known in war, this would be the worst.

———

Naoetsu was almost lethally cold. Each night of shivering ended before dawn, when Louie was forced outside for roll call in deep snow and howling wind.

By day, he huddled with Tinker and Wade, fighting worsening diarrhea and fever. The Naoetsu rations—mostly seaweed—didn't help him. Because all the guards smoked American cigarettes, the prisoners knew the Red Cross was sending relief boxes. The POWs got nothing.

Louie's transfer back to the Bird was no coincidence. Watanabe, whom the Aussies called "Whatabastard," had handpicked him, almost certainly to torment him. Almost the moment Louie walked into camp, the Bird was on him. Louie took his beatings with defiance, provoking the Bird to ever more violent attacks. He descended back into a state of profound stress.

And yet Louie was lucky. Naoetsu was a war production village, and the enlisted POWs were its slaves. Each day, they were marched to factories, a steel mill, and barges, doing dangerous, backbreaking labor in shifts of some eighteen hours. At the shifts' ends, Louie saw men rambling in, some so exhausted they had to be carried. The Japanese literally worked men to death at Naoetsu. Louie had much to bear, but because he was an officer, at least he didn't have that.

———

Winter faded; the snow melted. A pig appeared. All winter, he'd been living in a snow cavern, sustained by food dropped to him by an Australian. Louie looked at him in wonder. The animal's skin had become see-through.

When the ground thawed, the Bird announced he was sending the officers to a farm to labor. Though this violated the Geneva Convention, Fitzgerald knew it would keep his officers away from the Bird and couldn't be anything like the killing labor done by the enlisted men. He raised no protest.

Each morning, Louie and the other officers assembled, attended by a guard, Ogawa. They loaded a cart with *benjo* waste—used as fertilizer—yoked themselves to it, and pulled it to the farm, sometimes darting away to steal vegetables from fields while Ogawa's back was turned.

The six-mile walk was tiring, but the work, tending potatoes, was easy, and Ogawa was placid. And because they were working, the officers were granted full rations. Though rations were dwindling as Japan's fortunes fell, a full bowl of seaweed was better than half a bowl of seaweed.

April 13 was a bright day, the land bathed in sunshine, the sky wide and clear. Louie and the other officers were scattered over the farm, working, when the field suddenly went still and the men turned up their faces. At the same moment, all over Naoetsu, POWs and Japanese gazed up. High overhead, something was winking in the sunlight, white ribbons unfurling behind it. It was a B-29, the first to cross over Naoetsu.

Followed by innumerable eyes, the plane made a lonely arc from one horizon to the other. It dropped no bombs, but its appearance showed how far over Japan the Americans were venturing, and how little resistance the Japanese could offer. The POWs were elated. The Japanese were unnerved, none more than the Bird.

A few days later, Ogawa teased Watanabe about his lazy laborers. He meant no harm, but the remark sent the Bird into a fury. He shouted for the farm workers to line up, then stormed and frothed, thoroughly deranged.

Finally, he screamed his punishment: from now on, all officers would do hard labor on coal barges. If they refused, he'd execute every one of them. One look at the Bird told Fitzgerald this was an order he couldn't fight.

The next morning, as the officers were marched into slavery, the Bird watched. He was smiling.

———

The officers were taken to the river and crowded onto a barge heaped with coal. Six were given shovels; Louie and the rest had large baskets strapped to their backs. On the guards' orders, the shovelers began heaving coal into the baskets. A cubic foot of coal can weigh as much as sixty pounds, so the bearers were soon staggering. With the guards screaming at them, they were hounded off the barge and up the riverbank to a railcar, where they wobbled up a narrow ramp, dumped the coal, and returned to have their baskets refilled.

All day, the men labored. By the time they were allowed to stop, they were utterly spent: by Wade's estimate, each basket bearer had carried well over four tons of coal.

So began a daily routine. Each time the men finished one barge, another arrived. Then one day they were loaded onto an empty barge and taken into the Sea of Japan. The barge drew alongside a coal ship, the sea heaving, water spraying over the deck. A guard gestured to a net slung over the side of the ship. Jump onto the net, he said, then climb to the deck.

The POWs were appalled. The two vessels were crashing together and rolling apart, and the net was a rapidly moving target. The men balked, but the guards forced them forward, and POWs began jumping. Louie, terrified, sprang across and climbed clear.

He was hustled into the ship's hold, to a giant dome of coal beside a large hanging net. He was given a shovel, and the guards were suddenly teeming around him, cracking him with clubs. Hour after hour, Louie stooped over his shovel in a swirl of shouting guards and black dust, heaving coal into the net. At last, at day's end, the work was halted. The POWs were so caked in coal that they were indistinguishable.

Every morning, the men were sent to their shovels again. Every night, they dragged back to the barracks, black ghosts trudging in and falling onto their bunks, weary to their bones, spitting black saliva. Occasionally, Louie was switched from coal to industrial salt; the work was just as taxing, and the salt liquefied in his sweat and ran down his back, burning cracks in his skin.

Tragedy was inevitable. One day, as Louie stood on the barge, awaiting his jump to the ship, the man ahead mistimed his leap. Crushed between the vessels, he crumpled onto the barge. The guards hardly paused, pushing Louie to step past the man and jump. Louie never learned whether the man survived.

———

Slavery swallowed men's souls, but the POWs scored little victories. On the barges, they'd sneak to the galleys and stuff food into their clothes. The guards' lunch boxes kept vanishing; an overseer's cigarettes, set down as he turned away, were gone when he turned back. The POWs stole anything they could, risking their necks for something as trivial as a pencil box. The box itself was nothing; the theft of it, a tiny act of defiance, was everything.

In the *benjo* one day, Louie noticed something blocking a knothole in the wall. Looking closer, he realized it was a rice sack in a storage room on the other side of the wall. Remembering the Omori sugar thieves, he searched camp, found a hollow reed, and sharpened the end. That night, he donned his camp-issued pajamas, fitted with ankle strings. He tied the strings tight, headed into the *benjo*, jammed one end of the reed through the knothole, piercing the rice sack, then put the other end into his pajamas. Rice streamed through the reed and into his pants.

Louie left the *benjo*, moving as naturally as he could with ten pounds of rice in his pajamas. He strolled past the guards and into the barracks, where Fitzgerald waited, a blanket spread before him. Louie stepped on the blanket, untied his ankle strings, and let the rice spill out. Fitzgerald quickly folded the blanket, then hid the rice in socks and compartments he'd made in the walls. When the guards left the building, Louie and Fitzgerald rushed the rice to the heating stove, boiled it, and shared it with other POWs.

In Naoetsu's POW insurgency, perhaps the greatest feat was pulled off by Ken Marvin, a marine captured at Wake. When Marvin's one-eyed slave guard, Bad Eye, asked Marvin to teach him his language, Marvin began teaching Bad Eye catastrophically bad English. From that day forward, when asked "How are you?" Bad Eye would smilingly reply, "What the f**k do you care?"

———

Disaster struck Louie in April. He was lugging a load of salt up the railcar ramp when a guard started walking down. The guard threw out his elbow, sending Louie tumbling off the ramp. Landing feet first, Louie felt a tearing sensation, then scorching pain in his ankle and knee.

Louie couldn't walk. He hopped back to camp and was removed from salt duty. He would now be the only officer trapped in camp with the Bird all day, and his rations would be halved.

Louie lay in the barracks, ravenous, crippled by his injured leg, diarrhea, and a 104-degree fever. To get his rations restored, he had to find work he could do on one leg. Desperate, he begged the Bird for work.

The Bird savored his plea. From now on, he said, Louie would care for the pig. He'd get full rations, but there was a catch: he'd have to use his bare hands to clean the sty.

Emaciated and seriously ill, Louie was condemned to crawl on the ground, picking up feces and cramming handfuls of the pig's feed into his mouth to save himself from starving to death.

If anything's going to shatter me, Louie thought, *this is it.*

CHAPTER 29

Two Hundred and Twenty Punches

On May 5, 1945, the growl of four huge engines echoed over Naoetsu. A B-29 was circling the steel mill. Sirens sounded, but in the mill, the foreman kept the POWs working. There was a sudden, massive crash, and it began snowing very hard inside the mill.

It wasn't snow, but dust falling from the rafters. The Japanese fled. The panicked POWs crowded together, praying they wouldn't get hit.

The bombs missed, blowing gaping craters in a field nearby. But for the POWs, there was much more to this raid than holes in the ground. If the Americans were attacking a lone steel mill in a place as obscure as Naoetsu, did this mean they had already destroyed the big strategic cities?

The answer came ten days later, when four hundred new POWs shuffled through the gates. The Bird delivered his standard harangue.

"You must be sincere! You must work for earnest! You must obey! I have spoken."

"Who the hell is Ernest?" muttered a POW.

The new men said they'd come from slave camps in the vast war production cities of Kobe and Osaka. Weeks before, B-29s had swept over the cities in three-hundred-plane swarms, showering them in firebombs. Of no use to

B-29 bombing Osaka.

Japan in razed cities, the POWs had been shipped to Naoetsu to continue slaving for the Empire. The new men had one other piece of news: Germany had fallen. The whole weight of the Allies was now thrown against Japan.

———

By June, Louie's leg was healed enough for him to walk, and he was sent back to slavery. He was growing sicker. When he begged for rest while burning with a 103-degree fever, the Bird refused.

One day, Louie was shoveling on a barge when the foreman discovered fish was missing from the galley. If the thieves didn't turn themselves in, he said, he'd report it to the Bird. The culprits confessed, but the foreman, suspecting more men were involved, told the Bird anyway.

The Bird called the work party out and ordered the thieves to stand in front. He then yanked out Wade, Tinker, Louie, and two other officers. These officers, he said, were responsible for the thieves' acts. His punishment: each enlisted man would punch each officer and thief in the face, with maximum force. The chosen men were horrified: there were some one hundred enlisted men. Any POW who refused to punch the chosen men, the Bird said, would also be beaten.

The enlisted men had no choice. At first, some hit softly, but they were immediately clubbed by the guards, then set upon by the Bird, screeching at them and forcing them to hit their victims more and more. Louie began whispering to each man to just do it, and hit hard.

For the first few punches, Louie stayed upright. But soon his legs wavered, and he collapsed. He pulled himself up, but fell again with the next punch, and the next. Eventually he blacked out. When he woke, the Bird forced the men to resume punching him, barking, *"Next! Next! Next!"* In Louie's whirling mind, the voice began to sound like the tramping of feet. The sun sank. For two hours, the beating went on.

The victims had to be carried to the barracks. Louie's face was so swollen that for several days he could barely open his mouth. By Wade's estimate, each man had been punched in the face some 220 times.

———

June 1945 became July. Every night, great forests of B29s passed over, air-raid sirens screaming their arrival. Sometimes, the men could hear soft booming in the darkness.

Louie was sick and demoralized. He lay on his plank, daydreaming of the Olympics, clinging to them as a shining promise. He prayed ceaselessly for rescue. His nightmares of the Bird were endless. His will was fraying.

The food situation was increasingly dire. With the import of the new POWs, the population had more than doubled, but the rations hadn't. Now the rations were still smaller, usually nothing but seaweed.

Fall was coming, and Louie and the other POWs were scared. They were told their rations and supplies of heating fuel would be cut more in winter, and might be discontinued. Many men were barely hanging on. In the barracks one day, a young POW dragged in from slave work, lay down, asked Louie to wake him for dinner, and went still. At chow time, Louie kicked his foot. The man didn't move. He was dead. Few POWs, in Naoetsu or anywhere else, thought they'd live to see another spring.

There was a worry greater still. Even in isolated Naoetsu, it was obvious Japan was staggering. Watching B-29s flying unopposed, the POWs knew Japan's air defenses were gutted, and the Americans were very close. Civilians were in shocking condition: the limbs of the adults were grotesquely swollen from beriberi; the children were gaunt. The POWs were so disturbed by the famine among civilians that they stopped stealing. Japan had long ago lost this war.

But for Japan, surrender was unthinkable. If a massively destructive air bombardment couldn't end the war, invasion seemed the only possibility. POWs saw women holding sharpened sticks, practicing lunges, and small children being drilled with wooden mock guns. Japan was preparing to fight to the last man, woman, and child.

Invasion seemed inevitable and imminent. The POWs, knowing of the kill-all order, were terrified. At one camp, which held two thousand POWs and civilian captives, villagers told the prisoners of hundreds of POW bodies lying in the jungle. A notoriously sadistic camp official began speaking of his sympathy for the POWs, and how they'd soon be taken to a new camp where there was ample food, medical care, and no more slavery. The POWs knew it was a lie. In the camp office sat written orders for all captives to be "liquidated" on September 15. Women and children would be poisoned; civilian men would be shot; the sick would be bayoneted. The five hundred POWs would be marched into the jungle, shot, and burned.

At camps across Japan, things looked just as ominous. At Omori, some Japanese warned the POWs that plans were set for prisoners to be shot. At other camps, machine guns and barrels of accelerant were brought in, and POWs' dog tags were confiscated in an apparent effort to "not . . . leave any traces." Prisoners were ordered to dig mysterious tunnels, and at several camps, friendly guards warned POWs that mines, ditches, and tunnels were going to be used as death chambers.

At Phil and Fred Garrett's camp, officials suddenly announced that American POWs were being moved to a pleasant new camp, for their safety. The men were taken by train across Japan, through rivers of refugees and charred cities. The air smelled of burned bodies.

After dark, they reached a remote area and were told to walk up a trail winding up a mountain. In a crashing rainstorm, they climbed for hours. Garrett, his stump still unhealed, labored on his crutches, and the guards wouldn't allow anyone to help him. The Japanese drove the group on for eleven miles. Men fainted from exhaustion.

At two a.m., they reached a collection of wooden shacks high on the mountain. There, they collapsed. This was their new camp, Rokuroshi. No one explained why they'd been taken to a place so remote. The POW physician looked around and came to a conclusion: *They'll kill us here.*

At Naoetsu, officials announced that POWs would soon be taken into the mountains to protect them from air raids. The guards told a different story, saying the army had issued orders to kill the POWs in August. This might have been dismissed as a lie, but a friendly civilian warned that an execution date was set. The same date was reportedly mentioned to prisoners in at least two other camps.

All Naoetsu POWs, the civilian said, would be killed on August 22.

CHAPTER 30

The Boiling City

No one in Naoetsu was sleeping. B-29s crossed over every night, sirens wailed, and the Bird spun deeper into madness.

As the bombers thundered over, the Bird would crash into the barracks, ordering the Americans out. Shouting and swinging clubs, kendo sticks or rifles, he'd shove them into two lines and make them slap each other's faces. Sometimes he'd make them stand with arms raised for hours, pounding them when their arms sagged. During one beating, Louie was clubbed on his injured ankle, leaving it so painful he could barely walk. And on at least one night, the Bird beat Louie to unconsciousness.

Louie's job as pig custodian was over. Barge work had also been canceled; so many Japanese ships had been sunk that none came to Naoetsu anymore. Louie was back on half rations. Limping, ill, and starved, he pleaded with the Bird for work to get full rations. The Bird brought him a sickly, paper-thin goat.

"Goat die, you die."

Louie nursed the goat, and at night, tied him in a grain shack. The goat got sicker.

One morning, the Bird ordered Louie to come before him. He said the goat had escaped, gorged himself on grain, and become deathly ill, and it was Louie's fault. Louie knew his knot had been secure. If the goat had gotten loose, someone had untied him. He knew that person was almost certainly the Bird himself.

The goat died. Terrified of retribution, Louie hid in the barracks, but his diarrhea was killing him. Risking being seen by the Bird, he snuck out, trying to get to the camp doctor. The Bird spotted him and ran him down.

The Bird hustled Louie across the compound. Lying on the ground was a heavy wooden beam, some six feet long. Pick it up, the Bird said. Louie hoisted it, and the Bird ordered him to lift it over his head. Louie heaved it up. The Bird called a guard. If the prisoner lowers his arms, the Bird said, ram him with your gun. He walked to a nearby shack, climbed on the roof, and settled in to watch.

Louie stood in the sun, holding the beam. The Bird stretched over the roof, calling to passing guards, pointing to Louie and laughing. Louie locked his eyes on the Bird's face, seething.

Minutes passed. Louie stood, eyes on the Bird. The beam felt heavier and heavier. The Bird stared, mocking him. Nearby, Wade and Tinker watched anxiously. Wade had looked at the camp clock when Louie had lifted the beam. He was increasingly conscious of how much time was passing.

Five more minutes passed, then ten. Louie's arms went numb. He shook. The beam tipped. The guard jabbed him, and he straightened. He began to feel confused, the camp swimming around him. All he knew was a single thought: *He cannot break me.*

Time ticked on, and still Louie remained, the beam over his head, his eyes on the Bird's face, enduring long past when he should have collapsed. The Bird stopped laughing.

Frustrated and furious, the Bird jumped down, charged across the compound, and rammed his fist into Louie's stomach. Louie crumpled in agony, and the beam dropped, striking his head. He flopped to the ground.

When he woke, Wade was crouched by him. He had no idea how long he'd stood there, but Wade had looked at the clock when Louie had fallen.

Louie had held the beam for thirty-seven minutes.

On the night of August 1, the sirens suddenly began blasting and the air filled with a shattering roar. Above was an awesome spectacle: wave after wave of B-29s, part of the biggest raid, by tonnage, of WWII. As they swept overhead, the Bird raced into the barracks and shouted for all Americans to get out. The men hurried outside, and the Bird began smashing them over their heads with his kendo stick. Men started falling. Louie went down, and the Bird pounced on him. Woozy, Louie lay there as the Bird clubbed him. The planes roared and the Bird and the sirens screamed.

Then the planes were gone, the sirens quiet. Dawn broke, and the Bird went still. Louie stumbled to his feet and looked northeast. The horizon was glowing with fire.

That same night, B-29s showered leaflets over thirty-five Japanese cit-

One of more than five million leaflets dropped over thirty-five Japanese cities on the night of August 1–2, 1945, warning civilians that heavy bombing was coming and that they needed to evacuate.

ies, warning of bombings and urging civilians to evacuate. The Japanese government ordered civilians to turn the leaflets in to authorities, forbade them to share the warnings with others, and arrested anyone with leaflets in their possession.

———

The next morning, Louie's diarrhea was extremely severe. He was dangerously dehydrated and struggling to force food down.

The B-29s raked the sky, and the Bird rampaged. As Louie crossed camp, the Bird collared him and dragged him to the overflowing *benjo* pit with several other men. He forced them to their stomachs, atop the waste pits, and ordered them to do push-ups. When the exhausted men faltered, the Bird used his rifle butt to grind their faces into the excrement.

Then came the day Louie had been dreading. He was filling a tub of water when the Bird barked at him to come, then gestured toward the water.

"Tomorrow I'm going to drown you."

Louie spent a day gripped in fear, looking for the Bird, thinking about drowning. When the Bird found him, he was terrified.

"I have changed my mind," the Bird said. He lunged at Louie and began punching his face, alternating right and left fists in a violent ecstasy. Then he stopped, suddenly serene.

"I will drown you tomorrow," he said. Then he strolled away.

———

Louie could take no more. He joined about a dozen officers in a secret meeting. They decided to kill the Bird.

The plan was simple. They'd leap on the Bird and pull him to the barracks' top floor, overlooking the river. There, they'd lash him to a rock and shove him out the window. When the Bird struck the water, the rock would carry him under. He'd never draw another breath.

The officers divvied up the tasks. One group would make a plan to capture the Bird. Others would find a heavy rock and sneak it upstairs. Louie was tasked with stealing rope to lash the rock to the Bird.

The rock crew somehow got a large boulder into the barracks without discovery. Louie couldn't find a rope long enough, so he stole shorter ropes and tied them together. They looped it around the rock, a dangling end ready to be lashed around the Bird.

The conspirators discussed who would join the group that would capture the Bird and throw him to his death. Louie volunteered.

———

On the morning of August 6, 1945, a B-29 skipped off a runway on Tinian Island, next to Saipan. Pilot Paul Tibbets guided it north, toward Japan. In his pocket were poison cyanide capsules. If the plane crashed and the men were captured, they'd swallow the capsules and kill themselves to avoid revealing the new, world-changing secret weapon that sat in the bomb bay: a twelve-foot-long, nine-thousand-pound bomb called Little Boy. It was an atomic bomb.

Crossing the Inland Sea, Tibbets saw a city ahead: Hiroshima. As the plane crossed over it, the crew donned shaded goggles. Below, Tibbets saw a T-shaped bridge, the target. The bombardier lined up on it.

The B-29 Enola Gay, *bearing an atomic bomb called Little Boy, readies for takeoff on Tinian Island on August 6, 1945.*

At 8:15.17, the bomb slipped from the plane. Tibbets turned the plane sharply and dove to gain speed. It would take forty-three seconds for the bomb to reach detonation altitude. No one knew if in that brief time, the bomber could get far enough away to survive what was coming.

A crewman counted seconds in his head. He hit forty-three. Nothing happened. For an instant, he thought the mission had failed.

Exactly as the thought crossed his mind, the sky over the city ripped open in a storm of color, sound, and wind. A white light, ten times the intensity of the sun, enveloped the plane as the flash and noise and jolt of it skidded out in all directions. Tibbets's teeth began tingling, and his mouth tasted of lead. He would later be told that it was the metal in his fillings resonating with the radioactivity of the bomb. The entire sky was swirling in pink and blue. The copilot scribbled two words in his diary: "MY GOD!"

The tail gunner saw an eerie shimmering warp in the air, ripping toward them at one thousand feet per second. "Here it comes!" he said. The shock wave slammed into the plane, pitching the men into the air and down again. Then came a second wave, a consequence of the force of the explosion hitting the ground and ricocheting up, and the plane heaved again.

At a POW camp not far from Hiroshima, a prisoner felt a shudder, and the air warmed strangely. He looked up. A fantastically huge, roiling cloud, glowing bluish-gray, stood swaggering over the city. It was more than three miles tall. Below it, Hiroshima was boiling.

The aftermath of the atomic bombing of Nagasaki, August 9, 1945.

NAGASAKI ATOMIC BOMB MUSEUM/EPA/CORBIS

CHAPTER 31

The Naked Stampede

The POWs knew something big had happened. Guards paced around with stricken faces. Civilians walked past camp, eyes dazed, hands in fists.

A civilian told the POWs that one American bomb had destroyed an entire city. He used a word that sounded like "atomic." The word was unfamiliar, and no one knew how one bomb could wipe out a city.

At Omori, the shaken Japanese commander gathered the POWs. "One plane came," he said, "and a whole city disappeared." He asked if anyone knew what weapon could do such a thing. No one had an answer.

On August 9, the city of Nagasaki, like Hiroshima, disappeared.

———

Uneasy days passed. Everything in Naoetsu remained the same, and the POWs were still sent to labor in the war production factories. Clearly, something monumental had happened, but Japan hadn't given in.

For the POWs, time had all but run out. It was nearly mid-August, and the kill-all policy loomed. Even if Japan surrendered, many POWs believed the guards would murder them anyway, out of vengeance or to prevent them from testifying in war crimes trials. With officials talking about taking them to a new camp, the POWs believed the Japanese planned to murder them in the mountains, where no one would ever find them.

Louie lingered in his bunk, fading, praying. In nightmares, he and the Bird fought death matches, the Bird trying to beat him to death, Louie trying to strangle the sergeant. He'd been staying as far as he could from the Bird, but the sergeant always hunted him down.

Then, abruptly, the violence stopped. The Bird was gone. The guards said he was in the mountains, preparing the "new camp." The August 22 kill-all day was one week away.

———

On August 15, Louie woke gravely ill. He was having twenty bloody bowel movements a day. In one month, he'd lost thirteen pounds from a frame already dangerously thin. His legs were strangely swollen. He'd seen too many men die to be ignorant of what this meant. Potentially fatal beriberi was setting in.

In late morning, Louie crept from the barracks. With the Bird away, it was safer to walk in the open. He saw gentle Ogawa, the potato field overseer, one of the few Japanese he didn't fear. But when he saw Louie, Ogawa yanked out his club and struck him in the face. Louie reeled in astonishment, his cheek bleeding.

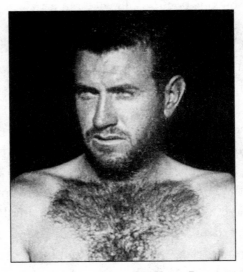

COURTESY OF LOUIS ZAMPERINI

A few minutes later, the compound was suddenly, eerily silent. The Japanese were all gone. In the factories, the POWs realized they were alone. The guards had left.

Frank Tinker walked through the deserted Naoetsu compound. Passing the guardroom, he glanced inside. There were the guards, crowded around a radio, listening to a small Japanese voice. Something of great importance was being said.

At the factories, the guards reappeared and told the POWs to get back to work. When Ken Marvin returned to his station, he found no one working. He spotted Bad Eye, the guard whom he'd been teaching bad English. Marvin asked why work had stopped. Bad Eye said there was no electricity. Marvin looked around, then turned to Bad Eye and told him the lights were on. Bad Eye replied solemnly.

"The war is over."

Marvin began sobbing.

As the workers marched to camp, Marvin hurried among them, sharing what Bad Eye had said. No one believed it. Everyone had heard this rumor before, and it had always turned out to be false. In camp, nothing had changed.

In the morning, the work crews were told there was no work and dismissed. The men began to wonder if Marvin was right.

The guards would say nothing. A day passed with no news. When night fell, the men saw the village glowing; the civilians had taken their blackout shades down. As a test, the POWs removed the shades on the barracks windows. The guards ordered them to put them back up. If the war really had ended, the guards were hiding it from the POWs. The kill-all date was five days away.

The next day, Louie was sicker still. He'd been vomiting for two days. He scrawled sad words in his diary: "Look like skeleton. Feel weak."

The Bird reappeared. Louie saw him outside. He watched the sergeant's back as he stepped into his office and closed the door.

———

On the seventeenth of August, at Rokuroshi POW camp on the frigid summit of a Japanese mountain, a telephone rang.

Phil, Fred Garrett, and the other Rokuroshi POWs were shivering through the summer. The guards had nailed the barracks doors shut. In this remote, deathly quiet camp, the telephone hardly ever rang, and the POWs noticed it. A few minutes later, the Japanese commander hurried down the mountain.

All summer, the Rokuroshi prisoners had been racked with tension. The sky was scratched with bomber vapor trails. One night in July, the horizon had lit up red, generating light so bright, the men could read by it. On August 15, the guards had suddenly become much more brutal.

After the commander left, something troubling happened. The guards began dividing the POWs into small groups and herding them deep in the forest, then back to camp. Later, the walks were repeated. The guards seemed to be habituating the men to this routine in preparation for something terrible.

———

On August 20, under a threatening sky, there was a shout in the Naoetsu compound: all POWs were to assemble outside. The camp commander spoke, a translator beside him.

"The war has come to a point of cessation."

There was no reaction from the POWs. Some believed it but kept silent for fear of reprisal. Others thought it was a trick.

With the POWs waiting in suspicious silence, the translator invited the men to bathe in the river. This was odd; the men had almost never been allowed in the river. Louie and the others dragged down to the water, dropping clothes, and waded in. They scattered, scrubbing their skin, unsure what was happening. Then they heard it.

It was the howl of an aircraft engine, huge, low, and close. The swimmers looked up and at first saw nothing but white sky. Then, there it was, bursting from the clouds: a torpedo bomber.

As the men watched, the bomber dove, leveled off, and skimmed over the water, engine screaming. It was headed straight toward the POWs.

In the instant before the plane shot overhead, the POWs could just make out the cockpit, and inside, the pilot, standing. Then the bomber was upon them. On each side of the fuselage there was a broad white star in a blue circle. The plane wasn't Japanese. It was American.

The plane's red code light blinked frantically. A POW read the signals and suddenly cried out.

"Oh! The war is over!"

In seconds, masses of naked men were stampeding up the hill. As the plane turned loops above, the POWs swarmed the camp, out of their minds with relief and rapture. Their fear of the guards, and the massacre they'd awaited, was gone, dispersed by the muscle of the bomber. The prisoners jumped, shouted, and sobbed. Some scrambled onto the roofs, waving and singing out to the pilot above. Others piled against the camp fence, sent it crashing over, and lit it on fire. The Japanese shrank back and withdrew.

In the midst of the celebrating men, Louie stood on wavering legs, wet, emaciated, and sick. In his tired mind, two words were repeating themselves, over and over.

I'm free! I'm free! I'm free!

A battered Australian was sitting at the water's edge, watching the bomber, when he saw something flit out of the cockpit and fall toward the river. He stood up and leaned far over the water, arms outstretched. The object, a wooden packet, dropped into his hands. Regaining his balance with the treasure in his grasp, he had a delightful thought: *Chocolate!*

He opened the packet and realized, to his immense disappointment, that it wasn't chocolate. It held a message from the pilot, saying he'd lead supply planes back the next day to drop food.

Captain Ray Hawkins, who piloted a torpedo bomber over Naoetsu to alert POWs that the war was over, dropped this note from the cockpit to the men below.

NATIONAL NAVAL AVIATION MUSEUM BY MICHAEL DUNCAN

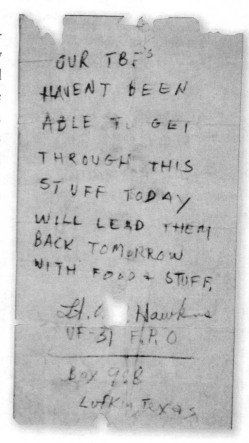

Before he flew off, the pilot dropped a candy bar with a bite taken out of it. Fitzgerald had it sliced into seven hundred slivers, and each man licked a finger, dabbed it on his bit of chocolate, and put it in his mouth. Louie's portion was the size of an ant.

Another American plane thrummed over, and a man fell from it. Down he fell, and no parachute opened. Everyone gasped. Then they realized it wasn't a man, it was a pair of pants, stuffed with something.

The officers retrieved the pants, and Louie stood by as they were opened. Inside were cigarettes and candy bars, and the compound was soon littered with wrappers and naked, skinny, smoking men. Also in the pants was an American magazine. On the cover was a photograph of an impossibly massive bomb cloud. The men fell silent, piecing together the rumors of one giant bomb vaporizing a city and the abrupt end to the war.

———

The rock still sat by the barracks window, Louie's rope around it. But the conspirators were too late; the Bird was gone. Sometime that day, or perhaps the day before, he'd slipped into the countryside and vanished.

CHAPTER 32

Cascades of Pink Peaches

On August 22, Phil and Fred Garrett sat in Rokuroshi, wondering what was happening. They'd been told nothing of the war's end. All they knew was that the Japanese commander had been gone for five days, and the guards had been leading them on ominous marches through the forest.

That afternoon, the Japanese commander walked into the barracks.

"The Emperor has brought peace to the world," he said. He surrendered his sword.

That night, the POWs threw a party to end all parties. Demolishing the fence, they built a gigantic pile of wood. They got a barrel of rice wine; drinking began, the bonfire was lit, an Alabaman transformed a huge can into a drum, and tipsy men began dancing. A conga line of crazy drunk POWs wrapped around camp, and one man did a terrible striptease. The revelry was so riotous that one POW was surprised everyone survived the night.

The following day, the hungover POWs walked down the mountain to find mostly ghost towns. The civilians had seen the bonfire and fled. The POWs hiked back up and waited for help to come.

At Naoetsu, the guards were suddenly fawning and submissive. Only the Japanese commander was defiant, haughtily refusing Fitzgerald's repeated demands for food for his starving men.

POWs celebrate the war's end. NAVAL HISTORY AND HERITAGE COMMAND

On the morning of August 26, six days after the war's end was announced in Naoetsu, American fighter planes arrived. The POWs charged outside, yelling. They painted two giant words on the ground in white lime: FOOD SMOKES. Messages dropped from the cockpits. The planes had been hauling emergency supplies to POW camps but had exhausted their loads. The pilots promised food would soon come.

Unable to feed the POWs, the pilots did the next best thing, putting on an air show while the prisoners shouted and wept. The show had a persuasive effect on the Japanese commander. Japanese trucks soon arrived, and out came rations, biscuits, and canned fruit.

That afternoon, more planes flew over, and as the POWs ran for their lives, bags began thumping down. Each man received half a tin of tangerines, one pack of biscuits, two cigarettes, and candy. Concerned that it wasn't nearly enough food, Fitzgerald had someone write 700 PWS HERE on the ground.

Someone waded into the river to grab an errant bag and in it found magazines. The war, the magazines said, had ended on August 15; the speaker Wade had heard on the guards' radio that day had been Emperor Hirohito. So for five days—seven, in the case of Rokuroshi—the Japanese had deceived the POWs to hide the fact that the war was over. The reason was almost certainly that they were awaiting instruction on whether to carry out the kill-all order.

Three days after the fighters flew over, the Americans sent in the big boys: six loaded B-29s. Giant pallets poured out, swinging under red, white, and blue parachutes. The first load hit the compound. Others fell into nearby rice paddies, pursued by hundreds of gleeful living skeletons. One canister bore a message written in chalk: *Bombed here in May 45—sorry I missed.* Boxes fell all over the landscape. Some civilians pulled them into their homes. Others, though in great hardship, dragged them into camp.

Pallets banged down and broke open. Cascades of pink peaches spilled over the countryside. A crate exploded, and the sky rained peas. Louie and Tinker just missed being totaled by a drum full of shoes that shot through the *benjo* roof. To prevent disaster, someone ran onto the road and wrote DROP HERE. Food, medicine, and clothing fell in such abundance that Fitzgerald asked a man to check that whoever had written 700 PWS HERE hadn't accidentally added a zero. Eventually someone climbed on a roof and wrote: NO MORE—THANKS.

Photograph of Naoetsu compound taken by a rescue plane just after war's end. The POWs had written messages for the pilots on the barracks roofs. NAVAL AVIATION MUSEUM

An orgy of eating commenced. Men crammed their stomachs full, then had seconds and thirds. Louie shoveled an entire can's worth of condensed soup into his mouth, too hungry to add water. Three men drank two *gallons* of cocoa.

At nightfall, the eating stopped. Men upended by swollen stomachs drifted off to sleep. Louie lay among them, swaddled in an American parachute.

———

In its rampage over the east, Japan had brought atrocity and death on a scale that staggers the imagination. In the midst of it were prisoners of war. Japan held some 132,000 POWs from America, Britain, Canada, New Zealand, Holland, and Australia. Of those, nearly 36,000 died, more than one in every four. Japan also held more than 215,000 POWs from other nations, and untold thousands of forced laborers; their death rates are unknown. Americans fared particularly badly; of the 34,648 Americans held by Japan, 12,935—more than 37 percent—died. By comparison, only 1 percent of Americans held by the Nazis and Italians died.

Japan murdered thousands of POWs on death marches and worked thousands of others to death in slavery. Thousands of other POWs were beaten, burned, stabbed, or clubbed to death, shot, beheaded, murdered in medical experimentation, and eaten alive in ritual acts of cannibalism. And as a result of being fed grossly inadequate and befouled food and water, thousands more died of starvation and easily preventable diseases.

Under the kill-all order, the Japanese massacred all five thousand Korean captives on Tinian, all the POWs on Ballale, Wake, and Tarawa, and all but eleven POWs at Palawan. They were evidently about to murder all the other POWs and civilian internees in their custody when the atomic bomb brought their empire crashing down.

On September 2, 1945, Japan signed its formal surrender. The Second World War was over.

———

For Louie, these were days of bliss. Though sick and weak, he glowed with euphoria. Days earlier, he would have killed the Bird without remorse. Now, the

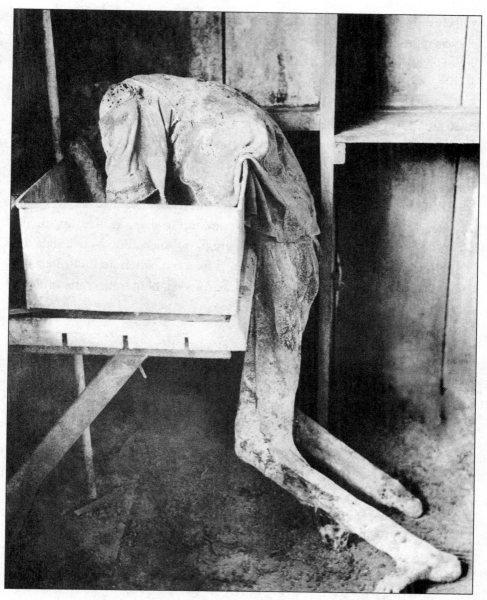

At a Japanese POW camp, this dead American was found near war's end, still standing, at a sink at which he was trying to drink. American soldiers and guerrillas went behind enemy lines to rescue the men at this camp, but they were too late. They found the bodies of 150 POWs, starved to death. ASSOCIATED PRESS

vengeful urge no longer had sure footing. The Bird was gone, and all Louie felt was rapture. He and other POWs doled out supplies to civilians; stood in circles of Japanese children, handing out chocolate; and brought food and clothing to the guards for their families.

Gorging brought consequences. Bodies that had spent years scraping by on seaweed were overwhelmed. Naoetsu became a festival of rapidfire diarrhea. The *benjo* lines wound everywhere, and men unable to wait began dropping their pants and fertilizing Japan wherever the spirit moved them. Then they resumed feasting.

All over Japan, more than one thousand planes saturated POW camps with nearly forty-five hundred tons of Spam and fruit cocktail, soup, chocolate, medicine, and countless other treasures. At Omori, Bob Martindale was sitting in the Bird's old office, savoring his freedom, when an enormous box sailed out of the sun, hit the ground, and exploded, obliterating the office in

American POWs upon liberation from a Japanese prison camp. GETTY IMAGES

a cataclysm of American cocoa powder. Martindale stumbled out, caked head to toe in cocoa but otherwise uninjured.

———

Everyone in camp was eager to get home, but Fitzgerald received a radio message telling him to wait for an evacuation team to arrive on September 4. So the POWs waited, eating, smoking, eating, celebrating, swimming, and eating more. Someone broke into a storehouse and discovered some fifteen hundred Red Cross boxes, hidden by the Japanese while the POWs starved. Louie ate voraciously, got stronger, and expanded in all directions, his body bloating from water retention.

September 4 arrived. The evacuation team never showed up. More than two weeks had passed since the men had learned the war was over, and Fitzgerald was sick of waiting. He walked to the train station and asked a Japanese official to arrange for a train to be there the next day. The official refused.

Commander Fitzgerald had been in Japanese custody since April 1943. For two and a half years, he'd been forced to grovel before sadists and imbeciles as he tried to protect his men. He'd been starved, beaten, waterboarded, and enslaved and had had his fingernails torn out. He was done negotiating. He hauled back and punched the station official in the face. The next morning, the train was there, right on time.

On September 5, Louie stepped from the barracks for the last time. Outside, the POWs were congregating, holding what few possessions they had. The British Commonwealth soldiers held the boxes bearing the remains of the sixty Aussies who had died in camp. Determined to leave this indecent place with dignity, the men assembled behind their nations' flags. Together, they marched through the gate, toward wives and sweethearts and Mom and Dad and home.

Louie glanced back. The sickest POWs remained behind, awaiting transport the next day. Fitzgerald stayed with them, unwilling to leave until the last of his men was liberated.

As he crossed over the bridge and Naoetsu passed out of view, Louie raised his arm and waved the war goodbye.

CHAPTER 33

Mother's Day

The Naoetsu POWs had control of the train. At each village, the train squealed to a stop and the men piled off, then piled back on, laden with wine. The men grew rowdier. A lieutenant told them to behave themselves: he didn't want any men falling overboard. His warning did no good. All afternoon, drunken POWs fell off the train. One of them was the lieutenant himself.

Across Japan, as POW trains snaked toward Yokohama, the men saw what the B-29s had done. Once-grand cities were now black stains. Seeing the destruction of the enemy that had enslaved and tormented them and murdered their friends, the POWs cheered. But after the first city there was another, then another, city after city razed, survivors drifting like specters. The cheering died away. On Louie's train, the silence came at Tokyo. A week after Louie left Omori, sixteen square miles of the city, and tens of thousands of souls, had been burned by B-29s.

Some trains rolled past Hiroshima. The city was simply gone. Virtually every POW believed its destruction had saved them from execution. They were almost certainly right.

———

As his train pulled into Yokohama, Tom Wade heard a woman's voice.

"Welcome back, boys."

"Before me in immaculate khaki uniform and cap stood an American girl with a magazine-cover smile, faultless makeup, and peroxide blonde hair," he wrote. "After three and a half years in prison camp, I had been liberated by the great American blonde!"

The POWs were blissfully enveloped in Red Cross nurses. To Ken Marvin, they all looked like goddesses.

Someone spotted a mess hall, and a stampede ensued. A journalist, Robert Trumbull, called out, asking if anyone had a good story. Tinker told him to talk to Louie Zamperini.

"Zamperini's dead," said Trumbull. The POW Tinker pointed to didn't even look like the famous runner, but Trumbull was curious enough to stop him. He asked Louie to prove his identity. Louie retrieved his wallet. In it, there were eight dollars, the newspaper illustration that had gotten him and Phil beaten up, and a USC pass inscribed with Louie's name.

Trumbull was astonished. He began asking questions, and as he scribbled notes, Louie told his story. When he finished, Trumbull asked him to reflect on his odyssey. Louie stood silent.

"If I knew I had to go through those experiences again," he finally said, "I'd kill myself."

The next morning, Louie was taken to an airfield to be flown to Okinawa. Finding a table stacked with K rations—meal boxes for servicemen—he crammed several under his shirt, ignoring an attendant who tried to assure him that no one would starve him anymore. Looking extremely pregnant, Louie boarded his plane.

In the bustle, he'd been separated from his friends. There were no good-byes. He was soon airborne, leaving Japan, he hoped, forever.

———

Frank Rosynek, a staff sergeant for Louie's 11th Bomb Group, stood on the Okinawa airfield, watching POWs arrive. He walked among them, marveling at how they savored the awful mess hall food, seeing them cry over photographs of wives and girlfriends who they hoped hadn't given them up for dead.

Rosynek's commanding officer asked him to come to the debriefing of a POW from the 11th. When Rosynek arrived, he saw a battered POW sitting before officers who were staring at him in shock. The colonel said the man was Louis Zamperini, and he'd disappeared in 1943. Everyone in the bomb group had thought he was dead. Rosynek was incredulous. It was his job to write next-of-kin letters, and he'd probably written to Zamperini's mother, but he didn't remember. There'd been so many such letters. Not one of those men had turned up alive, until now.

Later, the dead man walked into the 11th Bomb Group's quarters, startling everyone. But it wasn't the reunion Louie anticipated. He knew almost no one. Many of his friends, he learned, were dead. Of the sixteen young officers who'd shared his barracks on Oahu, only four, Louie and Phil included, were still alive.

Louie (right) and Fred Garrett, a few weeks after war's end. Gorging nonstop after their camps were liberated, both men had gained weight precipitously. COURTESY OF LOUIS ZAMPERINI

Doctors examined Louie. After gorging for weeks, he weighed 143 pounds. But thanks to dramatic water retention, it was a doughy, moonfaced weight. He still had volatile diarrhea and was as weak as a blade of grass. He was only twenty-eight, but his body was etched with twenty-seven months of abuse. The doctors, who knew what Louie had once been, gave him a solemn talk. After Louie left, a reporter asked about his running career.

"It's finished," he said, his voice sharp. "I'll never run again."

———

The Zamperinis were on edge. Louie's only message to reach home had been his radio broadcast ten months earlier. The letters he'd written after the Bird left Omori had still not arrived. The papers were full of stories about the Japanese murdering POWs, and the Zamperinis were scared.

On the morning of September 9, Pete was shaken awake by a hand on his shoulder. A friend was bending over him with a huge smile. Trumbull's story had appeared in the *Los Angeles Times*: "Zamperini Comes Back from Dead."

Pete bolted for a telephone and called home. Sylvia picked up. Pete asked if she'd heard the news.

"Did you hear the news?" she repeated to him. "Did I! Wow!" Pete asked to speak to his mother, but she was too overcome to talk.

Louise and Virginia rushed to church to give thanks, then raced back to prepare for the homecoming. Dusting trophies in Louie's room, Louise blinked away tears, singing out, "He's on the way home. He's on the way home."

"From now on," she said, "September ninth is going to be Mother's Day to me, because that's the day I learned for sure my boy was coming home."

———

Liberation was a long time coming for Phil at Rokuroshi. After learning the war was over, the POWs sat for ten days, waiting for someone to come. Finally, a wondrous sight: B-29s skimming over, pallets hitting the rice paddies so hard, the men had to dig them out. The POWs ate themselves silly, including one who devoured twenty pounds of food in one day.

On September 9, the Rokuroshi POWs were rescued. In Yokohama, a general broke down when he saw their condition. They were escorted aboard a ship for hot showers and pancakes. The ship set off for America.

On October 16, 1945, Russell Allen Phillips stepped off a train in Indiana. There, standing where he'd left her four years earlier, was the woman whose love had sustained him. Cecy was in his arms at last.

Four weeks later, in a wedding ceremony in Cecy's parents' house, the hero finally got the girl. Then, as he'd promised in a letter so long ago, Allen ran away with Cecy to a place where no one would find them.

———

On Okinawa, Louie had a grand time, eating, drinking, and making merry. He discovered a delightful upside to being believed dead: scaring the hell out of people. Learning that a former track recruiter from USC was on the island,

Russell Allen Phillips arrives at his mother's house.
On the back of this photo, someone wrote, "Home!" Courtesy of Karen Loomis

Louie prepares to board a flight home. Courtesy of Louis Zamperini

he asked a friend to tell the recruiter that he knew a college running prospect who could spin a mile in just over four minutes. The recruiter eagerly asked to meet the runner. When Louie appeared, the recruiter fell over backward in his chair.

On one of the series of flights that carried him home, Louie sat with the pilot, telling his story, from the crash to Kwajalein to Japan. As he spoke, the pilot landed on an island, stopped the plane, and asked Louie if he knew where he was. Louie looked around at a charred wasteland.

"This is Kwajalein," said the pilot.

This *couldn't* be Kwajalein, Louie thought. When he was a captive, it was a swath of intense green. Now he couldn't see a single tree. The fight for this place had ripped the jungle off the island. Louie wondered if kindhearted Kawamura had died here.

Louie and Pete, reunited. Courtesy of Louis Zamperini

There was, in fact, one tree still standing, and they went to see it. Staring at Kwajalein's last tree, with food in his belly, no one there to beat him, Louie felt as if he were in the sweetest of dreams.

———

Pete was so anxious to see Louie that he could hardly bear it. When he learned Louie was finally stateside, admitted to San Francisco's Letterman General Hospital to recover from his ordeal, he went AWOL. He bummed a plane ride to San Francisco, hitchhiked to Letterman, and walked in. At the front desk, he called Louie's room. A minute later, Louie bounded into the lobby.

Each was startled by the sight of the other. Expecting Louie to be emaciated, Pete was surprised to find him almost portly from water retention. Louie was disturbed by what years of worry had done to his brother. Pete was gaunt, and he'd gone largely bald. The brothers fell together, eyes shining.

Pete and Louie spent several days together while doctors finally cured Louie of his diarrhea. After reading the Trumbull article, Pete had worried Louie might be severely traumatized, but his fears faded. Louie was upbeat and chatty. He seemed so well that when reporters came in to interview Louie, they crowded around Pete, assuming that of the two men, this haggard one had to be the POW.

The army sent a bomber to bring Louie home. The plane rose over the clouds into a shining blue morning. Scared of flying, Pete tried to distract himself by staring out over a carpet of bright clouds, the upside of a rainstorm. He felt as if he could step from the plane and walk on them.

They sank into the rain and landed at Long Beach, where the rest of the family waited. The moment the plane stopped, Louie jumped down, ran to his sobbing mother, and folded himself around her.

"*Cara mamma mia,*" he whispered—"my dear mother." It was a long time before they let go.

Louie's homecoming, Long Beach Airport. Foreground, left to right: *Virginia, Sylvia, Louise, and Louie.* COURTESY OF LOUIS ZAMPERINI

PART

V

Louie reunited with his family.
Left to right: *Sylvia, Anthony, Louie, Louise, Pete, and Virginia.*

CHAPTER 34

The Shimmering Girl

On an October afternoon, Louie stood before his parents' house for the first time in more than three years.

"This little home," he said, "was worth all of it."

As his family filed into the house, Louie paused, overcome by a strange uneasiness. He had to push himself to walk up the steps.

The dining room table was heaped with food. Three years of Christmas and birthday presents sat ready for opening. There was a cake with *Welcome Home Louie* inscribed in icing.

The family ringed around Louie, eager to look at him and touch him. No one asked about prison camp. Louie said a little about it, and to everyone's relief, it seemed to carry little emotion for him. He seemed happy.

Sylvia had a surprise for him. She'd obtained a recording of his POW broadcast, treasured by the family because it had given them proof he was alive. As Louie sat nearby, relaxed and cheerful, Sylvia dropped the record on the turntable. The broadcast began to play.

Louie was suddenly screaming. Shaking violently, he shouted, *"Take it off! Take it off! I can't stand it!"* Sylvia snatched the record, and Louie yelled at her to break it. She smashed it and threw it away.

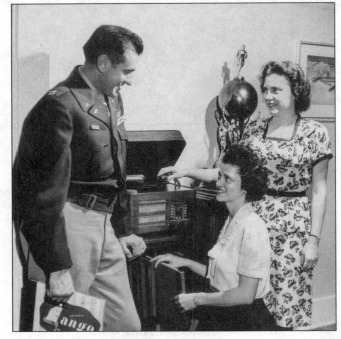

*Virginia (center) and Sylvia with Louie
at the family record player.* COURTESY OF LOUIS ZAMPERINI

Louie fell silent, trembling. His family stared in horror.

Louie walked upstairs and lay on his bed. When he finally drifted off, the Bird followed him into his dreams.

———

The same man was on many other minds that fall. In debriefings, war crimes investigators listened as POWs told of monstrous abuses and atrocities committed by the Japanese. Over and over, the same name was mentioned: Mutsuhiro Watanabe. Ultimately, prosecutors would gather some 250 affidavits concerning Watanabe's crimes. When Tom Wade gave the name, his interviewer exclaimed, "*Not* the same Watanabe! We've got enough to hang him six times already."

On September 11, General Douglas MacArthur, heading the occupation of Japan, ordered the arrest of forty war crimes suspects. While thousands of men would later be sought, this preliminary list included those accused of the worst crimes, including Hideki Tojo, mastermind of Pearl Harbor and the enslavement of POWs. Listed with them, reportedly seventh, was Watanabe.

When he got the news, the Bird was sitting in a bar in the village where his mother lived. He packed a trunk, jumped on a train, and fled to the city of Kofu. There, he heard a radio broadcast about wanted men and was shocked to hear himself listed with Tojo. If his case was considered comparable to Tojo's, he thought, arrest would mean execution.

He vowed to never let himself be captured. He would disappear forever. He slipped out of Kofu and vanished.

———

As Mutsuhiro fled, the hunt for him began. Police appeared at the home of his mother, Shizuka. She said he might be with his sister Michiko, in Tokyo. She gave them an address, and they converged on it. Not only was there no Michiko there, there was no house. B-29s had burned the neighborhood months earlier.

Shizuka's misdirection of the detectives may have been an honest mistake—Michiko had moved down the road, so the only change in the address was the door number—but the police now suspected her of deliberately misleading them to protect her son. They took her in for questioning. If she knew anything, she let nothing slip.

Detectives began tailing and regularly interrogating Shizuka. Her monetary transactions were tracked, her landlord questioned. Mutsuhiro's other relatives and acquaintances were investigated, questioned, and sometimes searched. Police intercepted the family's mail. They even had someone deliver a fake letter, apparently pretending it was from Mutsuhiro, in hopes the family would betray his whereabouts. His photograph was distributed to police in four prefectures, and countless special searches were conducted.

The police found only one clue. A man who'd seen Mutsuhiro at war's end said the sergeant had told him he'd rather kill himself than be captured. Perhaps the Bird was already dead.

———

As his tormenter disappeared in darkness, Louie was pulled into blinding light. Featured in the media, he was a national sensation. Two thousand people wrote him letters. Press photographers tailed him. He was buried in speaking invitations, most of which came with an award, so he couldn't decline. In his first weeks home, he gave ninety-five speeches.

The attention was overpowering. Louie was beginning to suffer from suffocating anxiety. Each time he told his story, his gut would wring. Every night, in his dreams, the Bird stood over him, screaming, *"Next! Next! Next!"*

Shortly after returning home, Louie attended a gala where he was slated to speak. He waited to be introduced, anxious. Drinks were set before him, and he sipped them and felt his nerves unwinding. By the time he rose to speak, he was in a haze. The alcohol brought him a pleasant numbness.

Soon after, as he fretted over another speech, he opened a bottle of whiskey and poured some in his coffee. It gave him a warm feeling, so he had another shot, then another. The whiskey floated him through that speech, too. From then on, when the harsh push of memory ran through Louie, he reached for his flask.

———

It was March 1946. Louie was at a club bar in Miami Beach, taking the two weeks' vacation awarded to servicemen. A door opened. Louie glanced up. Flitting into the club was a shimmering woman, arrestingly beautiful, her hair a tumble of blond. Louie took one long look and had the startling thought that he had to marry this girl.

The next day, Louie returned to the club, vaulted the fence surrounding its private beach, and lay down near two sunbathing women. When one of the women turned, Louie recognized the beauty from the bar. Louie chatted with her and thought her bright, lively, and very beautiful. When they parted, Louie said something about how she probably wouldn't want to see him again. "Maybe," she said playfully, "I want to see you again."

Her name was Cynthia Applewhite, and forests of men had gone down at the sight of her. She was wealthy and pedigreed, living in her parents' mansion and educated in private schools. But for all her polishing, she wasn't a buttoned-up girl. She dressed in bohemian clothes, penned novels, painted, and yearned to roam the world. She was passionate, impulsive, and irresistibly willful. Mostly, she was bored by the vanilla sort of boys who trailed her

Cynthia Applewhite, on the day after Louie met her. COURTESY OF LOUIS ZAMPERINI

around, and by Miami Beach. Along came Louie. He was a war hero, understood her fiercely independent personality, and was from nowhere near Miami Beach.

In the coming days, Louie and Cynthia whirled around town, racing through his hotel and streaming toilet paper out the windows, laughing, exhilarated by each other. For Louie, something about this girl seemed the answer to his suffering. Just before he was to leave, he asked her to marry him. She said yes.

After Louie left, Cynthia broke the news to her parents. The Applewhites were alarmed that their daughter, who'd just turned twenty, was leaping into marriage with a twenty-nine-year-old soldier she'd known for less than two weeks. Mrs. Applewhite refused to give Cynthia money to fly to California to get married. Cynthia vowed to get the money somehow.

Louie wrote Cynthia almost every day, and every morning waited for the mailman to bring Cynthia's pink letters. Though their letters were adoring, they revealed how little the two knew each other. Cynthia had no idea how deeply Louie was haunted by his war ordeal, or that he was turning to alcohol to cope. In critical ways, she was engaged to a stranger.

Cynthia vowed to help Louie forget the war, and he grasped her promise as a lifeline. "If you love me enough," he wrote back, "I'll have to forget it. How much can you love?"

———

Cynthia on her first date with Louie, March 1946. Courtesy of Louis Zamperini

Cynthia arrives in Los Angeles.
COURTESY OF LOUIS ZAMPERINI

In May, Cynthia's parents agreed to let her visit Louie, on the condition that they not marry until the fall. Cynthia raced to the airport. When her plane landed, Louie bounded up the steps to embrace her, then squired her home to meet his family. The Zamperinis fell for her, just as Louie had.

Driving away, Louie sensed Cynthia drawing backward. Maybe she'd seen something that hinted at all she didn't know, or maybe impulsive decisions were becoming too real. Thinking she was slipping away from him, Louie lost his temper and said they should end the engagement. Cynthia panicked, and they argued. When they calmed down, they made a decision.

A few days later, Louie and Cynthia drove to a church. One of Louie's friends walked Cynthia down the aisle, and the couple said their vows.

That night, Cynthia called home with the news. She hung on the phone all evening, crying, while her mother bawled her out. Unable to get her to hang up, Louie picked up a bottle of champagne, drank it dry, and went to sleep alone.

Phil, Cecy, Cynthia, and Louie at a dinner club in Hollywood, 1946.

CHAPTER 35

Coming Undone

One evening in 1946, Louie sat in a dinner club, with Cynthia nestled near him. Phil and Cecy were visiting, and Fred Garrett had joined them. Phil and Louie were grinning at each other. The last time they'd been together was in early 1944, when Phil was leaving Ofuna and they didn't know if they'd live to see each other again.

They were happy. Sporting a prosthetic leg, Fred bumped to the dance floor to prove he could still cut a rug. Phil and Cecy were moving to New Mexico, where Phil would open a plastics business. Louie and Cynthia were glowing from their honeymoon. As the men laughed and chatted, all they'd been through seemed forgotten. But then a waiter set a plate before Fred. On it, beside the entrée, was white rice. That was all it took. Fred was suddenly raving, furious, shouting at the waiter. Louie tried to calm him, but Fred had come undone.

The waiter hurried the rice away and Fred pulled himself together, but the spell was broken. For these men, nothing was ever going to be the same.

———

After World War II, former prisoners of the Japanese, known as Pacific POWs, came home. Physically, they were ravaged. The average army or army air forces POW had lost sixty-one pounds. They were severely malnourished, many were crippled, and nearly all were afflicted with serious diseases. Many would never fully recover. Some couldn't be saved.

The emotional injuries were even worse. Mental illnesses were among the most common diagnoses given to former Pacific POWs, and they proved lasting. Some forty years after the war, nearly 90 percent of former Pacific POWs in one study still suffered from post-traumatic stress disorder (PTSD), a devastating syndrome characterized in part by flashbacks, anxiety, and intense nightmares.

Postwar life was often tormented. Men sleepwalked, acting out prison camp traumas, and woke screaming or lashing out. One had a recurrent hallucination of seeing his dead POW friends walking past. Another, a wealthy physician, fought urges to scavenge in trash cans. One man regularly woke running outside, shouting for help, and avoided hotels because his screaming nightmares upset other guests. Sixty years after the war, he still hoarded clothes and food. Many men escaped by drinking: more than a quarter of former Pacific POWs became alcoholics. Seeing an Asian person, or hearing Japanese, left many men shaking, weeping, enraged, or lost in flashbacks. At one hospital just after the war, former POWs tried to attack a staffer who was of Japanese ancestry, not knowing he was an American veteran.

The Pacific POWs who went home in 1945 were torn-down men. Carrying unspeakable memories of torture and humiliation, they felt deeply vulnerable. Their dignity was gone, replaced with a sense of shame and worthlessness. The central struggle of postwar life was to restore their dignity. There was no one right way to peace; every man had to find his own path. Some succeeded. For others, the war never ended. For some, years of rage, terror, and humiliation concentrated into an obsession with revenge.

———

The honeymoon brought Louie a brief respite from his troubles. Sleeping beside Cynthia each night, he still saw the Bird lurking in his dreams, but now, the sergeant hung back. It was the closest thing to peace Louie had known since *Green Hornet* had hit the water.

Cynthia Zamperini on her honeymoon. COURTESY OF LOUIS ZAMPERINI

Louie and Cynthia rented an apartment in a cheap quarter of Hollywood. Louie's mother had been awarded his $10,000 life insurance payout when he was declared dead, and Louie was allowed to keep it. Investing it brought him a modest income, but the apartment was the best he could do. It was tiny, nothing like the mansion Cynthia had grown up in, but she did her best to make it homey.

On his first night there, Louie fell into a dream. As always, the Bird was there, but he was no longer hesitant. The sergeant towered over Louie, the belt flicking from his hand, lashing Louie's face. Every night, he returned. Louie was helpless once again.

Trying to cope with his nightmares and increasing anxiety, Louie began to feel an old pull. The summer Olympics, suspended since 1936, were set to return. They'd be held in London in July 1948, two years away. Louie began taking long hikes, borrowing a dog for company. His bad leg felt sturdy, his body healthy.

He began training. His strength returned, and his dodgy leg gave him no pain. He took it slowly, thinking always of London in '48. He began clocking miles in 4:18 with ease. He was coming all the way back.

But running wasn't the same. Once, he'd felt liberated by it, but now it felt forced and joyless. With no other answer to his turmoil, Louie doubled his workouts, and his body answered.

One day, Louie set off to see how fast he could turn two miles. He felt pain in his bad ankle, just where it had been injured at Naoetsu. He shouldn't have kept pushing, but pushing was all he knew now. As he completed the first mile, his ankle was crackling with pain. On he went, running for London.

Late in his last lap, there was an abrupt slicing sensation in his ankle. He half hopped to the line and collapsed. He'd run the year's fastest two-mile on the Pacific coast, but it didn't matter. A doctor confirmed he'd worsened his war injury disastrously. It was all over.

———

COURTESY OF LOUIS ZAMPERINI

Louie was wrecked. The quest that had saved him as a kid, that had sustained him through prison camp, was lost. The last barricade within him fell. By day, he obsessed about the Bird. In his nightmares, the sergeant lashed him. As the belt whipped him, Louie would grasp his attacker's throat and close his hands around it. No matter how hard he squeezed, the black eyes still danced at him. Louie regularly woke screaming and soaked in sweat. He was afraid to sleep.

He began going to bars and drinking hard, trying to drown the war. He often drank so much he passed out, but he welcomed it; it saved him from having to go to bed and wait for his monster. Cynthia couldn't talk him into giving it up. He left her alone each night while he went out to lose the war.

Rage consumed him. Once, he harassed a man for walking slowly in front of his car, and the man spat at him. Louie jumped out, and as Cynthia screamed for him to stop, beat the man to the ground. When another man accidentally let a door swing into him, Louie chested up to him and provoked a scuffle that ended with Louie grinding the man's face in the dirt.

His mind derailed. While sitting at a bar, he heard a sudden, loud sound, perhaps a car backfiring. Instantly, he was on the floor, cringing, as the bar fell silent and people stared. On another night, he was drinking, his mind drifting, when someone yelled something while joking with friends. In Louie's mind, it was *"Keirei!"* He leapt to attention, heart pounding, awaiting the flying belt buckle. The illusion cleared and he saw that again, everyone was looking at him. He felt foolish and humiliated.

One day, Louie was overcome by a strange feeling, and suddenly he was back in the war, not a memory, but the actual *experience*—the glaring and grating and stench and howl and terror of it. When he emerged, he was confused and frightened. It was his first flashback. After that, if he glimpsed blood or saw a tussle in a bar, everything would reassemble itself as prison camp. Sometimes he felt imaginary lice and fleas wiggling on his skin. He drank harder.

And then he saw a newspaper story that riveted his attention. A former POW had walked into a store, spotted one of his captors, and had him arrested. Louie's fury crystallized. He saw himself finding the Bird and overpowering him, strangling him slowly, making him feel all the pain, fear, and helplessness that Louie felt. His veins beat with an electric urgency.

Louie had no idea where the Bird was but felt sure that if he could return to Japan, he could hunt him down. This would be his reply to the Bird's effort to extinguish his dignity: *I am still a man.* He saw no other way to save himself.

Louie had found a quest to replace his lost Olympics. He was going to kill the Bird.

CHAPTER 36

The Body on the Mountain

In the first winter after the war, a police officer trudged through a remote village in Japan's Nagano prefecture, knocking on doors. The hunt for Mutsuhiro Watanabe now involved every police force in Japan. In one prefecture alone, 9,100 officers participated.

The officer reached the largest house in the village. Inside, he found an old farmer, his wife, and their laborer. As the laborer prepared pickles, a traditional gift to visitors, the officer showed a photograph of Watanabe. Did they recognize him? None of them did.

The officer left. He had no idea that the fugitive he was seeking had just been standing in front of him, holding a plate of pickles.

———

The Bird had come to Nagano the previous September. He grew a mustache and chose an alias, Saburo Ohta, a name unlikely to attract notice. He told people he was a refugee from Tokyo whose relatives were dead, a common story. He met the old farmer and offered himself as a laborer in exchange for room and board. The farmer agreed.

At night, lying on the farmer's floor, Watanabe couldn't sleep. Thousands of other soldiers were being arrested and tried for war crimes. Many were given death sentences. On the pages on which he poured out his emotions, Watanabe wrote of feeling guilty when he thought of those soldiers. He pondered his behavior toward the POWs. "Am I guilty?" he wrote. He didn't answer his question but expressed no remorse.

Listening to radio reports on fugitive war crimes suspects, Watanabe watched his hosts, worried that they'd suspect him. The newspapers called the fugitives "enemies of human beings," wounding Watanabe's feelings. It seemed to him outrageous that the Allies who "would not forgive" would oversee trials of Japanese. "I wanted to cry out," he wrote, "'That's not fair!'"

The tension wore on him. He had to work himself to exhaustion to bring sleep on. He wondered if he should surrender.

One night, as the fire died in the hearth, Watanabe told the farmer who he was. The farmer listened, his eyes on the fire, his tongue clicking on his teeth.

"People say to control your mouth, or it brings evil," the farmer said. "You should be careful of your speech."

He said nothing else and turned away.

———

Watanabe waited out a bitter winter. The policeman's visit shook him. The farmer's wife eyed him with what seemed to be suspicion. When night fell, Watanabe lay awake, mulling capture and execution.

When summer came, Watanabe was asked to accompany the farmer's son as he toured the country, selling leather. The tour would take them through major cities where he was surely being sought, but he was living on the farmer's good graces and had to accept. Watanabe donned glasses to obscure his features and headed off, filled with anxiety.

In the cities, no one gave Watanabe a second look. As his fear of being caught eased, he became bolder. He longed to see his family. They would now be in Tokyo, on their regular visit to his elder sister Michiko's home. Watanabe took out fortune-telling cards his little sister had given him just before he'd fled. The cards told him if he went to his family, he'd be safe.

On a sweltering day in the summer of 1946, Mutsuhiro boarded a train for Tokyo. His timing couldn't have been worse. Doubling their efforts to find him, the police were scouring the city for him. Watanabe was walking into the manhunt.

The Watanabe family was sitting in Michiko's house when the front door opened and in walked Mutsuhiro. The room fell silent as the startled family members looked at Mutsuhiro and then at each other. Mutsuhiro, overwhelmed and dizzy from the heat, wavered, afraid he'd faint. The family broke into celebration.

For two hours, Mutsuhiro listened to his family tell of being arrested, questioned, followed, and searched. He said nothing of where he'd been, believing they'd fare better if they didn't know.

There was shuffling outside. Someone looked and saw detectives. The Watanabes sprang up. Someone tossed Mutsuhiro's belongings into a closet. Someone else whisked their teacups into the sink. Mutsuhiro raced into a tearoom. Behind him, he heard the detectives enter and begin questioning his family.

His heart racing, Mutsuhiro tried to decide whether to run or conceal himself here. The room was tiny, but there was a closet. Slowly, slowly, he opened the closet door and squeezed in. He decided not to close the door, as it risked making noise. He stood there, a hand over his mouth to smother the sound of his breath.

The tearoom door opened. A detective looked in, and there was a pause as he looked about. If he only turned his eyes to the closet, he'd see Mutsuhiro. "It is tidy," he said. The door closed. The detectives left.

Mutsuhiro had planned to stay overnight, but the scare changed his mind. He told his mother he'd try to see her again in two years. Then he left, walking back, he wrote, "into the lonesome world."

———

Watanabe returned to the village and waited tables in the farmer's son's coffee shop. The farmer approached him with a proposition. Arranged marriage was still common in Japan, and the farmer had found a young woman for him.

Watanabe was tempted; he was lonely and unhappy, and liked the idea of marrying. But marriage now seemed impossible. He said no.

The woman eventually came to him. When the farmer's son fell ill, she visited, and Watanabe went in to meet her. He liked her. Part of him seemed to want to fall for her, and he believed that love "could save my daily life."

The woman was taken with the handsome waiter and lingered in the coffee shop to be near him. He kept his identity secret from her. She told her parents about him in hopes of winning their blessing for a wedding. After much thought, Watanabe decided he had to leave her. All he told her was that he had a burden that would make her unhappy.

He quit his job, hiked into the countryside, and took a job as a cowherd. He was despondent. At sunset, he lifted his eyes to the Asama volcano, watching a ribbon of smoke unspooling from its summit, the cattle grazing below.

In Japan's Okuchichibu Mountain range stands the holy peak of Mitsumine. In the fall of 1946, the bodies of a man and a woman were found there, a suicide pistol lying with them. No one knew who they were.

The police drove Shizuka Watanabe to Mitsumine and led her to the bodies. Shizuka looked down at the lifeless form of the young man.

Japanese newspapers ran the sensational story: Mutsuhiro Watanabe, one of Japan's most wanted men, was dead. He and a woman, probably a lover, had killed themselves.

CHAPTER 37

Twisted Ropes

Louie knew nothing of the Bird's death. When the bodies were found on Mt. Mitsumine, he was in Hollywood, falling to pieces. He was drinking heavily, slipping into flashbacks, screaming through nightmares, lashing out. Murdering the Bird was his fevered obsession, and he gave his life to it. He spent hours slamming his hatred into a punching bag, preparing for the confrontation he believed would save him. He walked around with murder in his head.

Throughout 1947 and 1948, he jumped into scheme after scheme to raise money to return to Japan. A man talked him into investing $7,000 in an earthmoving equipment business, then stole the money. Plans to found a boat company and a movie production company failed. He even considered working as a mercenary bombardier in a coup in a Caribbean country, but the coup was called off. He and a partner cut a deal with Mexican officials to issue fishing licenses to Americans. The partner was in a car wreck, and the deal died with him. Each time Louie got money together, it was lost, and his return to Japan had to be put off.

Drinking made him unrecognizable. As he sat at a bar one night, stinking drunk, he groped a woman. Next he knew, he was outside, his jaw thumping with pain, and a friend was chewing him out. The woman's boyfriend had knocked him unconscious.

On another night, after drinking what he'd remember as only one beer, he felt oddly light and stepped outside. Then he was in his car, driving, with no idea where he was. He weaved through the streets, disoriented, stopped the car, and rolled out. There was a tree before him, and he relieved himself against it.

When he turned back for his car, he couldn't find it. He stumbled along all night, scared and lost.

At sunrise, he realized he was in front of his apartment building. There was Cynthia, frantic with worry. He toppled into bed. When he woke and dressed, he had no memory of the night before and couldn't understand why

Louie, after the war. Courtesy of Frank Tinker

the heels of his new shoes were worn down. He couldn't find his car, so he reported it stolen. Two days later, the police found the car. He went to it, and memories of his night came back to him, carrying the ethereal quality of a nightmare.

Cynthia pleaded with Louie to stop drinking. It did no good.

―――――

The further Louie fell, the less he could hide it. Friends spoke to him about his drinking, but they made no impact. Pete, too, was worried but knew only of Louie's financial woes. He had no idea that Louie had slid into alcoholism and that he planned to kill a man.

Cynthia was distraught over what her husband had become. In public, his behavior was frightening and embarrassing. In private, he was often prickly and harsh. Cynthia couldn't bring Louie back. Her pain became anger, and she and Louie had bitter fights. She slapped him and threw dishes at him; he grabbed her so forcefully he left her bruised. While she cooked dinner on a friend's docked yacht, Louie was so snide to her, in front of their friends, that she walked off the boat. He chased her down and grabbed her by the neck. She slapped him, and he let her go. She fled to his parents' house.

Cynthia eventually came back, and the two struggled on together. His money gone, Louie tapped a friend for a thousand-dollar loan, staking his car as collateral. The money ran out, the loan came due, and Louie had to turn over his keys.

When Louie was a small child, he'd tripped and fallen on a flight of stairs. When he'd gotten up, he'd fallen again, then again. He'd risen convinced that God was toying with him. Now he had the same thought. When he heard preaching on the radio, he angrily turned it off. He forbade Cynthia to go to church.

In the spring of 1948, Cynthia became pregnant. Louie was excited, but the prospect of more responsibility filled him with guilt and despair. He drank ever harder. His only hope of pulling himself together, he believed, was to kill the man who'd taken everything from him.

―――――

One night in late 1948, Louie dreamed beside Cynthia. The Bird rose over him, the belt unfurled, and Louie felt the buckle cracking into his head, pain like lightning. Around and around the belt whirled, lashing Louie's skull.

Louie raised his hands to the Bird's throat, his fingers clenching around it. Now he was on top of the Bird, and the two thrashed.

There was a scream. Louie fought on, trying to crush the life from the Bird. On his knees with the Bird under him, he looked down. The Bird's shape shifted.

Louie was straddling Cynthia's chest, hands locked on her neck. Through her closing throat, she was screaming. Louie was strangling his pregnant wife.

He let go and leapt off of Cynthia. She recoiled, gasping, crying out. He sat beside her, horrified, his nightclothes heavy with sweat. The sheets were twisted into ropes around him.

———

Cissy Zamperini was born two weeks after Christmas. Louie was enraptured, but Cissy couldn't cleave him from alcoholism or his murderous obsession. In the sleepless stress of caring for a newborn, Louie and Cynthia fought furiously. Louie drank without restraint.

One day, Cynthia found Louie gripping a crying Cissy in his hands, shaking her. With a shriek, she pulled the baby away. Appalled at himself, Louie went on bender after bender. Cynthia packed up, took the baby, and walked out. Louie was alone. All he had left was his alcohol and his rage.

———

On the other side of the world, Shizuka Watanabe sat in a Tokyo restaurant. Outside, the street was lively with shoppers. Shizuka watched people drifting past.

It was there that she saw him. Just outside the door, gazing in at her, was her dead son.

CHAPTER 38

The Promise

For Shizuka Watanabe, the sight of her son answered a desperate hope. Two years earlier, she'd been taken to see a dead man who looked just like Mutsuhiro. Everyone, even her relatives, believed it was he. But Shizuka had felt a trace of doubt. In secret, she clung to a promise Mutsuhiro had made when he'd last seen her: on October 1, 1948, he'd meet her at a Tokyo restaurant.

As she waited, others began to question whether Mutsuhiro was really dead. His army sidearm didn't match the suicide gun. Mutsuhiro could easily have used another gun, but an examination of the body found features that seemed different from those of the fugitive. The detectives couldn't confirm definitively that the dead man was Mutsuhiro. They descended again on the Watanabes.

For two years, Shizuka endured intense scrutiny. Her visitors were tailed and investigated. When she ran errands, detectives followed and questioned those who encountered her. She was frequently interrogated but answered questions about her son by referring to the suicides on Mitsumine. Then, when the October 1948 day came, she went to the restaurant, eluding her pursuers. There was her son, a living ghost.

The sight of him brought as much fear as joy. Appearing in public, he was taking a huge risk. She spoke to him only briefly, in hushed tones. Mutsuhiro said he'd return in two years, then slipped away.

More than a year passed. Shizuka heard nothing from him. Rumors abounded. One had him shot by Americans; another had him struck by a train after an American soldier tied him to the track. Many stories ended in his suicide, by gunshot, by *hara-kiri* (stabbing), by a leap into a volcano. There seemed only one conclusion to draw from the failure of the search. He must be dead.

Whether Shizuka believed this is unknown. But in his last meeting with her, Mutsuhiro had given her one troubling clue: I'll see you in two years, he'd said, *if I am alive.*

———

In September 1949, an obscure young minister named Billy Graham walked into a vacant parking lot in Los Angeles. He and his friends threw up a giant tent, set out folding chairs, hammered together a stage the size of a fairly spacious backyard, and began a campaign to bring Christianity to Los Angeles.

At first, Graham preached to a half-empty tent. But his sermons got people talking. Soon, ten thousand people a night were coming to hear him, leaving hundreds standing in the street, straining to hear him over the traffic. In a city hardly bashful about sinning, Graham had kicked off a religious revival.

Louie knew nothing of Graham. Four years after the war, he was still in the dingy apartment, lost in alcohol and plans to murder the Bird. Cynthia had returned but was only staying until she could arrange a divorce. The two lived in grim coexistence.

One day that October, Cynthia and Louie passed a new tenant in the hall. They chatted, and it was at first a pleasant conversation. Then the man mentioned that a minister named Billy Graham was preaching downtown. Louie turned abruptly and walked away.

Cynthia stayed in the hall. When she returned to the apartment, she asked Louie to take her to hear Graham speak. Louie refused.

Cynthia went alone. When she came home, she was alight. She told Louie she wasn't going to divorce him. The news filled Louie with relief, but when Cynthia said she'd experienced a religious awakening, he was appalled.

For several days, Cynthia badgered Louie to see Graham. Louie angrily refused; he wanted nothing to do with God. They argued. Exhausted by her persistence, he finally agreed to go.

———

When Louie and Cynthia entered the tent, Louie insisted on staying far in the rear. He'd wait out the sermon, go home, and be done with it.

As the service began, Louie was sullen and resentful. Graham began speaking, and Louie paid little notice. But then Graham posed a question: Why is God silent while good men suffer? Louie was suddenly wide awake.

Graham's answer was that God is not silent. "If you look into the heavens tonight, on this beautiful California night, I see the stars and can see the footprints of God," he said. "My heavenly father hung them there with a flaming fingertip and holds them there with the power of his omnipotent hand,

The tent in Los Angeles where Billy Graham preached in the fall of 1949.
COURTESY OF LOUIS ZAMPERINI

and he runs the whole universe, and he's not too busy running the whole universe to count the hairs on my head and see a sparrow when it falls, because God is interested in me. . . . God spoke in creation."

A memory suddenly came to Louie: he and Phil, starving on the raft, drifting into the doldrums, a seascape so overpoweringly beautiful that Louie had forgotten his thirst and hunger, forgotten even that he was dying, and felt only gratitude. That day, he'd believed such beauty had to be the work of God, a gift of compassion. Realizing he'd forgotten that gift, forgotten his gratitude, Louie wound tight.

Graham went on. He spoke of God reaching into the world through miracles. God sends blessings, he said, that give men strength to outlast their sorrows. "God works miracles one after another. . . . God says, 'If you suffer, I'll give you the grace to go forward.'"

Unbidden, memory after memory swept over Louie. He felt again the moment he'd woken in the sinking hull of *Green Hornet*, the wires that had trapped him a moment earlier now, impossibly, gone. He remembered the machine guns riddling the rafts with bullets and yet not one bullet striking him, Phil, or Mac. He'd fallen into unbearably cruel worlds, and yet he'd borne them. When he turned these memories in his mind, the only explanation he could find was that he had been graced with miracles.

Louie shone with sweat. This stranger seemed to be speaking directly to him, knowing his history, knowing all he'd forgotten. Louie felt spooked, accused, guilty, angry. Beneath it all was fear. There was another, long-buried memory pushing its way to the surface. Louie wanted to run away before he saw it. He felt a frantic urge to flee.

Graham asked his listeners to come forward to declare their faith. Louie grabbed Cynthia's arm, stood up, and bulled his way toward the exit. His mind was tumbling.

As he reached the aisle, he stopped. Everything around him disappeared. The memory he'd long beaten back, the memory from which he was fleeing, was upon him. He fell into a flashback.

He was on the raft. There was gentle Phil crumpled up before him, Mac's breathing skeleton, endless ocean, the sun lying over them, the cunning bodies of the sharks, waiting, circling. He was a body on a raft, dying of thirst. He felt words whisper from his swollen lips. It was a promise thrown to God, a promise he hadn't kept, a promise he'd allowed himself to forget until this instant: *If you'll save me, I'll serve you forever.* And then, standing under a tent on a clear night in Los Angeles, Louie felt rain falling on his face.

It was the last flashback he'd ever have. Louie let go of Cynthia and turned toward Graham. He began walking.

———

Cynthia watched Louie all the way home. When they entered the apartment, Louie went straight to his liquor, carried the bottles to the kitchen, and emptied them into the sink.

In the morning, he woke feeling cleansed. For the first time in five years, the Bird hadn't come into his dreams. The Bird would never come again.

Louie found the Bible issued to him by the air corps and sent to his mother when he was believed dead. He walked to a park, sat under a tree, and began reading.

Resting in the shade and the stillness, Louie felt profound peace. When he thought of the war, he thought not of all he'd suffered, but the divine love he believed had intervened to save him. He was not the worthless, broken, forsaken man the Bird had tried to make of him. His rage, his humiliation, his helplessness, had fallen away. His dignity had returned. That morning, he believed, he was a new creation.

Softly, he wept.

Louie (right) at Sugamo, 1950. Courtesy of Louis Zamperini

CHAPTER 39

Daybreak

On a chilly fall morning in 1950, Louie walked up a long road, toward a complex of buildings. His whole body tingled. On the entrance archway were painted the words SUGAMO PRISON, and beyond it waited Louie's POW camp guards. Louie had returned to Japan.

In the year since he'd entered Billy Graham's tent, Louie had worked to keep a promise. He'd become a Christian speaker, telling his story all over America. He'd scraped together just enough money for a down payment on a house but was still so poor that Cissy's crib was the house's only furniture, and Louie and Cynthia slept in sleeping bags. They were barely getting by, but their connection had been renewed and deepened. They were blissful together.

For more than four years after the war, a return to Japan had been Louie's obsession, the path to killing the man who'd ruined him. But thoughts of murder no longer had a home in him. He'd come here not to avenge himself, but to answer a question.

Louie had been told that all the men who'd tormented him had been arrested, convicted, and imprisoned in Sugamo. He could speak and think of his captors, even the Bird, without bitterness now, but a question tapped in

271

his mind: If he saw them again, would the peace he'd found prove resilient? He'd resolved to go to Sugamo and find out.

On the evening before, Louie had written to Cynthia to tell her what he was about to do. He asked her to pray for him.

———

The former guards sat on the floor of a common room. Louie looked out over the faces.

At first he recognized no one. Then he saw a face he knew, then another and another. One was missing: Louie couldn't find the Bird. When he asked where Watanabe was, he was told he wasn't there. Over five years, tens of thousands of policemen had hunted for him, but they'd never found him.

As Louie was packing to come to Japan, the long-awaited day had arrived in the life of Shizuka Watanabe: October 1, 1950, the day her son had promised to come to her, if he was still alive. He'd told her he'd meet her in Tokyo, at the restaurant where they'd met two years earlier. That morning, Shizuka boarded a train for Tokyo. At the restaurant, Mutsuhiro apparently never showed up.

Shizuka went to the city of Kofu and checked into a hotel, staying alone, taking no visitors. For four days, she wandered the city. Then she left abruptly, without paying her hotel bill. Police questioned the hotel matron. Asked if Shizuka had spoken of her son, the matron said yes.

"Mutsuhiro," Shizuka had said, "has already died."

In her house, Shizuka kept a shrine to Mutsuhiro, a tradition among bereaved Japanese families. Each morning, she left an offering in his memory.

———

In Sugamo, Louie asked what had happened to the Bird. He was told it was believed the former sergeant, hunted, exiled, and despairing, had stabbed himself to death.

The words washed over Louie. In prison camp, Watanabe had forced him to live in incomprehensible degradation, humiliation, and violence, leaving Louie lost in darkness and hate. But on an October night in Los Angeles, Louie had found, said a friend, "daybreak." That night, the sense of shame and powerlessness that had driven his hatred of the Bird had vanished. The Bird was no longer his monster. He was only a man.

As he was told of Watanabe's fate, all Louie saw was a lost person, a life now beyond redemption. He felt something he'd never felt for his captor before. With a shiver of amazement, he realized it was compassion.

At that moment, something shifted sweetly inside him. It was forgiveness, beautiful, effortless, and complete. For Louie Zamperini, the war was over.

———

Before Louie left Sugamo, his escort asked Louie's former guards to come forward. The prisoners shuffled into the aisle, moving hesitantly, looking up at Louie with small faces.

Louie was seized by giddy exuberance. Before he realized what he was doing, he was bounding down the aisle. In bewilderment, the men who had abused him watched him come to them, his hands extended, a radiant smile on his face.

Louie rappels down a cliffside. COURTESY OF LOUIS ZAMPERINI

Epilogue

In the California mountains on a June day in 1954, a mess of boys tumbled from a truck and stood blinking in the sunshine. They were quick-fisted, hard-faced boys, most of them veterans of juvenile hall. Louie stood with them, watching them feel earth without pavement, space without walls. He felt as if he were watching his own youth again.

So opened the great project of Louie's life, Victory Boys Camp. Beginning with only an idea and very little money, he'd found a campsite, talked businesses into donating materials, and spent two years building the camp himself.

At Victory, lost boys found themselves. Louie took them fishing, skiing, swimming, and camping. He led them on hikes, letting them talk out their troubles, and rappelled down cliffs beside them. At each day's end, he sat with them by a campfire, speaking of his youth, the war, and the road that led him to peace. He went easy on Christianity but laid it before them. Some were convinced, some were not, but either way, boys who arrived at Victory as ruffians often left it renewed and reformed.

When he wasn't with his campers, Louie was walking the world, telling his story everywhere from classrooms to stadiums. On the side, he worked in a local church, supervising the senior center.

His body gave no quarter to age or punishment. In time, even his injured leg healed. When Louie was in his sixties, he was running the mile in less than six minutes. When he was in his seventies, he discovered skateboarding. At eighty-five, he returned to Kwajalein on a quest, ultimately unsuccessful, to find the bodies of the marines whose names had been etched in his cell wall. When he was ninety, his neighbors saw him high in a tree, chain saw in hand. "When God wants me, he'll take me," he told Pete. "Why the hell are you trying to help him?" Pete replied. Well into his tenth decade, he could still be seen perched on skis, merrily cannonballing down mountains.

He remained invariably cheerful. His belief that everything happened for a reason and would come to good gave him a laughing, infectious joy even in hard times. "I never knew anyone," Pete once said, "who didn't love Louie."

———

Left: *Louie carries the torch before the 1984 Los Angeles Olympics.* Right: *Louie took up skateboarding in his seventies.* PHOTOS COURTESY OF LOUIS ZAMPERINI

Russell Allen Phillips with his children, Chris and Karen, bedtime, 1952.

With the war over, Phil dropped his wartime nickname and became Allen again. He and Cecy eventually moved to his boyhood hometown in Indiana, where they taught in a junior high and raised two children.

Allen rarely mentioned the war. Other than the scars on his forehead, only his habits spoke of what he'd endured. Having lived for weeks on raw albatross and tern, he tended to avoid poultry. He liked to eat food straight out of cans, cold. And the onetime daredevil pilot wouldn't go near an airplane. As the jet age overtook America, he stayed in his car.

He never returned to Japan, and seemed, outwardly, free of bitterness. Though almost always treated as a footnote in what was celebrated as Louie's story, he bore it graciously. He spoke fondly of Zamp for the rest of his life.

In 1998, shortly before Allen died, the staff of his retirement home learned

In 1996, two years before his death, Phil sat at the controls of a B-24 once more.
COURTESY OF LOUIS ZAMPERINI

his war story and scheduled an event to honor him. For the first time in his life, Allen became an open book. As people hushed to hear him speak, his daughter, Karen, saw a lovely light coming to her father's face. There was, she said, "a little grin underneath."

———

Pete devoted his life to the work he was born to do, coaching high school track and football, with enormous success. Coach Zamperini retired in 1977.

"I'm retired; my wife is just tired," Pete loved to say. But retirement never really took. At ninety, Pete had the littlest kids in his neighborhood in training, fashioning dumbbells out of cement and cans, as his dad had done for Louie. He'd cheer the kids through sprints, awarding a dime for each race, a quarter for a personal best.

He remained deeply devoted to his brother. In old age, he still proudly remembered every detail of Louie's races, seventy-five years after Louie had run them. He was haunted by Louie's war experiences. Asked to join a 1992 fishing trip, he brought a dazzling assortment of safety items, including a plastic bag to use as a flotation device, a lanyard, a whistle, and a pocketknife that he imagined flailing at sharks. He spent the trip staring uneasily at the ocean. Describing Louie's ordeal to an audience gathered to honor him, he broke down. It was some time before he could go on.

In May of 2008, the brothers said goodbye. Pete was dying of melanoma. Their sister Virginia had died a few weeks before; Sylvia would follow months later. Cynthia, gorgeous as ever, had died of cancer in 2001, drifting away as Louie pressed his face to hers, whispering *I love you*. Louie, declared dead more than sixty years earlier, would outlive them all.

Pete was on his bed, eyes closed. Louie sat beside him. Softly, he spoke of their lives, tracing the paths they'd taken since coming to California in 1919. The two ancient men lingered together as they had as boys, lying side by side, waiting for the *Graf Zeppelin*.

Louie spoke of what a wild boy he'd been, and how Pete had rescued him. He told of the bountiful lives he and Pete had found in guiding children. All those kids, Louie said, "are part of you, Pete."

Pete's eyes opened, and with sudden clarity, rested on the face of his little brother for the last time. He couldn't speak, but he was beaming.

In late 1996, in Louie's church in Hollywood, a telephone rang. Louie, then a nudge short of eighty, answered.

The caller was Draggan Mihailovich, a CBS-TV producer. The 1998 Winter Olympics had been awarded to Japan, and Louie had accepted an invitation to run the torch past Naoetsu. Mihailovich was filming a profile of Louie, to be aired during the Olympics, and had gone to Japan to prepare. There, while chatting with a man over a bowl of noodles, he'd made a shocking discovery.

Mihailovich asked Louie if he was sitting down. Louie said yes. Mihailovich told him to grab hold of his chair.

"The Bird is alive."

Louie nearly hit the floor. When he collected himself, the first thing he said was that he wanted to see him.

———

The dead man had walked out of the darkness one night in 1952. He stepped off a train, walked through a city, and stopped before a house. Under a gate light, he saw his mother's name.

In the seven years in which he'd been thought dead, he'd been hiding in the countryside, selling ice cream and fish and laboring in rice paddies. Then one day, he'd seen a newspaper story that startled him. As part of America's effort to reconcile with Japan, the arrest order for war crimes suspects had been dropped. There on the page was his name. He was free to go home.

Watanabe rang the bell, the gate swung open, and there was his youngest brother, whom he hadn't seen since the latter was a boy. His brother threw his arms around him, then pulled him inside, shouting that Mutsuhiro was home.

Watanabe's exile was over. He married, had two children, opened a successful insurance business, and lived in a luxurious Tokyo apartment. He never faced prosecution. Late in his life, when asked about what he'd done to POWs, he admitted to having been "severe," and was sometimes apologetic, but always with absurd justifications, self-serving lies, self-pity, and even apparent pride.

He never forgot Louie. Asked about him in a 1997 CBS interview, he knew the name instantly. "Six hundred prisoner," he said. "Zamperini number one."

"Zamperini was well known to me," he said. "If he says he was beaten by Watanabe, then such a thing probably occurred at the camp." He called beatings "unavoidable." Told that Louie wished to come to offer forgiveness, Watanabe said he would see him and apologize.

———

One day a few months later, Louie sat at his desk for hours, thinking. Then he began to write.

To Matsuhiro [sic] Watanabe,

As a result of my prisoner of war experience under your unwarranted and unreasonable punishment, my post-war life became a nightmare. It was not so much due to the pain and suffering as it was the tension of stress and humiliation that caused me to hate with a vengeance.

Under your discipline, my rights, not only as a prisoner of war but also as a human being, were stripped from me. It was a struggle to maintain enough dignity and hope to live until the war's end.

The post-war nightmares caused my life to crumble, but thanks to a confrontation with God through the evangelist Billy Graham, I committed my life to Christ. Love replaced the hate I had for you. Christ said, "Forgive your enemies and pray for them."

As you probably know, I returned to Japan in 1952 [sic] . . . I asked then about you, and was told that you probably had committed Hara Kiri [sic], which I was sad to hear. At that moment, like the others, I also forgave you and now would hope that you would also become a Christian.

Louis Zamperini

Louie carried the letter to Japan, intending to give it to the Bird. The meeting was not to be. Asked if he'd see Zamperini, as he'd agreed, Watanabe practically spat his reply: the answer was no.

When Louie arrived at Naoetsu, he still had the letter. Someone took it, promising to get it to Watanabe. If Watanabe received it, he never replied.

Watanabe died in April 2003.

———

On the morning of January 22, 1998, snow sifted gently over Naoetsu. Louis Zamperini, four days short of his eighty-first birthday, stood in a swirl of white. His body was worn and weathered, his skin scratched in lines, mapping the miles of his life. His riot of black hair was now a translucent scrim of white, but his blue eyes still threw sparks. On his right hand, a scar was still visible, the last mark *Green Hornet* had left in the world.

It was time. Louie extended his hand, and in it was placed the Olympic torch. His legs could no longer reach and push as they once had, but they were still sure beneath him. He began running.

All he could see, in every direction, were smiling Japanese faces. There were children in hooded coats, men who'd once worked beside the POW slaves, civilians clapping and cheering, and two columns of Japanese soldiers, parting to let him pass. Louie ran through the place where cages had once held him, where a black-eyed man had crawled inside him. But the cages were long gone, and so was the Bird. There was no trace of them here among the voices, the falling snow, and the old and joyful man, running.

In Conversation

Laura Hillenbrand and Louie Zamperini

Running

What did you learn from your older brother, Pete?

If it hadn't been for Pete, I don't know where I would have ended up. I was a thief, I was a juvenile delinquent, my whole life was to figure out how to get something for nothing. Pete pinned me down and said, "Do you want to be a bum all your life or do you want to amount to something?" He was my older brother, so I kind of worshipped him, wished I could be like him. It's important that you have a role model. Then you have to make a decision to try to be like your role model. I loved my brother and I accepted him as my mentor.

He introduced you to running and taught you discipline.

Yeah, he taught me discipline. He said you can be a champion or you can be a flop. He kept on me until finally I started to want to be a winner, to want to be a champion. The desire I had in trying to get away with evil was channeled into running. I told my brother, "Yes, I want to be an athlete," and after that, boy, I tell you, I was a fanatic.

Why did running appeal to you?

The most important thing to me was recognition. That's probably why I was always in trouble: I never got any recognition for being an athlete or student or anything else, so I got mine from stealing from the bootleggers, stealing pies from the bakery, stealing whatever I could get my hands on.

In my second race, there were three runners ahead of me, and coming down the homestretch, I gunned it. I didn't intend to win, I just wanted to pass somebody. But the students were screaming, "Come on, Louie! Come on, Louie!" I was nobody, and then all of a sudden, even though it was a race nobody had ever heard of, here were the kids calling my name, and I had no idea they even knew my name. That was recognition, and I thought, "Golly!" I looked at all these kids in the grandstand and I didn't know them but I loved them because they were cheering for me.

When I started running and got some recognition, I wanted more recognition. So I did everything I could to get it, and I got in the best shape of my life. I kept doubling my training and got to the All City Finals. I came in fifth and got a medal, and they gave me a little pin to put on my sweater. Oh boy, that was like an Olympic gold for me. I wore that proudly around school. I had gotten self-esteem from fighting other boys, but I got more self-esteem as a runner because I was doing something legitimate and good.

The Crash and the Raft

When Green Hornet was falling out of the sky, what did it feel like to be in a plane that was about to crash?

A terrible, hollow feeling in my stomach. You're just bracing yourself, hoping that there's one chance in a million you're going to survive, and that's the way it was until we hit the water. But you're petrified, because at that speed, and with a wing tipping over, you know the plane's going to blow up, and you just assume that you're going to die. But there's always a hope that you might not, and that little bit of hope is with you until the crash. But you have a hollow feeling in your stomach when you know this is it.

After you crashed, you knew that very few raftbound men were rescued, and you knew that you were two thousand miles from land, so your chances of surviving were almost zero. But you never thought you were going to die. Why not?

That's part of my life as an athlete. You never give up. That's one thing that's good about competition—you want to win no matter who you're running against. On the raft, I was running against nature, storms, hot sun, cold nights, starvation, thirst. There are so many things that are against you, and you really have to use your mind and try to adjust the best you can and take advantage of every situation.

What were your emotions when you encountered the huge great white shark in the middle of the night?

We were there, three of us huddled, hardly breathing. That great white, he had to be eighteen to twenty feet long, and he kept splashing water in on us to see if we were something he could eat. He kept throwing water on us at both sides of the raft, and we just kept silent until he decided that we were nothing edible, gave up, and disappeared. But boy, you talk about being frightened. That shark was so big he would only have had to bite through the raft once.

Historically, a lot of starving castaways have resorted to cannibalism, deciding that the only way that anyone will survive is if someone is sacrificed. Why was that something you could never consider?

I think that as a human being you have a respect for other human beings, whether they're alive or dead. Cannibalism never, ever crossed my mind. I'd rather be dead than live with that on my conscience. To me it was repulsive. We all thought the same way.

What are your thoughts about Mac, who panicked and ate all the chocolate on the raft on the first night but later tried hard to help out?

At first, I thought, wow, I've got a real problem with him. But every time he did something right I knew I had to compliment him, and he just kept changing and changing. One day the sharks were jumping on the raft trying to take me out, two of them, one right after the other. I'm pushing them back into the water with my hand on the ends of their noses. And then Mac grabs an oar and the two of us were punching them out with the oars, and they finally gave up. Well, boy, I really complimented Mac, and he kept getting better and better. He just turned out beautifully, and it was breaking my heart to see him dying.

He asked me if he was going to die, and I said, "Yeah, Mac, you're going to die tonight." I gave him a swig of water, and he lay back and waited. He died that night. It was pathetic. He finally became a real man, a hero, and then he's dying. But it was precious to me to see the radical change in him, how he was willing to help doing everything now, which he wasn't to begin with.

Prison Camp

When you were in Kwajalein and the POW camps, the guards, especially the Bird, treated you in a terribly dehumanizing way. What does it do to your spirit to be stripped of your dignity?
It's the worst thing of all. You can't believe another human being can treat you so subnormally, like you're some kind of creeping thing on the ground. We had never run into anybody that would dehumanize you like the Japanese. They treated us like dirt. You feel like you want to kill these guys. It's the worst feeling ever. But what can you do? You just lay there, helpless.

I learned one thing: Accept everything and try to stay alive. But I was just totally humiliated. The Bird treated me like a nonentity, and that is the hardest thing in the world to accept. That's the way he treated me and that's the way I felt. It strips you of your dignity. The only way we could maintain our dignity was among ourselves; that's why there was so much cooperation among the POWs. We didn't fall apart in prison camp because we knew if we didn't support one another, they had us.

In camp, you played a trick on a particularly vicious guard called the Weasel, shaving his eyebrows so he looked like a woman. You took a huge risk in doing this. Why did you do it?

I loved humor, and I saw a chance to draw some humor with the Weasel and it worked. It raised morale. If you're ill and you go to a doctor, he gives you a shot and puts you back on your feet, so that was like a shot. It really put me back on my feet.

When you were at your lowest moment, what thought helped you go on?

In running, you're at your lowest moment coming down the homestretch, but you just get yourself to think, "I've got to win." If you know you can't win, you've got to think, "I've got to finish." I think being an athlete is a great asset to a prisoner of war because you always have that desire to come out on top. Your mind is always working to see what you can do to stay alive. You just have to go on. On the raft, there was no way I was going to give up. In prison camp, I was the same way.

What else helped you survive?

Survival training. I advise people to take survival training on land, sea, and in the air. Because when you wind up against a real foreign situation, it's so important to be able to adapt. Taking survival courses makes you more adapt-able to something foreign, even when the training is not directly related to the survival moment.

What did you miss most about home?

The first thing you think about is freedom and food. I thought of the love and concern of my family. And I thought of my mom, the greatest cook in the world. I thought of all those great dinners where she'd make her dishes— lasagna, risotto, and her pasta, her cookies.

The Bird wanted you to give in to him, and if you had, maybe he would have punished you less. But you couldn't bring yourself to give in, keeping your fists clenched, looking the Bird straight in the eyes, refusing to fall down when he hit you. Why couldn't you give in?

Pride. I think we all have pride. I'm an Olympic athlete. I'm congratulated constantly on my athletic ability. I've earned the love and affection of students in school. And then I came up against a guy like Watanabe and it was hard for me to take.

When I was a kid, being punished, I wouldn't let anybody make me cry. I wouldn't show fear in my eyes, and that was a big mistake. But that's the way I was. I would never give anybody the satisfaction of seeing me cry. If I cried, then they might stop punishing me, but I didn't care. I didn't care if I got punched more and more, I said, "They're not going to make me cry."

It was the same way with the Bird. My buddies said, "Hey, what are you clenching your fists for?" and I said, "I want to punch the guy and I want to strangle him." All the other prisoners told me to give in. But I looked defiantly at him and he'd just keep working me over. I would stand my ground, too proud to fall down.

How far would you have gone to avoid becoming a propaganda prisoner or giving away military secrets in interrogation?

I would have died before I'd give in. I couldn't. I'd rather be dead, because if I did it, I couldn't live with myself the rest of my life. And I'd rather end it and not have the shame embedded in my mind and my heart.

Coming Home, Forgiveness, and Looking Back at a Remarkable Life

How did you feel when you were free, you stepped off the plane in California, and you finally saw your family again?

I had a fantastic family. We were a big family of helping one another and loving one another. When I got off the plane and there was my mom, my dad, my two sisters, and my brother, my emotions almost cracked. That's an emotion I can never explain. It was just phenomenal.

If you had killed the Bird, do you think you would have gotten over the war?
I don't think so. He treated me so brutally that I thought, "I've got to get even," and I figured I could get away with it. But I don't know what kind of satisfaction that would be.

I'm glad that I got over my post-traumatic stress and forgave all the guards, including the Bird. That was a great moment in my life. I'll never forget it. Since then, I've never had a slight inkling of post-traumatic stress, no visions of the war at all. Everything has left my mind. I can think now, "Yeah, I remember the bombing mission," but those visions never enter my mind. I can sit down and reminisce.

Why is it important to forgive the people who hurt you?
Because if you don't forgive, that's eating at your soul. Forgiveness must be completely a hundred percent, with everything. If you haven't forgiven, that's gnawing on you, that's gnawing on your soul, and it's going to keep gnawing on you. And that's why, when I forgave all the guards, including the Bird, I felt like I had just had a nice, clean shower.

How do you feel about the Bird now?
I feel sorry for him. I think he had a miserable life. I really feel sorry for him because he knows what he did and I think it got into him. When the amnesty was signed, he came out a free man. But to me he never could feel free because of all the damage he did, taking out his frustrations and his failures on prisoners of war.

Are you a hero?
I don't like that word, *hero*. I'm a survivalist. If I can help somebody along the way, I'll help them. That is a reward to me, a big reward. A survivalist will use his survival skills to help somebody else who needs help, and that's the most gratifying thing in the world. To me a hero would be somebody who gave his life on the spot to save somebody else. All I was doing was using my training and my talent to survive and along the way helping everyone I could.

If the war hadn't happened, it's very likely that you would have been the world's first four-minute miler and the 1940 Olympic 1,500-meter gold medalist. When you look back, do you feel frustrated that the war took those chances from you?

Well, it's a thing of the past, and all we can do is think about it, dream about it. I've had a great life, no matter what, no matter if I had won at the Olympics or not. I don't think anybody in the world has had as adventurous a life as I have.

——

Louie Zamperini died peacefully in his sleep on July 2, 2014.
He was ninety-seven years old.

ACKNOWLEDGMENTS

"I'll be an easier subject than Seabiscuit," Louie once told me, "because I can talk."

When I finished writing my first book, *Seabiscuit: An American Legend*, I felt certain that I would never again find a subject that fascinated me as did the Depression-era racehorse and the men who campaigned him. When I had my first conversation with the infectiously effervescent and apparently immortal Louie Zamperini, I changed my mind.

That conversation began my seven-year journey through Louie's unlikely life. I found his story in the memories of Olympians, former POWs and airmen, Japanese veterans, and the family and friends who once formed the home front; in diaries, letters, essays, and telegrams, many written by men and women who died long ago; in military documents and hazy photographs; in unpublished memoirs buried in desk drawers; in deep stacks of affidavits and war-crimes trial records; in forgotten papers in archives as far-flung as Oslo and Canberra. By the end of my journey, Louie's life was as familiar to me as my own. "When I want to know what happened to me in Japan," Louie once told his friends, "I call Laura."

In opening his world to me, Louie could not have been more gracious. He sat through some seventy-five interviews, answering thousands of questions with neither impatience nor complaint. He was refreshingly honest, quick to confess his failures and correct a few embellished stories that journalists have written about him. And his memory was astounding; nearly every time I cross-checked his accounts of events against newspaper stories, official records, and other sources, his recollections proved accurate to the smallest detail, even when the events took place some eighty-five years ago.

A superlative pack rat, Louie has saved seemingly every artifact of his life, from the DO NOT DISTURB sign that he swiped from Jesse Owens in Berlin to the paper number that he wore as he shattered the interscholastic mile record in 1934. One of his scrapbooks, which covers only 1917 to 1938, weighs *sixty-three* pounds. This he volunteered to send me, surrendering it to my friend Debie Ginsburg, who somehow manhandled it down to a mailing service. Along with it, he sent several other scrapbooks (fortunately smaller), hundreds of photographs and letters, his diaries, and items as precious as the stained newspaper clipping that was in his wallet on the raft. All of these things were treasure troves to me, telling his story with immediacy and revealing detail. I am immensely grateful to Louie for trusting me with items so dear to him, and for welcoming me into his history.

Pete Zamperini, Sylvia Zamperini Flammer, and Payton Jordan didn't live to see this book's completion, but they played an enormous role in its creation, sharing a lifetime of memories and memorabilia. There were many joys for me in writing this book; my long talks with Pete, Sylvia, and Payton ranked high among them. I also thank Louie's daughter, Cynthia Garris; Harvey Flammer; Ric Applewhite; and Marge Jordan for telling me their stories about Louie and Cynthia.

Karen Loomis, the daughter of Russell Allen Phillips and his wife, Cecy, walked me through her family's history and sent her father's wartime love letters to her mother, scrapbooks, photographs, clippings, and her grandmother's memoir. Thanks to Karen, I was able to peer into the life of the quiet, modest pilot known as Phil and uncover the brave and enduring man underneath. Someday I'll make it down to Georgia for long-promised muffins with Karen. My thanks also go to Bill Harris's daughter Katey Meares, who sent family photographs and told me of the father she lost far too soon, remembering him standing on his head in his kitchen to summon giggles from his girls. I also thank Monroe and Phoebe Bormann, Terry Hoffman, and Bill Perry for telling me about Phil and Cecy.

For the men who endured prison camp, speaking of the war is often a searing experience, and I am deeply grateful to the many former POWs who shared their memories, sometimes in tears. I shall never forget the generosity of Bob Martindale, Tom Wade, and Frank Tinker, who spent many hours bringing POW camp and the Bird to life for me. Milton McMullen described Omori, the POW insurgency, and the day he knocked over a train. Johan Arthur Johansen told of Omori and shared his extensive writings on POW camp. Ken Marvin spoke of the last pancakes he ate on Wake before the Japanese came, Naoetsu under the Bird, and teaching a guard hilariously offensive English. Glenn McConnell spoke of Ofuna, Gaga the duck, and the beating of Bill Harris. John Cook told me of slavery at Naoetsu and shared his unpublished memoir. I also send thanks to former POWs Fiske Hanley, Bob Hollingsworth, Raleigh "Dusty" Rhodes, Joe Brown, V. H. Spencer, Robert Cassidy, Leonard Birchall, Joe Alexander, Minos Miller, Burn O'Neill, Charles Audet, Robert Heer, and Paul Cascio, and POW family members J. Watt Hinson, Linda West, Kathleen Birchall, Ruth Decker, Joyce Forth, Marian Tougas, Jan Richardson, Jennifer Purcell, Karen Heer, and Angie Giardina.

Stanley Pillsbury spent many afternoons on the phone with me, reliving his days aboard his beloved *Super Man*, the Christmas raid over Wake, and the moment when he shot down a Zero over Nauru. Frank Rosynek, a born raconteur, sent his unpublished memoir, "Not Everybody Wore Wings," and wrote to me about the bombing of Funafuti and Louie's miraculous return from the dead on Okinawa. Lester Herman Scearce and pilots John Joseph Deasy and Jesse Stay told of Wake, Nauru, Funafuti, and the search for the lost crew of *Green Hornet*. Martin Cohn told of squadron life on Hawaii; John Krey told of Louie's disappearance and reappearance. Byron Kinney described the day he flew his B-29 over Louie at Naoetsu and listened to the Japanese surrender as he flew back to Guam. John Weller described the fearfully complex job of a B-24 navigator.

I am deeply indebted to several Japanese people who spoke candidly of a dark hour in their nation's history. Yuichi Hatto, the Omori camp accountant and a friend to POWs, was an indispensable source on the Bird, Omori, and life as a Japanese soldier, answering my questions in writing, in his second language, when we were unable to speak on the telephone. Yoshi Kondo told me about the founding of the Joetsu Peace Park, and Shibui Genzi wrote to me about Japanese life in Naoetsu. Toru Fukubayashi and Taeko Sasamoto, historians with the POW Research Network Japan, answered my questions and pointed me toward sources.

The delightful Virginia "Toots" Bowersox Weitzel, Louie's childhood friend, made me cassette tapes of the most popular songs at Torrance High in the 1930s, narrating them with stories from her days as a school cheerleader. Toots, who passed away just before the adult edition of this book went to press, told of tackling Louie on his sixteenth birthday, cheering him on as he ran the Torrance track with Pete, and playing football with him in front of Kellow's Hamburg Stand in Long Beach. She was the only ninetysomething person I knew who was obsessed with *American Idol*. Iris Cummings Critchell and Velma Dunn Ploessel vividly described their experiences as competitors at the 1936 Olympics. Draggan Mihailovich told me of his remarkable encounter with the Bird. Georgie Bright Kunkel wrote to me about her brother, the great runner Norman Bright.

As I traced Louie's path through history, many people went out of their way to help me find information and make sense of it. Photographer David Mackintosh flew to California to pore over Louie's scrapbooks, diaries, and memorabilia, taking masterly shots of artifacts and never-before-seen family photographs that could not leave Louie's home. He hunted far and wide for arresting images to illustrate the paperback and the young-reader editions of *Unbroken* and painstakingly restored all the photos in this book, most of which are many decades old. He has my endless gratitude. Many thanks also to the immensely kind Cynthia Garris, who was so helpful to David in gathering photos and memorabilia, and Debbie Hays, first vice president of the Torrance Historical Society, for generously giving David access to the THS Zamperini archives and helping him find artifacts to photograph.

With the assistance of former USAAF bombardier Robert Grenz, William Darron of the Army Air Forces Historical Association brought a Norden bombsight to my house, set it up in my dining room, put a rolling screen of Arizona beneath it, and taught me how to "bomb" Phoenix. As I worked on my book, Bill was always happy to answer my questions. Gary Weaver of Disabled American Veterans climbed all over a B-24 to film the interior for me; thanks to Gary Sinise for putting me in contact with Mr. Weaver. Charlie Tilghman, who flies a restored B-24 for the Commemorative Air Force, taught me about flying the Liberator.

When I was too ill to get to the National Archives, Peggy Ann Brown and Molly Brose went there for me, wading into voluminous POW and war-crimes records and coming back with some of my most critical material. John Brodkin typed up my citations to save me from my vertigo and climbed on my dining room table to photograph images out of Louie's scrapbook. Nina B. Smith translated POW documents from Norwegian, and Noriko Sanefuji translated my letters to and from Japanese sources. Julie Wheelock transcribed many of my interviews, straining to hear elderly voices taped on my nearly-as-elderly recorder. Gail Morgan of the Torrance High School Alumni Association dug through the school archives in search of photographs of Louie.

I also want to send thanks to Draggan Mihailovich, Christopher Svendsen, and Sean McManus of CBS, who kindly got me permission to view unaired videotape from CBS's 1998 feature on Louie. Roger Mansell's Center for Research, Allied POWs Under the Japanese (mansell.com/pow-index.html) was a comprehensive source of information on POW camps; thanks also to historian Wes Injerd, who works with Mansell's site. Jon Hendershott, associate editor at *Track and Field News,* helped me decipher confusing 1930s mile records. Paul Lombardo, author of *The One Sure Cure: Eugenics, the Supreme Court and Buck v. Bell,* and Tony Platt, author of *Bloodlines: Recovering Hitler's Nuremberg Laws,* taught me about eugenics. Rick Zitarosa of the Naval Lakehurst Historical Society answered questions about the *Graf Zeppelin.* Janet Fisher of the Northeast Regional Climate Center, Janet Wall of the National Climatic Data Center, and Keith Heidorn, PhD, of the Weather Doctor (islandnet.com/~see/weather/doctor .htm), answered weather-related questions. Fred Gill, MD, helped me understand Phil's head injury. Charles Stenger, PhD, cleared up my confusion on POW statistics.

Working with Yvonne Kinkaid and Colonel J. A. Saaverda (Ret.) of the Reference Team, Analysis and Reference Division, Air Force Historical Research and Analysis, Bolling Air Force Base, the wonderfully helpful Colonel Frank Trippi (Ret.) unearthed heaps of AAF documents for me. I am also grateful to Lieutenant Colonel Robert Clark, USAF (Ret.), at the Air Force Historical Studies Office, Bolling Air Force Base; Will Mahoney, Eric Van Slander, and Dave Giordano of the National Archives; Cathy Cox and Barry Spink of the Air Force Historical Research Agency, Maxwell Air Force Base; and Carol Leadenham, assistant archivist for reference at the Hoover Institution Archives. I also thank my dear friend Colonel Michael C. Howard, USMC (Ret.), who worked with Captain William Rudich, USN (Ret.), Lieutenant Colonel Todd Holmquist, USMC, Major Heather Cotoia, USMC, Boatswain's Mate Chief Frank Weber, USN (Ret.), and Jim Heath, PhD, professor emeritus, Portland State University, to find information on Everett Almond, the navigator who was killed by a shark while trying to save himself and his pilot.

Thanks also to Pete Golkin, Office of Communications, National Air and Space Museum; Midge Fischer, EAA Warbirds of America; Patrick Ranfranz, Greg Babinski, and Jim Walsh of the 307th Bomb Group Association; Lieutenant Commander Ken Snyder of the National Naval Aviation Museum; Rich Kolb and Mike Meyer of the Veterans of Foreign Wars; Helen Furu of the Norwegian Maritime Museum; Siri Lawson of WarSailors.com; Phil Gudenschwager, 11th Bomb Group historian; Justin Mack, Web developer, 11th Bomb Group; Bill Barrette, Sugamo historian; Wayne Weber of the Billy Graham Center archives at Wheaton College; Melany Ethridge of Larry Ross Communications; Tess Miller and Heather VanKoughnett of the Billy Graham Evangelistic Association; Shirley Ito, librarian, LA84 Foundation; Victoria Palmer, Georgetown Public Library; Edith Miller, Palo Alto High School; Wayne Wilson, vice president, Amateur Athletic Foundation of Los Angeles; Lauren Walser of USC *Trojan Family* magazine; Cheryl Morris, Alumni Records, Princeton; Parker Bostwick of the *Torrance News Torch*; and Eric Spotts of Torrance High School.

Others who assisted me include my dear friend Alan Pocinki, who has helped me in more ways than I can count; Linda Goetz Holmes, author of *Unjust Enrichment*; Hampton Sides, author of *Ghost Soldiers*; Morton Janklow; Dave Tooley; Karen and Russ Scholar; William Baker, professor emeritus, University of Maine; John Powers of NorthChinaMarines.com; Ken Crothers; Christine Hoffman; Bud Ross; John Chapman; Robin Rowland; Ed Hotaling; Morton Cathro; Chris McCarron; Bob Curran; Mike Brown; Richard Glover; Jim Teegarden of pbyrescue.com; Tom Gwynne of *Wingslip*; Cheryl Cerbone, editor, *Ex-POW Bulletin*; Clydie Morgan, Ex American Prisoners of War; Mike Stone of accident-report.com; Dr. Stanley Hoffman; Kathy Hall; Jim Deasy; Captain Bob Rasmussen, USN (Ret.); Thorleif Andreassen; Janet McIlwain; Gary Staffo; Lynn Gamma; Patrick Hoffman; and Gene Venske.

Adapting my book for younger readers was unknown terrain to me, and as I set out, I sought the advice of librarians, teachers, and other authors of books for young adults. I am so grateful to Vickie Weiss, Martha Betcher, Jim Rodgers, Jane Wallace, Barbara Webb, Paula Lewis, Kathie Weinberg, and Annette Klause for answering my many questions and sharing their wisdom. Thank you to my long-suffering college roommate, Sarah Wilsman, now a children's librarian, who did so much to guide me in this process.

In assembling questions for my Q&A with Louie, I solicited the input of students, who sent me hundreds of thought-provoking questions, from which I crafted my interview with Louie. I thank John Pratt, history teacher at Greensburg High School in Greensburg, Indiana, and his students: Darreyn Burritt, Morgan Stagge, Megan McDole, Madison Bower, Sarah Amberger, Chelsie Ruble, Torrie Brogan, Annalie Scheidler, Tori Abplanalp, Breonica McQueary, Riley Burkert, Daniel Santiago, Morgan Hahn,

Katie Bennett, Collin Rigney, Aliya Morrow, Kelsey Etherington, Devin Rathburn, Courtland Ramech, David Booker, Brianna Armstrong, Sarah Meredith, Kaylie Wood, Bryant McIntosh, Tori Giddings, Katelyn Rhea, Jurney Mozingo, Claire Welage, Bryce Bennett, Tye Fleetwood, Paige Moore, Devin Workman, Becca Mcdole, Adam Budinski, Matt Scheumann, Brandi Combs, Katherine Teague, Olivia Beverly, Mikayla Delay, Tom Lawrence, Chaz Smiley, Alli Phillips, Andy Meadows, and Whitney Keller. I also thank Eileen M. Mize, director of communications at Justin-Siena High School in Napa, California, and her students: Austin Connolly, Laurie Cruz, Maddie Osgood, Isaiah Herrera, Khloe Kim (Yegyeong), Christin Estes, Vida Jaffe, Givino Rossini, Nick Best, Singa Danle, Santiago Madrigal, Sean Piatti-Sanders, and Sam Sheekey. Finally, I thank the young readers who submitted questions through the Internet: Sam Reilly, Nick Shaughnessy, Wesley Sturgill, Shahriar Bayat, Mitch Beber, Kathy Riley Miller, Blake Jones, and Rosie Richards.

There are several people to whom I owe special thanks. My brother John Hillenbrand, a longtime private pilot, reviewed the aircraft and flying sections of my book with an extraordinarily careful eye and helped me understand the arcane details of aeronautics. My sister, Susan Avallon, read and reread the manuscript, offered invariably brilliant suggestions, and talked me through the places that had me stumped. Susan and John, I am so lucky to be your little sister. I also thank *EQUUS* magazine editor Laurie Prinz and my old Kenyon friend Chris Toft, who read my manuscript and gave me insightful suggestions.

Phil Scearce, the author of the beautifully written *Finish Forty and Home: The Untold Story of B-24s in the Pacific*, knows the world of the AAF's Pacific airmen better than any other historian. As I wrote this book, Phil was singularly generous, sharing his voluminous research, directing me to sources, and helping me sort through many a quandary. I am forever in his debt.

I have great gratitude for B-29 navigator and former POW Raymond "Hap" Halloran. As I wrote this book, Hap became my almost daily email correspondent, offering me research help, sharing his photographs, telling of his experiences, sending gifts to cheer my sister's children after their father's death, and simply being my friend. Very few human beings have seen humanity's dark side as Hap did, and yet he was ever buoyant, ever forgiving. Hap's resilient heart is my inspiration.

From the beginning of this project, I worked with two translators in Japan. They did so much more for me than mere translation, teaching me about their culture, helping me to understand the war from the Japanese perspective, and offering their thoughts on my manuscript. Because the war remains a highly controversial issue in Japan, they have asked me not to identify them, but I will never forget what they have done for me and for this book.

If I had a firstborn, I'd owe it to my editor, Jennifer Hershey. Jennifer was infinitely kind and infinitely patient, offering inspired suggestions on my manuscript, making countless accommodations for my poor health, and ushering me from first draft to last. I am also so grateful to my young reader editors, Judith Haut and Beverly Horowitz, as well as Barbara Marcus, Isabel Warren-Lynch, Trish Parcell, Colleen Fellingham, and Tim Terhune, who guided me in the daunting leap to a new edition. And as always, I thank the brilliant Gina Centrello, president and publisher of the wonderful Random House.

I also thank my spectacularly talented agent, Tina Bennett, who guides me through authordom with a sure and supportive hand, and my former editor, Jon Karp, who saw the promise in this story from the beginning. I can't send enough thanks to my genius publicist, Sally Marvin, who exhausted herself to bring this book to the world. Thanks also to associate editor Joey McGarvey, who was enormously helpful in so many ways. And I am ever thankful to Tina's assistant, Svetlana Katz, and Jennifer's assistant, Courtney Moran.

In the many moments in which I was unsure if I could bring this book to a happy completion, Borden Flanagan was there to cheer me on. He spent long hours at the kitchen table, poring over my manuscript and making it stronger, and, when illness shrank my world to the upper floor of my house, filled that little world with joy. Thank you, Borden, for your boundless affection, for your wisdom, for your faith in me, and for always bringing me sandwiches.

Finally, I wish to remember the millions of Allied servicemen and prisoners of war who lived the story of the Second World War. Many of these men never came home; many others returned bearing emotional and physical scars that would stay with them for the rest of their lives. I come away from this book with the deepest appreciation for what these men endured, and what they sacrificed, for the good of humanity. It is to them that this book is dedicated.

Laura Hillenbrand
Spring 2014

INDEX

Note: Italic page numbers refer to illustrations.

Army Air Forces, U.S. (AAF), 66, 70, 73, 75–77, 108–109. *See also specific planes*

B-24 Liberators. *See also specific planes*
  in crashes and ditchings, 68, 69–77, *70, 72, 73*
  parts of, *54*
  Funafuti air raid, 89–90, *90*
  performance of, 54–56
  photographs of, *48, 70, 74, 278*
  range limitations of, 184
  short runways and, 71–72, *71*
  survival equipment, 97, 104
  Wake Atoll raid and, 64, 65
B-29 Superfortresses
  atomic bombing of Japan, 216–217, *216*
  Japanese fighters and, 191–192
  leaflets and, 214–215, *214*
  in overflights and air raids over Japan, 183–184, 191–193, 197–198, 203, 207, *208, 209,* 212, 214–215, 232
  photograph of, *182*
  relief airdrops by, 227, 235
Bad Eye (Japanese guard), 205, 221
Bright, Norman, 24, 26, 28
Brooks, Harry, 54, 71, 81–85, *85,* 91

China, 44, 76–77, 183–184
Corpening, Clarence, 95, *95,* 96, 107
Cunningham, Glenn, 16–17, 22, 41–52, *44*

Cuppernell, Charleton Hugh, 62–63, *62,* 71, 79–82, 85, 91, 95–99, 110

Daisy Mae (B-24 Liberator), 96–97, 107, 108–109, *109*
Deasy, Joe, 87, 96, 107, 162–163
Douglas, Clarence, 53, *53,* 81, 83–85, 91, 111

Enola Gay (B-29 Superfortress), *216*

Fitzgerald, John, 152, 166, 196, 198–199, 201–202, 205, 224–227, 231
Flammer, Harvey, *51*
Funafuti Atoll, 72, 78, 83–85, *86,* 87–91, *90*

Garrett, Fred, 157–158, 211, 222, 225, *234,* 251
Geneva Convention, 176–177, 179, 202
Germany, 32–33, 36–37, 44–45, 208. *See also* Olympic Games of 1936
Glassman, Frank, 53, *53,* 81, 91
Graf Zeppelin, 5–6, 60
Graham, Billy, 266–269, *267,* 271
Green Hornet (B-24 Liberator)
  crash of, 93, 96–100, *96,* 104, 106, 107–108, 110, 163, 194, 281, 286–287
  safety concerns about, 93, *94,* 97
Green Hornet castaways. *See also* McNamara, Francis "Mac"; Phillips,

Russell Allen "Phil"; Zamperini, Louis
Silvie "Louie"
capture by Japanese, 132–134
crash injuries of, 99–100, 103–104, 106
damaged rafts of, 1–2, 115
distance drifted by, 122–123, 133
escape from wreckage by, 99–100
families' reactions to news of loss, 110–111
health of, 109, 112, 115
hunger and thirst suffered by, 109,
112–117, 126, 129–130
inflated raft survival record, 113–114,
128–129, 132
Japanese bomber's strafing of, 118–121,
119, 124
Mac's binge on rations, 107–108,
112–113, 128, 287
rationing of supplies by, 105–106,
107–108
search for, 107–110
sharks and, 1–2, 106, 107, 112–115, 118,
120–122, 125–128, 269, 287–288
storms encountered by, 131–132

Harris, William, 152–153, *153*, 158, 165,
166, 168–170, *169*, 196, 198
Hawaii
Japanese aggression, 44
Pearl Harbor attack, 46, 49, 60
372nd Bomb Squadron stationed in,
60–64, *60, 61, 64*, 69, 77, 91, 95, 110,
111, 234
Hiroshima, 216–217, 228, 232
Hitler, Adolf, 6, 33, 36–38, 44–45
Höckert, Gunnar, 33–34, 36

Japan. *See also specific cities*
atomic bombing of, 216–217, *216, 218,*
219–221, 224, 228, 232
cultural fear of shame and humiliation
in, 140–141
deaths of POWs held by, 228, *229*
Geneva Convention and, 176–177

invasion of territories by, 44, 49–50, 76
leaflets and, 214–215
shame of capture in, 150–151, 210
Japanese guards. *See also* Watanabe,
Matsuhiro "the Bird"; *specific POW
camps and interrogation centers*
abuse and beatings of prisoners, 134,
139–140, 142, 145, 148–149, 151,
152, 154, 157, 158, 167, 170
execution of POWs and, 197
kindness shown by, 142, 151
Louie's forgiveness of, 273, 291
Louie's return to Japan and, 271–273
at Naoetsu POW camp, 202–205, 213,
219–221, 225, 227
at Omori POW camp, 177, 184
reaction to B-29 raids, 184, 191, 193,
197
at Rokuroshi POW camp, 222, 225
theft of POW rations, 156, 167, 194,
202, 231
Japanese military. *See also* Japanese guards;
*See also specific POW camps and
interrogation centers*
culture of brutality in, 149–151
debasement of POWs, 140–141
enslavement of native populations, 132
Funafuti air raid and, 87–91
"kill-all" rule, 151, 166, 168, 197,
210–211, 219–221, 228
medical experiments on POWs, 143
Nauru and, 78
numbers of POWs held by, 228
POW officers' slave labor exemption,
177, 179, 202
Rape of Nanking and, 76–77
shame of capture in, 150–151
torture of Fitzgerald, 152, 231
Wake Atoll and, 49–50, 65–66

Kawamura (Japanese guard), 142, 144, 236
"kill-all" rule, 151, 166, 168, 197, 210–211,
219–221, 228

Kwajalein Atoll
    abuse of prisoners at, 134, 139–141, 142
    bombed-out remains of, 237–238
    execution of POWs, 77, 139, 191
    Green Hornet castaways moved to,
        134–135, 162–163
    interrogations at, 141–144
    Louie's cell at, 134–135, 158

Lambert, Ray, 54, 81, 91
Lash, Don, 24, 26, *27*, 28, 34, 36
Lehtinen, Lauri, 33–34, 36
life rafts
    conditions in, 76, *124*
    Green Hornet castaways and, 1–2, 97–99,
        102, 103–110, 112–123, *124*, 125–132
    sharks and, 75, 122, 125–128
Little Boy (atomic bomb), 216

Marshall Islands, 109, 122–123, 133, 157
Martindale, Bob, 176–177, 184, 186, 192,
    230–231
Marvin, Kevin, 205, 221, 233
Matheny, William, 61, 63, 65, 67
McNamara, Francis "Mac." *See also Green
        Hornet* castaways
    binge on rations, 107–108, 112–113, 128
    as castaway, 103–106, 107–109,
        112–117, 118–123, 125–130, *127*,
        268–269, 287–288
    as crew member, 93, *105*
    despair of, 105, 109, 114, 115
    Japanese bomber's strafing raft of,
        118–121, *124*
    redeeming acts of, 122, 125–126, 128,
        287–288
    responsibility for survival supplies,
        97–98, 104
    sharks and, 107, 112, 114, 118, 121–122,
        125–128, 269, 287–288
Midway, 44, 49, 64, 67
Mitchell, Robert, 53, *53*, 61, 79–80, 91,
    98, 110
Moznette, George, Jr., 54, 61, 69, 70

Nagasaki, *218*, 219
Naoetsu POW camp
    air raid on, 207
    atomic bombing of Japan and, 219–221,
        224
    conditions at, 201–202
    end of war at, 221, 221–224, 222–228,
        230
    "kill-all" order and, 211, 219–221
    liberated POWs gorging on food at, 228,
        230–231
    Louie's arrival at, 198–199, *200*
    notes and relief supplies dropped on,
        223–224, *223*, 226–228, *227*,
        230–231
    Olympic torch in, 281–282
    plot to kill Watanabe, 215–216
    POWs' move to Yokahama, 232–233
    POW thievery at, 202, 204–205
    rations at, 202, 205–206, 209–210, 212,
        226
    slave labor at, 202–205, 208, 210, 219,
        282
Nauru, 78–83, *80*, 111, 162
NCAA Championships, 42–44, *43*

Ofuna interrogation center
    abuse and beatings of POWs, 147–149,
        151, 152, 154, 158, 167, 170
    enforced silence at, 147, 152, 154, 196
    illness and malnutrition at, 147, 149,
        151, 156–157, 165–166
    POW defiance, 154–156
    POW escape plans, 165, 168
Ogawa (Japanese guard), 202–203, 220
Ohta, Saburo. *See* Watanabe, Mutsuhiro
    "the Bird"
Olympic Games of 1936
    Louie's 5,000-meter race, 33–35, *34*, *35*,
        36–37
    Louie's Berlin voyage, *25*, 31–32, 38
    Louie's Nazi flag–stealing escapade,
        37–39
    Louie's propaganda value, 191

qualifying for, 22–26, *27*, 28–29
Olympic Games of 1940, 39, 41, 44, 45
Olympic Games of 1948, 253
Olympic Games of 1984, *276*
Omori POW camp
    aerial views of, *178*, *185*
    air raids on Tokyo, 197–198, 232
    atomic bombing of Japan and, 219
    B-29 raids and, 184, 191–193
    beatings of prisoners, 173–174
    Christmas play at, 194–195
    "kill-all" order and, 210
    Louie moved to, 170, 171
    Louie's first encounter with Watanabe,
      171, *172*, 173
    rations at, 177, 178, 179
    relief airdrops, 230–231
    slave labor at, 176–177, 180
    thievery by POWs at, 180–181, 205
    Watanabe's transfer, 196–197
Osaka, 207, *208*

Pacific POWs. *See also specific POW camps
    and interrogation centers*
    celebrations at war's end, 225, 226, *226*,
      228, 230
    dignity of, 140–141, 156, 181, 231, 252,
      256, 269, 281, 288
    Hiroshima and, 217, 228, 232
    "kill-all" rule, 151, 166, 168, 197,
      210–211, 219–221, 228
    Nanking executions, 76–77
    propaganda prisoners, 186, 191, 290
    PTSD of, 252
    reaction to liberation, 233–236, *234*
    relief airdrops, 230
    as slave labor, 176–177, 197
    at Wake Atoll, 50
    weight loss of, *146*, 156–157, *230*,
      251–252
Palmyra island, 96, 97, 107
Pearl Harbor attack, 46, 49, 60, *60*
Phillips, Cecile Perry "Cecy"
    care packages from, 63

Phil's courtship of, 51, 53, 59, 77
Phil's disappearance and, 163, 193–194
Phil's letters, 77, 110, 158–159
Phil's talismans and, 77, 104
Phil's thoughts of, 114
photograph of, *193*
postwar life with Phil, 236, *250*, *251*,
    277
Phillips, Chris, *277*
Phillips, Karen, *277*, *278*
Phillips, Kelsey, 110, *193*, 194
Phillips, Russell Allen "Phil." *See also
    Green Hornet castaways*
    capture by Japanese, 132–134
    as castaway, 103–108, 112–123,
      125–130, 131–132, 268
    with children, *277*
    crash injuries of, 103–104, 106
    at Ephrata air base, 51, *52*, 53–54, *53*,
      55, *57*, 58–59, *58*
    family's notification of disappearance,
      110–111
    Funafuti air raid and, 87–89, 91
    Green Hornet crash and, 96–99, 114, 154
    Hawaiian base life of, 61–63, 77, 91, 95,
      110
    homecoming of, 235–236, *236*
    hunger and thirst suffered by, 112,
      129–130
    with children, *277*
    Japanese bomber's strafing raft of,
      118–121, *124*
    kindness of captors and, 133–134
    Kwajalein imprisonment of, 134–135,
      139–144, 162–163
    letters home of, 77, 110, 158–159
    marriage of, 236, *250*, *251*, 277
    move from Kwajalein to Japan, 144, 145,
      163
    Nauru air raid, 79–85
    at Ofuna interrogation center, *148*, 154,
      158–159
    old age of, 277–278, *278*
    piloting close calls, 66–67, 70–71

postwar life with Cecy, 236, *250*, 277
at Rokuroshi POW camp, 211, 222, 225, 235–236
sharks and, 106, 107, 112, 114, 118, 121–122, 126–128, 269
Wake Atoll raid and, 65–67
War Department death declaration of, 163–164, 194
in Zentsuji POW camp, 193, 211
Pillsbury, Stanley, 53, *53*, 57, 59, 71, 78–85, *82*, 88, 91, 111
Postman Calls (radio program), 186–189, 190, 191, 243
post-traumatic stress disorder (PTSD), 252, 255, 261, 264, 291

Quack (Japanese guard), 154, 167–170, *167*, 196

Radio Tokyo, 186–187, 190
Rape of Nanking, 76–77
Red Cross, 147, 161, 178, 194, 196, 202, 231, 233
Reynolds, James, *116*
Rickenbacker, Eddie, 113–114, *115*, 116
Rokuroshi POW camp, 211, 222, 225, 227, 235–236
Rosynek, Frank, 72, 89, 233–234

Saipan, 166–167, 183, 184
Salminen, Ilmari, 33–34, 36
search and rescue missions, 76, 95–97, 108–109
sharks
    downed airmen and, 69, 75
    Green Hornet castaways and, 1–2, 106–107, 112–115, 118, 120–122, 125–128, 269, 287–288
Stay, Jesse, 87–88
Strong, Robert, 73, 75
Sugamo Prison, *270*, 271–273
Super Man (B-24 Liberator), 58, 59, 62–63, 65–67, 70, 78–86, *84*, 91, *92*

Tarawa Atoll, 151, 228
372nd Bomb Squadron of the 307th Bomb Group, Seventh Air Force. *See also Super Man* (B-24 Liberator)
    departure for the Pacific, 64–65
    at Ephrata air base, 54, 56–57
    Hawaiian barracks and base life of, 60–64, *60*, *61*, *64*, 69, 77, 91, 95, 110, 111, 234
    injuries and casualties, 69–70
    Nauru air raid, 78–85, *80*
    sea search patrols and, 61–63
    Wake Atoll raid, 64–67
Tibbets, Paul, 216–217
Tinian Island, 216, *216*, 228
Tinker, Frank, 158, 165, 168, 170, 171, 193, 198, 209, 221, 227, 233
Tojo, Hideki, 244, 245
Tokyo
    Allied air raids on, 181, 183–184, 191–192, 197–198, 232
    Graf Zeppelin overflight of, 60
    Olympics of 1940 and, 39, 41
    Omori POW camp and, 170–171
    Postman Calls broadcast, 187–188
    Watanabe's postwar activities, 245, 257–259, 264–265, 272
Torrance, California
    Graf Zeppelin's flight over, 5–6
    high school, 13, 15, 17
    Louie's childhood and youth in, 7–11
    Louie's track feats as pride of, 21–22, 24, *25*, 28, 39
Trumbull, Robert, 233, 235

UCLA's Southern California Cross-Country meet, 18–19, *18*
University of Southern California, 23, 40, 41–44, *42*

Wade, Tom
    B-29 raids and, 184
    coal barge slave labor and, 203

Japanese surrender message, 227
Japanese theft of Red Cross boxes and, 194
liberation of, 233
move to Naoetsu POW camp, 198, 202
on Watanabe, 174, 176–177, 244
Watanabe's abuse and beatings of POWs, 209, 213
Wake Atoll, 44, 49–50, 151, 228
war criminals, 219, 244–245, 257–258. *See also* Japanese guards; Japanese military
Watanabe, Michiko, 258–259
Watanabe, Mutsuhiro "the Bird"
beatings of prisoners by, 173–175, 178–179, 185–186, 191–193, 202, 209, 212–215
emotional torture of prisoners by, 173, 174–175, 179, 185–186, 192–193, 203, 215
as fugitive, 245, 257–260, 265–266, 272
Louie as vicious fixation of, 175, 178–179, 181, 185–186, 191, 193, 199, 201–202, 205–206, 209, 212–214, 220, 228–230
Louie's desire for revenge on, 228, 230, 255–256, 261, 263, 266, 271, 291
in Louie's dreams, 209, 220, 246, 252–253, 255, 261, 264, 269, 281
Louie's first encounter with, 171, *172*, 173
Louie's forgiveness of, 269, 271–273, 280–282, 291
meeting with Shizuka Watanabe, 264, 265–266, 272
at Naoetsu POW camp, 199, 221, 224, 230, 235
POW sentry system monitoring, 177
promise to apologize to Louie, 280–281
reaction to B-29 raids, 184, 191–193, 203, 212, 214–215
reaction to theft of fish, 208–209
reported suicide of, 260, 261, 265, 266, 280

staged propaganda photographs and, 194
transfer from Omori, 195
as war criminal, 244–245
Watanabe, Shizuka, 264, 265–266, 272
Weasel (Japanese guard), 154, 166, 289
World War II
Army Air Force planes lost in, 70
atomic bombing of Japan, 216–217, *216*, *218*, 219–221, 224, 228, 232
fall of Germany, 208
Japanese Funafuti air raid, 86, 87–91, 90
Japan's invasion of territories in, 44, 49–50, 76
Nauru air raid, 78–83, *80*, 111, 162
Pearl Harbor attack, 46, 49, 60
surrender of Japan, 210, 219, 225, 228

Yokahama, 232–233, 236–237

Zamperini, Anthony (father)
Louie's childhood and youth and, 10, 15–16
Louie's disappearance and, 111, 160, 161, 164
Louie's homecoming and, *242*, 290
Louie's track career and, 28
Louie's wartime goodbye to, 50, *51*
Zamperini, Cynthia Applewhite (wife)
Louie's courtship of, 246, *247*, 248–249, *248*, *249*, 250, 251–253
Louie's religious reawakening and, 266–269
Louie's return to Japan and, 272
marriage of, 249, *250*, 251, 253, 254, 262–266, 271
Zamperini, Cynthia "Cissy" (daughter), 264, 271
Zamperini, Louise (mother)
attachment to Louie's airman's wings, 59
comparison of Louie and Pete, 10, 12
letters from Kelsey Phillips, 194
Louie at USC and, 41

Louie's death declaration and, 163–164,
  164, 234
Louie's disappearance and, 111, 160,
  162, 164, 235, 289
Louie's homecoming and, 235, 239, *239*,
  242, 290
Louie's track career and, 22, 26
Louie's wartime goodbye to, 50, *51*
Postman Calls broadcast and, 187–189
troubles with Louie as youth, 6–7,
  10–11, 15–16
Zamperini, Louis Silvie "Louie"
alcohol use and, 7, 16, 32, 37, 246, 255,
  261–264, 266, 269
as athletic in old age, *274*, *276*, *276*
bullying of, 10, 181
capture by Japanese, 132–134, 160
care of wounded compatriots by, 104, 106
as castaway, 1–2, 103–110, 112–123,
  125–130, *130*, 131–134, *148*, 268–269,
  286–288
childhood and youth of, *4*, 5–11, *7*, *8*,
  12, 15–16, *17*
civilian jobs of, 45
courtship and marriage of, 246, 248–249,
  249, *250*, 251–253, *253*
desire for revenge on Watanabe, 228,
  230, 255–256, 261, 263, 266, 271, 291
diaries of, *94*, 96, 155–156, *155*
at Ephrata air base, 50–51, 53, *53*,
  56–59, *56*
ethnicity of, 6, 10
flashbacks and, 255, 261, 268–269
in forced prison exercise and races, 152,
  153, 157, 158
forgiveness of Watanabe, 269, 271–273,
  280–282, 291
Funafuti air raid and, 87–91, *92*
Green Hornet crash, *94*, 95–100
Hawaiian base life of, 61–64, *61*, 69, 91,
  110, 111, 234
homecoming of, 237–239, *237*, *238*,
  239, *242*, *244*, *262*, 290

illness in captivity, 139–140, 156–157,
  202, 205, 213, 215, 220–221, 235,
  238
imprisonment's effect on track career of,
  235
injuries of, 43, 99–100, 106, 145, 205,
  209, 212, 254
Japanese bomber's strafing raft of,
  118–121, *124*
kindness of captors and, 133–134
Kwajalein imprisonment of, 134–135,
  139–144, 163, 191, 237–238, 288
leaving Naoetsu, 231
letters home of, 196, 235
media attention focused on, 38, 245
medical experiments performed on, 143
military training of, 45–46, *45*, 50, 56,
  57–59
at Naoetsu POW camp, 198–199,
  201–224, *220*
Nauru air raid, 78–85, *80*
nightmares of, 209, 220, 246, 252–253,
  255, 261, 264, 269, 281
at Ofuna interrogation center, 147–151,
  150, 152–158, 165–170, 191, 196
in Okinawa, 233–237
Olympic aspirations and training of,
  22–26, *25*, *27*, 28–29, 39, 41, 44,
  253–254
at Omori POW camp, 171–198
Pete's involvement in track career of, 13,
  15–18, *18*, *20*, 21, 23, 24, 26, 28–29,
  33, 34, 36, 39, 42, 285
plot to kill Watanabe, 215–216, 224
Postman Calls broadcast by, 186–189,
  190–191, 243
as potential propaganda tool, 147, 154,
  186, 191, 290
PTSD and, 255, 261, 264, 291
quest for four-minute mile, 41–42, 292
relief supplies dropped on Naoetsu POW
  camp and, 227–228
religion and spirituality of, 77, 115, 117,

128, 140, 142, 186, 220, 262, 266–269, 275, 277, 281

return to Japan, 270, 271–273, 281–282, 283

running for wartime stress relief, 77, 91, 95

running in postwar life, 253–254, 254

sharks and, 1–2, 69, 75, 106, 107, 112, 114, 115, 116, 118, 120–122, 125–128, 269, 287–288

skill as bombardier, 79

slave labor as POW, 204, 205, 208

temperamental outbursts of, 10, 243–244, 249

thievery of, 8–9, 22, 31, 37–38, 165, 166, 168–170, 285–286

thirst and hunger suffered by, 104–105, 108, 109, 112–117, 129–130, 149, 156–157, 165–166, 194, 202, 205, 212–213, 233, 269

Tokyo's wartime conditions and, 183, 198–199

track career as Olympian, 1–2, 30, 31–34, 34, 35, 36–39, 191, 289

track career in college, 23, 40, 41–44, 42, 43

track career in high school, 13, 14, 15–19, 20, 21–23, 22, 23, 286

track records broken by, 17–19, 18, 21, 22, 22, 44

Victory Boys Camp and, 274, 275

Wake Atoll raid and, 65–67

War Department death declaration of, 163–164, 164, 186, 188, 233–234, 253

Watanabe's vicious fixation on, 175, 178–179, 181, 185–186, 191, 193, 195, 199, 201–202, 205–206, 209, 212–214, 220, 228–230

Zamperini, Pete (brother)
childhood and youth of, 5, 7, 8, 8, 9–10, 11
letters to Louie, 110
Louie's disappearance and, 111, 161, 164, 235
Louie's financial woes and, 263
Louie's homecoming and, 237–238, 238, 242, 290
Louie's optimism and, 276
Louie's track career and, 13, 15–18, 18, 20, 21, 23, 24, 26, 28–29, 33, 34, 36, 39, 42, 285
Louie's wartime goodbye to, 50, 51
old age and death of, 278–279
Postman Calls broadcast and, 189

Zamperini, Sylvia (sister)
childhood of, 9, 10
death of, 279
Louie's departure for war and, 51
Louie's disappearance and, 111, 160–162, 164
Louie's homecoming and, 239, 239, 242, 244, 290
Postman Calls broadcast and, 189, 243

Zamperini, Virginia (sister)
childhood of, 8, 9
death of, 279
Louie's departure for war and, 51
Louie's disappearance and, 161
Louie's homecoming and, 235, 239, 242, 244, 290

Zamperini family, 110, 111, 160–164, 186, 188–189, 194, 235

Zentsuji POW camp, 193

Zero aircraft, 66, 78–83, 91